Human rights in international law

Basic texts

Council of Europe Press, 1992

French edition:
Droits de l'homme en droit international. Textes de base

ISBN 92-871-2038-2

Cover illustration:
René Magritte (1898-1967), *Le Retour,*
Musées royaux des beaux-arts de Belgique, Brussels

Strasbourg, Council of Europe, Publishing and Documentation Service
First printed 1992
Reprinted 1993
ISBN 92-871-2039-0
Printed in the Netherlands

Table of contents

Preface

The purpose of this collection is to provide a selection of the major international texts relating to human rights.

Considering the growing interest of students, lawyers, teachers, diplomats and other professional groups, and, more generally, the public as a whole, it has been thought necessary to make available a collection which can be used both as an introduction to the vast subject of human rights and as a working tool.

Obviously a compilation of this kind cannot claim to be exhaustive and the Directorate of Human Rights has been faced with the difficult problem of making a selection of texts. However, even though it cannot be considered to embrace all international texts on the subject, it is hoped that this collection of basic texts in the field of human rights will provide all interested circles with a reference book capable of providing a maximum of relevant information in an objective and precise manner.

Directorate of Human Rights

A. **Universal protection of human rights**

Texts prepared within the United Nations

1. Universal Declaration of Human Rights

Adopted and proclaimed by General Assembly Resolution 217 A (III) of 10 December 1948

Preamble

Whereas recognition of the inherent dignity and of the equal and inalienable rights of all members of the human family is the foundation of freedom, justice and peace in the world,

Whereas disregard and contempt for human rights have resulted in barbarous acts which have outraged the conscience of mankind, and the advent of a world in which human beings shall enjoy freedom of speech and belief and freedom from fear and want has been proclaimed as the highest aspiration of the common people,

Whereas it is essential, if man is not to be compelled to have recourse, as a last resort, to rebellion against tyranny and oppression, that human rights should be protected by the rule of law,

Whereas it is essential to promote the development of friendly relations between nations,

Whereas the peoples of the United Nations have in the Charter reaffirmed their faith in fundamental human rights, in the dignity and worth of the human person and in the equal rights of men and women and have determined to promote social progress and better standards of life in larger freedoms,

Whereas member States have pledged themselves to achieve, in co-operation with the United Nations, the promotion of universal respect for and observance of human rights and fundamental freedoms,

Whereas a common understanding of these rights and freedoms is of the greatest importance for the full realization of this pledge,

Now, therefore,

The General Assembly,

Proclaims this Universal Declaration of Human Rights as a common standard of achievement for all peoples and all nations, to the end that every individual and every organ of society, keeping this Declaration constantly in mind, shall strive by teaching and education to promote respect for these rights and freedoms and by progressive measures, national and international, to secure their universal and effective recognition and observance, both among the peoples of member States themselves and among the peoples of territories under their jurisdiction.

Article 1

All human beings are born free and equal in dignity and rights. They are endowed with reason and conscience and should act towards one another in a spirit of brotherhood.

Article 2

1. Everyone is entitled to all the rights and freedoms set forth in this Declaration, without distinction of any kind, such as race, colour, sex, language, religion, political or other opinion, national or social origin, property, birth or other status.

2. Furthermore, no distinction shall be made on the basis of the political, jurisdictional or international status of the country or territory to which a person belongs, whether it be independent, trust, non-self-governing or under any other limitation of sovereignty.

Article 3

Everyone has the right to life, liberty and security of person.

Article 4

No one shall be held in slavery or servitude; slavery and the slave trade shall be prohibited in all their forms.

Article 5

No one shall be subjected to torture or to cruel, inhuman or degrading treatment or punishment.

Article 6

Everyone has the right to recognition everywhere as a person before the law.

Article 7

All are equal before the law and are entitled without any discrimination to equal protection of the law. All are entitled to equal protection against any discrimination in violation of this Declaration and against any incitement to such discrimination.

Article 8

Everyone has the right to an effective remedy by the competent national tribunals for acts violating the fundamental rights granted him by the constitution or by law.

Article 9

No one shall be subjected to arbitrary arrest, detention or exile.

Article 10

Everyone is entitled in full equality to a fair and public hearing by an independent and impartial tribunal, in the determination of his rights and obligations and of any criminal charge against him.

Article 11

1. Everyone charged with a penal offence has the right to be presumed innocent until proved guilty according to law in a public trial at which he has had all the guarantees necessary for his defence.

2. No one shall be held guilty of any penal offence on account of any act or omission which did not constitute a penal offence, under national or international law, at the time when it was committed. Nor shall a heavier penalty be imposed than the one that was applicable at the time the penal offence was committed.

Article 12

No one shall be subjected to arbitrary interference with his privacy, family, home or correspondence, nor to attacks upon his honour and reputation. Everyone has the right to the protection of the law against such interference or attacks.

Article 13

1. Everyone has the right to freedom of movement and residence within the borders of each State.

2. Everyone has the right to leave any country, including his own, and to return to his country.

Article 14

1. Everyone has the right to seek and to enjoy in other countries asylum from persecution.

2. This right may not be invoked in the case of prosecutions genuinely arising from non-political crimes or from acts contrary to the purposes and principles of the United Nations.

Article 15

1. Everyone has the right to a nationality.

2. No one shall be arbitrarily deprived of his nationality nor denied the right to change his nationality.

Article 16

1. Men and women of full age, without any limitation due to race, nationality or religion, have the right to marry and to found a family. They are entitled to equal rights as to marriage, during marriage and at its dissolution.

2. Marriage shall be entered into only with free and full consent of the intending spouses.

3. The family is the natural and fundamental group unit of society and is entitled to protection by society and the State.

Article 17

1. Everyone has the right to own property alone as well as in association with others.

2. No one shall be arbitrarily deprived of his property.

Article 18

Everyone has the right to freedom of thought, conscience and religion; this right includes freedom to change his religion or belief, and freedom, either alone or in community with others and in public or private, to manifest his religion or belief in teaching, practice, worship and observance.

Article 19

Everyone has the right to freedom of opinion and expression; this right includes freedom to hold opinions without interference and to seek, receive and impart information and ideas through any media and regardless of frontiers.

Article 20

1. Everyone has the right to freedom of peaceful assembly and association.

2. No one may be compelled to belong to an association.

Article 21

1. Everyone has the right to take part in the government of his country, directly or through freely chosen representatives.

2. Everyone has the right to equal access to public service in his country.

3. The will of the people shall be the basis of the authority of government; this will shall be expressed in periodic and genuine elections which shall be by universal and equal suffrage and shall be held by secret vote or by equivalent free voting procedures.

Article 22

Everyone, as a member of society, has the right to social security and is entitled to realization, through national effort and international co-operation and in accordance with the organization and resources of each State, of the economic, social and cultural rights indispensable for his dignity and the free development of his personality.

Article 23

1. Everyone has the right to work, to free choice of employment, to just and favourable conditions of work and to protection against unemployment.

2. Everyone, without any discrimination, has the right to equal pay for equal work.

3. Everyone who works has the right to just and favourable remuneration ensuring for himself and his family an existence worthy of human dignity, and supplemented, if necessary, by other means of social protection.

4. Everyone has the right to form and to join trade unions for the protection of his interests.

Article 24

Everyone has the right to rest and leisure, including reasonable limitation of working hours and periodic holidays with pay.

Article 25

1. Everyone has the right to a standard of living adequate for the health and well-being of himself and of his family, including food, clothing, housing and medical care and necessary social services, and the right to security in the event of unemployment, sickness, disability, widowhood, old age or other lack of livelihood in circumstances beyond his control.

2. Motherhood and childhood are entitled to special care and assistance. All children, whether born in or out of wedlock, shall enjoy the same social protection.

Article 26

1. Everyone has the right to education. Education shall be free, at least in the elementary and fundamental stages. Elementary education shall be compulsory. Technical and professional education shall be made generally available and higher education shall be equally accessible to all on the basis of merit.

2. Education shall be directed to the full development of the human personality and to the strengthening of respect for human rights and fundamental freedoms. It shall promote understanding, tolerance and friendship among all nations, racial or religious groups, and shall further the activities of the United Nations for the maintenance of peace.

3. Parents have a prior right to choose the kind of education that shall be given to their children.

Article 27

1. Everyone has the right freely to participate in the cultural life of the community, to enjoy the arts and to share in scientific advancement and its benefits.

2. Everyone has the right to the protection of the moral and material interests resulting from any scientific, literary or artistic production of which he is the author.

Article 28

Everyone is entitled to a social and international order in which the rights and freedoms set forth in this Declaration can be fully realized.

Article 29

1. Everyone has duties to the community in which alone the free and full development of his personality is possible.

2. In the exercise of his rights and freedoms, everyone shall be subject only to such limitations as are determined by law solely for the purpose of securing due recognition and respect for the rights and freedoms of others and of meeting the just requirements of morality, public order and the general welfare in a democratic society.

3. These rights and freedoms may in no case be exercised contrary to the purposes and principles of the United Nations.

Article 30

Nothing in this Declaration may be interpreted as implying for any State, group or person any right to engage in any activity or to perform any act aimed at the destruction of any of the rights and freedoms set forth herein.

2. International Covenant on Economic, Social and Cultural Rights

Adopted and opened for signature, ratification and accession by General Assembly Resolution 2200 A (XXI) of 16 December 1966

Entry into force: 3 January 1976, in accordance with Article 27

Preamble

The States Parties to the present Covenant,

Considering that, in accordance with the principles proclaimed in the Charter of the United Nations, recognition of the inherent dignity and of the equal and inalienable rights of all members of the human family is the foundation of freedom, justice and peace in the world,

Recognizing that these rights derive from the inherent dignity of the human person,

Recognizing that, in accordance with the Universal Declaration of Human Rights, the ideal of free human beings enjoying freedom from fear and want can only be achieved if conditions are created whereby everyone may enjoy his economic, social and cultural rights, as well as his civil and political rights,

Considering the obligation of States under the Charter of the United Nations to promote universal respect for, and observance of, human rights and freedoms,

Realizing that the individual, having duties to other individuals and to the community to which he belongs, is under a responsibility to strive for the promotion and observance of the rights recognized in the present Covenant,

Agree upon the following Articles:

Part I

Article 1

1. All peoples have the right of self-determination. By virtue of that right they freely determine their political status and freely pursue their economic, social and cultural development.

2. All peoples may, for their own ends, freely dispose of their natural wealth and resources without prejudice to any obligations arising out of international economic co-operation, based upon the principle of mutual benefit, and international law. In no case may a people be deprived of its own means of subsistence.

3. The States Parties to the present Covenant, including those having responsibility for the administration of Non-Self-Governing and Trust Territories, shall promote the realization of the right of self-determination, and shall respect that right, in conformity with the provisions of the Charter of the United Nations.

Part II

Article 2

1. Each State Party to the present Covenant undertakes to take steps, individually and through international assistance and co-operation, especially economic and technical, to the maximum of its available resources, with a view to achieving progressively the full realization of the rights recognized in the present Covenant by all appropriate means, including particularly the adoption of legislative measures.

2. The States Parties to the present Covenant undertake to guarantee that the rights enunciated in the present Covenant will be exercised

without discrimination of any kind as to race, colour, sex, language, religion, political or other opinion, national or social origin, property, birth or other status.

3. Developing countries, with due regard to human rights and their national economy, may determine to what extent they would guarantee the economic rights recognized in the present Covenant to non-nationals.

Article 3

The States Parties to the present Covenant undertake to ensure the equal right of men and women to the enjoyment of all economic, social and cultural rights set forth in the present Covenant.

Article 4

The States Parties to the present Covenant recognize that, in the enjoyment of those rights provided by the State in conformity with the present Covenant, the State may subject such rights only to such limitations as are determined by law only in so far as this may be compatible with the nature of these rights and solely for the purpose of promoting the general welfare in a democratic society.

Article 5

1. Nothing in the present Covenant may be interpreted as implying for any State, group or person any right to engage in any activity or to perform any act aimed at the destruction of any of the rights or freedoms recognized herein, or at their limitation to a greater extent than is provided for in the present Covenant.

2. No restriction upon or derogation from any of the fundamental human rights recognized or existing in any country in virtue of law, conventions, regulations or customs shall be admitted on the pretext that the present Covenant does not recognize such rights or that it recognizes them to a lesser extent.

Part III

Article 6

1. The States Parties to the present Covenant recognize the right to work, which includes the right of everyone to the opportunity to gain his living by work which he freely chooses or accepts, and will take appropriate steps to safeguard this right.

2. The steps to be taken by a State Party to the present Covenant to achieve the full realization of this right shall include technical and vocational guidance and training programmes, policies and techniques to achieve steady economic, social and cultural development and full and productive employment under conditions safeguarding fundamental political and economic freedoms to the individual.

Article 7

The States Parties to the present Covenant recognize the right of everyone to the enjoyment of just and favourable conditions of work which ensure, in particular:

a. remuneration which provides all workers, as a minimum, with:
   i. fair wages and equal remuneration for work of equal value without distinction of any kind, in particular women being guaranteed conditions of work not inferior to those enjoyed by men, with equal pay for equal work;
   ii. a decent living for themselves and their families in accordance with the provisions of the present Covenant;

b. safe and healthy working conditions;

c. equal opportunity for everyone to be promoted in his employment to an appropriate higher level, subject to no considerations other than those of seniority and competence;

d. rest, leisure and reasonable limitation of working hours and periodic holidays with pay, as well as remuneration for public holidays.

Article 8

1. The States Parties to the present Covenant undertake to ensure:

a. the right of everyone to form trade unions and join the trade union of his choice, subject only to the rules of the organization concerned, for the promotion and protection of his economic and social interests. No restrictions may be placed on the exercise of this right other than those prescribed by law and which are necessary in a democratic society in the interests of national security or public order or for the protection of the rights and freedoms of others;

b. the right of trade unions to establish national federations or confederations and the right of the latter to form or join international trade-union organizations;

c. the right of trade unions to function freely subject to no limitations other than those prescribed by law and which are necessary in a democratic society in the interests of national security or public order or for the protection of the rights and freedoms of others;

d. the right to strike, provided that it is exercised in conformity with the laws of the particular country.

2. This Article shall not prevent the imposition of lawful restrictions on the exercise of these rights by members of the armed forces or of the police or of the administration of the State.

3. Nothing in this Article shall authorize States Parties to the International Labour Organisation Convention of 1948 concerning Freedom of Association and Protection of the Right to Organize to take legislative measures which would prejudice, or apply the law in such a manner as would prejudice, the guarantees provided for in that Convention.

Article 9

The States Parties to the present Covenant recognize the right of everyone to social security, including social insurance.

Article 10

The States Parties to the present Covenant recognize that:

1. The widest possible protection and assistance should be accorded to the family, which is the natural and fundamental group unit of society, particularly for its establishment and while it is responsible for the care and education of dependent children. Marriage must be entered into with the free consent of the intending spouses.

2. Special protection should be accorded to mothers during a reasonable period before and after childbirth. During such period working mothers should be accorded paid leave or leave with adequate social security benefits.

3. Special measures of protection and assistance should be taken on behalf of all children and young persons without any discrimination for reasons of parentage or other conditions. Children and young persons should be protected from economic and social exploitation. Their employment in work harmful to their morals or health or dangerous to life or likely to hamper their normal development should be punishable by law. States should also set age limits below which the paid employment of child labour should be prohibited and punishable by law.

Article 11

1. The States Parties to the present Covenant recognize the right of everyone to an adequate standard of living for himself and his family, including adequate food, clothing and housing, and to the continuous improvement of living conditions. The States Parties will take appropriate steps to ensure the realization of this right, recognizing to this effect the essential importance of international co-operation based on free consent.

2. The States Parties to the present Covenant, recognizing the fundamental right of everyone to be free from hunger, shall take, individually and through international co-operation, the measures, including specific programmes, which are needed:

a. to improve methods of production, conservation and distribution of food by making full use of technical and scientific knowledge, by disseminating knowledge of the principles of nutrition and by developing or reforming agrarian systems in such a way as to achieve the most efficient development and utilization of natural resources;

b. taking into account the problems of both food-importing and food-exporting countries, to ensure an equitable distribution of world food supplies in relation to need.

Article 12

1. The States Parties to the present Covenant recognize the right of everyone to the enjoyment of the highest attainable standard of physical and mental health.

2. The steps to be taken by the States Parties to the present Covenant to achieve the full realization of this right shall include those necessary for:

a. the provision for the reduction of the stillbirth-rate and of infant mortality and for the healthy development of the child;

b. the improvement of all aspects of environmental and industrial hygiene;

c. the prevention, treatment and control of epidemic, endemic, occupational and other diseases;

d. the creation of conditions which would assure to all medical service and medical attention in the event of sickness.

Article 13

1. The States Parties to the present Covenant recognize the right of everyone to education. They agree that education shall be directed to the full development of the human personality and the sense of its dignity, and shall strengthen the respect for human rights and fundamental freedoms. They further agree that education shall enable all persons to participate effectively in a free society, promote understanding, tolerance and friendship among all nations and all racial, ethnic or religious groups,

and further the activities of the United Nations for the maintenance of peace.

2. The States Parties to the present Covenant recognize that, with a view to achieving the full realization of this right:

a. primary education shall be compulsory and available free to all;

b. secondary education in its different forms, including technical and vocational secondary education, shall be made generally available and accessible to all by every appropriate means, and in particular by the progressive introduction of free education;

c. higher education shall be made equally accessible to all, on the basis of capacity, by every appropriate means, and in particular by the progressive introduction of free education;

d. fundamental education shall be encouraged or intensified as far as possible for those persons who have not received or completed the whole period of their primary education;

e. the development of a system of schools at all levels shall be actively pursued, an adequate fellowship system shall be established, and the material conditions of teaching staff shall be continuously improved.

3. The States Parties to the present Covenant undertake to have respect for the liberty of parents and, when applicable, legal guardians to choose for their children schools, other than those established by the public authorities, which conform to such minimum educational standards as may be laid down or approved by the State and to ensure the religious and moral education of their children in conformity with their own convictions.

4. No part of this Article shall be construed so as to interfere with the liberty of individuals and bodies to establish and direct educational institutions, subject always to the observance of the principles set forth in paragraph 1 of this Article and to the requirement that the education given in such institutions shall conform to such minimum standards as may be laid down by the State.

Article 14

Each State Party to the present Covenant which, at the time of becoming a Party, has not been able to secure in its metropolitan territory or other territories under its jurisdiction compulsory primary education, free of charge, undertakes, within two years, to work out and adopt a detailed plan of action for the progressive implementation, within a reasonable number of years, to be fixed in the plan, of the principle of compulsory education free of charge for all.

Article 15

1. The States Parties to the present Covenant recognize the right of everyone:

a. to take part in cultural life;
b. to enjoy the benefits of scientific progress and its applications;
c. to benefit from the protection of the moral and material interests resulting from any scientific, literary or artistic production of which he is the author.

2. The steps to be taken by the States Parties to the present Covenant to achieve the full realization of this right shall include those necessary for the conservation, the development and the diffusion of science and culture.

3. The States Parties to the present Covenant undertake to respect the freedom indispensable for scientific research and creative activity.

4. The States Parties to the present Covenant recognize the benefits to be derived from the encouragement and development of international contacts and co-operation in the scientific and cultural fields.

Part IV

Article 16

1. The States Parties to the present Covenant undertake to submit in conformity with this part of the Covenant reports on the measures which

they have adopted and the progress made in achieving the observance of the rights recognized herein.

2.a. All reports shall be submitted to the Secretary General of the United Nations, who shall transmit copies to the Economic and Social Council for consideration in accordance with the provisions of the present Covenant;

b. The Secretary General of the United Nations shall also transmit to the specialized agencies copies of the reports, or any relevant parts therefrom, from States Parties to the present Covenant which are also members of these specialized agencies in so far as these reports, or parts therefrom, relate to any matters which fall within the responsibilities of the said agencies in accordance with their constitutional instruments.

Article 17

1. The States Parties to the present Covenant shall furnish their reports in stages, in accordance with a programme to be established by the Economic and Social Council within one year of the entry into force of the present Covenant after consultation with the States Parties and the specialized agencies concerned.

2. Reports may indicate factors and difficulties affecting the degree of fulfilment of obligations under the present Covenant.

3. Where relevant information has previously been furnished to the United Nations or to any specialized agency by any State Party to the present Covenant, it will not be necessary to reproduce that information, but a precise reference to the information so furnished will suffice.

Article 18

Pursuant to its responsibilities under the Charter of the United Nations in the field of human rights and fundamental freedoms, the Economic and Social Council may make arrangements with the specialized agencies in respect of their reporting to it on the progress made in achieving the observance of the provisions of the present Covenant falling within the scope of their activities. These reports may include particulars of decisions and recommendations on such implementation adopted by their competent organs.

Article 19

The Economic and Social Council may transmit to the Commission on Human Rights for study and general recommendation or, as appropriate, for information the reports concerning human rights submitted by States in accordance with Articles 16 and 17, and those concerning human rights submitted by the specialized agencies in accordance with Article 18.

Article 20

The States Parties to the present Covenant and the specialized agencies concerned may submit comments to the Economic and Social Council on any general recommendation under Article 19 or reference to such general recommendation in any report of the Commission on Human Rights or any documentation referred to therein.

Article 21

The Economic and Social Council may submit from time to time to the General Assembly reports with recommendations of a general nature and a summary of the information received from the States Parties to the present Covenant and the specialized agencies on the measures taken and the progress made in achieving general observance of the rights recognized in the present Covenant.

Article 22

The Economic and Social Council may bring to the attention of other organs of the United Nations, their subsidiary organs and specialized agencies concerned with furnishing technical assistance any matters arising out of the reports referred to in this part of the present Covenant which may assist such bodies in deciding, each within its field of competence, on the advisability of international measures likely to contribute to the effective progressive implementation of the present Covenant.

Article 23

The States Parties to the present Covenant agree that international action for the achievement of the rights recognized in the present Covenant includes such methods as the conclusion of conventions, the adoption of recommendations, the furnishing of technical assistance and the holding of regional meetings and technical meetings for the purpose of consultation and study organized in conjunction with the Governments concerned.

Article 24

Nothing in the present Covenant shall be interpreted as impairing the provisions of the Charter of the United Nations and of the constitutions of the specialized agencies which define the respective responsibilities of the various organs of the United Nations and of the specialized agencies in regard to the matters dealt with in the present Covenant.

Article 25

Nothing in the present Covenant shall be interpreted as impairing the inherent right of all peoples to enjoy and utilize fully and freely their natural wealth and resources.

Part V

Article 26

1. The present Covenant is open for signature by any State member of the United Nations or member of any of its specialized agencies, by any State Party to the Statute of the International Court of Justice, and by any other State which has been invited by the General Assembly of the United Nations to become a party to the present Covenant.

2. The present Covenant is subject to ratification. Instruments of ratification shall be deposited with the Secretary General oft the United Nations.

3. The present Covenant shall be open to accession by any State referred to in paragraph 1 of this Article.

4. Accession shall be effected by the deposit of an instrument of accession with the Secretary General of the United Nations.

5. The Secretary General of the United Nations shall inform all States which have signed the present Covenant or acceded to it of the deposit of each instrument of ratification or accession.

Article 27

1. The present Covenant shall enter into force three months after the date of the deposit with the Secretary General of the United Nations of the thirty-fifth instrument of ratification or instrument of accession.

2. For each State ratifying the present Covenant or acceding to it after the deposit of the thirty-fifth instrument of ratification or instrument of accession, the present Covenant shall enter into force three months after the date of the deposit of its own instrument of ratification or instrument of accession.

Article 28

The provisions of the present Covenant shall extend to all parts of federal States without any limitations or exceptions.

Article 29

1. Any State Party to the present Covenant may propose an amendment and file it with the Secretary General of the United Nations. The Secretary General shall thereupon communicate any proposed amendments to the States Parties to the present Covenant with a request that they notify him whether they favour a conference of States Parties for the purpose of

considering and voting upon the proposals. In the event that at least one-third of the States Parties favours such a conference, the Secretary General shall convene the conference under the auspices of the United Nations. Any amendment adopted by a majority of the States Parties present and voting at the conference shall be submitted to the General Assembly of the United Nations for approval.

2. Amendments shall come into force when they have been approved by the General Assembly of the United Nations and accepted by a two-thirds majority of the States Parties to the present Covenant in accordance with their respective constitutional processes.

3. When amendments come into force they shall be binding on those States Parties which have accepted them, other States Parties still being bound by the provisions of the present Covenant and any earlier amendment which they have accepted.

Article 30

Irrespective of the notifications made under Article 26, paragraph 5, the Secretary General of the United Nations shall inform all States referred to in paragraph 1 of the same Article of the following particulars:

a. signatures, ratifications and accessions under Article 26;

b. the date of the entry into force of the present Covenant under Article 27 and the date of the entry into force of any amendments under Article 29.

Article 31

1. The present Covenant, of which the Chinese, English, French, Russian and Spanish texts are equally authentic, shall be deposited in the archives of the United Nations.

2. The Secretary General of the United Nations shall transmit certified copies of the present Covenant to all States referred to in Article 26.

3. **International Covenant on Civil and Political Rights**

Adopted and opened for signature, ratification and accession by General Assembly Resolution 2200 A (XXI) of 16 December 1966

Entry into force: 23 March 1976,
in accordance with Article 49

Preamble

The States Parties to the present Covenant,

Considering that, in accordance with the principles proclaimed in the Charter of the United Nations, recognition of the inherent dignity and of the equal and inalienable rights of all members of the human family is the foundation of freedom, justice and peace in the world,

Recognizing that these rights derive from the inherent dignity of the human person,

Recognizing that, in accordance with the Universal Declaration of Human rights, the ideal of free human beings enjoying civil and political freedom and freedom from fear and want can only be achieved if conditions are created whereby everyone may enjoy his civil and political rights, as well as his economic, social and cultural rights,

Considering the obligation of States under the Charter of the United Nations to promote universal respect for, and observance of, human rights and freedoms,

Realizing that the individual, having duties to other individuals and to the community to which he belongs, is under a responsibility to strive for the promotion and observance of the rights recognized in the present Covenant,

Agree upon the following Articles:

Part I

Article 1

1. All peoples have the right of self-determination. By virtue of that right they freely determine their political status and freely pursue their economic, social and cultural development.

2. All peoples may, for their own ends, freely dispose of their natural wealth and resources without prejudice to any obligations arising out of international economic co-operation, based upon the principle of mutual benefit, and international law. In no case may a people be deprived of its own means of subsistence.

3. The States Parties to the present Covenant, including those having responsibility for the administration of Non-Self-Governing and Trust Territories, shall promote the realization of the right of self-determination, and shall respect that right, in conformity with the provisions of the Charter of the United Nations.

Part II

Article 2

1. Each State Party to the present Covenant undertakes to respect and to ensure to all individuals within its territory and subject to its jurisdiction the rights recognized in the present Covenant, without distinction of any kind, such as race, colour, sex, language, religion, political or other opinion, national or social origin, property, birth or other status.

2. Where not already provided for by existing legislative or other measures, each State Party to the present Covenant undertakes to take

the necessary steps, in accordance with its constitutional processes and with the provisions of the present Covenant, to adopt such legislative or other measures as may be necessary to give effect to the rights recognized in the present Covenant.

3. Each State Party to the present Covenant undertakes:

a. to ensure that any person whose rights or freedoms as herein recognized are violated shall have an effective remedy, notwithstanding that the violation has been committed by persons acting in an official capacity;
b. to ensure that any person claiming such a remedy shall have his right thereto determined by competent judicial, administrative or legislative authorities, or by any other competent authority provided for by the legal system of the State, and to develop the possibilities of judicial remedy;
c. to ensure that the competent authorities shall enforce such remedies when granted.

Article 3

The States Parties to the present Covenant undertake to ensure the equal right of men and women to the enjoyment of all civil and political rights set forth in the present Covenant.

Article 4

1. In time of public emergency which threatens the life of the nation and the existence of which is officially proclaimed, the States Parties to the present Covenant may take measures derogating from their obligations under the present Covenant to the extent strictlx reqtired by the exigencies of the situation, provided that such measures are not inconsistent with their other obligations under international law and do not involve discrimination solely on the ground of race, colour, sex, language, religion or social origin.

2. No derogation from Articles 6, 7, 8 (paragraphs 1 and 2), 11, 15, 16 and 18 may be made under this provision.

3. Any State Party to the present Covenant availing itself of the right of derogation shall immediately inform the other States Parties to the present Covenant, through the intermediary of the Secretary General of the United Nations, of the provisions from which it has derogated and of the reasons by which it was actuated. A further communication shall be made, through the same intermediary, on the date on which it terminates such derogation.

Article 5

1. Nothing in the present Covenant may be interpreted as implying for any State, group or person any right to engage in any activity or perform any act aimed at the destruction of any of the rights and freedoms recognized herein or at their limitation to a greater extent than is provided for in the present Covenant.

2. There shall be no restriction upon or derogation from any of the fundamental human rights recognized or existing in any State Party to the present Covenant pursuant to law, conventions, regulations or custom on the pretext that the present Covenant does not recognize such rights or that it recognizes them to a lesser extent.

Part III

Article 6

1. Every human being has the inherent right to life. This right shall be protected by law. No one shall be arbitrarily deprived of his life.

2. In countries which have not abolished the death penalty, sentence of death may be imposed only for the most serious crimes in accordance with the law in force at the time of the commission of the crime and not contrary to the provisions of the present Covenant and to the Convention on the Prevention and Punishment of the Crime of Genocide. This penalty can only be carried out pursuant to a final judgement rendered by a competent court.

3. When deprivation of life constitutes the crime of genocide, it is understood that nothing in this Article shall authorize any State Party to the present Covenant to derogate in any way from any obligation assumed under the provisions of the Convention on the Prevention and Punishment of the Crime of Genocide.

4. Anyone sentenced to death shall have the right to seek pardon or commutation of the sentence. Amnesty, pardon or commutation of the sentence of death may be granted in all cases.

5. Sentence of death shall not be imposed for crimes committed by persons below eighteen years of age and shall not be carried out on pregnant women.

6. Nothing in this Article shall be invoked to delay or to prevent the abolition of capital punishment by any State Party to the present Covenant.

Article 7

No one shall be subjected to torture or to cruel, inhuman or degrading treatment or punishment. In particular, no one shall be subjected without his free consent to medical or scientific experimentation.

Article 8

1. No one shall be held in slavery; slavery and the slave-trade in all their forms shall be prohibited.

2. No one shall be held in servitude.

3. a. No one shall be required to perform forced or compulsory labour;
b. Paragraph 3.*a* shall not be held to preclude, in countries where imprisonment with hard labour may be imposed as a punishment for a crime, the performance of hard labour in pursuance of a sentence to such punishment by a competent court;
c. For the purpose of this paragraph the term 'forced or compulsory labour' shall not include:

i. any work or service, not referred to in subparagraph *b*, normally required of a person who is under detention in consequence of a lawful order of a court, or of a person during conditional release from such detention;
ii. any service of a military character and, in countries where conscientious objection is recognized, any national service required by law of conscientious objectors;
iii. any service exacted in cases of emergency or calamity threatening the life or well-being of the community;
iv. any work or service which forms part of normal civil obligations.

Article 9

1. Everyone has the right to liberty and security of person. No one shall be subjected to arbitrary arrest or detention. No one shall be deprived of his liberty except on such grounds and in accordance with such procedure as are established by law.

2. Anyone who is arrested shall be informed, at the time of arrest, of the reasons for his arrest and shall be promptly informed of any charges against him.

3. Anyone arrested or detained on a criminal charge shall be brought promptly before a judge or other officer authorized by law to exercise judicial power and shall be entitled to trial within a reasonable time or to release. It shall not be the general rule that persons awaiting trial shall be detained in custody, but release may be subject to guarantees to appear for trial, at any other stage of the judicial proceedings, and, should occasion arise, for execution of the judgement.

4. Anyone who is deprived of his liberty by arrest or detention shall be entitled to take proceedings before a court, in order that that court may decide without delay on the lawfulness of his detention and order his release if the detention is not lawful.

5. Anyone who has been victim of unlawful arrest or detention shall have an enforceable right to compensation.

Article 10

1. All persons deprived of their liberty shall be treated with humanity and with respect for the inherent dignity of the human person.

2.a. Accused persons shall, save in exceptional circumstances, be segregated from convicted persons and shall be subject to separate treatment appropriate to their status as unconvicted persons;
b. Accused juvenile persons shall be separated from adults and brought as speedily as possible for adjudication.

3. The penitentiary system shall comprise treatment of prisoners the essential aim of which shall be their reformation and social rehabilitation. Juvenile offenders shall be segregated from adults and be accorded treatment appropriate to their age and legal status.

Article 11

No one shall be imprisoned merely on the ground of inability to fulfil a contractual obligation.

Article 12

1. Everyone lawfully within the territory of a State shall, within that territory, have the right to liberty of movement and freedom to choose his residence.

2. Everyone shall be free to leave any country, including his own.

3. The above-mentioned rights shall not be subject to any restrictions except those which are provided by law, are necessary to protect national security, public order *(ordre public)*, public health or morals or the rights and freedoms of others, and are consistent with the other rights recognized in the present Covenant.

4. No one shall be arbitrarily deprived of the right to enter his own country.

Article 13

An alien lawfully in the territory of a State Party to the present Covenant may be expelled therefrom only in pursuance of a decision reached in accordance with law and shall, except where compelling reasons of national security otherwise require, be allowed to submit the reasons against his expulsion and to have his case reviewed by, and be represented for the purpose before, the competent authority or a person or persons especially designated by the competent authority.

Article 14

1. All persons shall be equal before the courts and tribunals. In the determination of any criminal charge against him, or of his rights and obligations in a suit at law, everyone shall be entitled to a fair and public hearing by a competent, independent and impartial tribunal established by law. The press and the public may be excluded from all or part of a trial for reasons of morals, public order *(ordre public)* or national security in a democratic society, or when the interest of the private lives of the Parties so requires, or to the extent strictly necessary in the opinion of the court in special circumstances where publicity would prejudice the interests of justice; but any judgement rendered in a criminal case or in a suit at law shall be made public except where the interest of juvenile persons otherwise requires or the proceedings concern matrimonial disputes of the guardianship of children.

2. Everyone charged with a criminal offence shall have the right to be presumed innocent until proved guilty according to law.

3. In the determination of any criminal charge against him, everyone shall be entitled to the following minimum guarantees, in full equality:

a. to be informed promptly and in detail in a language which he understands of the nature and cause of the charge against him;
b. to have adequate time and facilities for the preparation of his defence and to communicate with counsel of his own choosing;
c. to be tried without undue delay;

d. to be tried in his presence, and to defend himself in person or through legal assistance of his own choosing; to be informed, if he does not have legal assistance, of this right; and to have legal assistance assigned to him, in any case where the interests of justice so require, and without payment by him in any such case if he does not have sufficient means to pay for it;

e. to examine, or have examined, the witnesses against him and to obtain the attendance and examination of witnesses on his behalf under the same conditions as witnesses against him;

f. to have the free assistance of an interpreter if he cannot understand or speak the language used in court;

g. not to be compelled to testify against himself or to confess guilt.

4. In the case of juvenile persons, the procedure shall be such as will take account of their age and the desirability of promoting their rehabilitation.

5. Everyone convicted of a crime shall have the right to his conviction and sentence being reviewed by a higher tribunal according to law.

6. When a person has by a final decision been convicted of a criminal offence and when subsequently his conviction has been reversed or he has been pardoned on the ground that a new or newly discovered fact shows conclusively that there has been a miscarriage of justice, the person who has suffered punishment as a result of such conviction shall be compensated according to law, unless it is proved that the non-disclosure of the unknown fact in time is wholly or partly attributable to him.

7. No one shall be liable to be tried or punished again for an offence for which he has already been finally convicted or acquitted in accordance with the law and penal procedure of each country.

Article 15

1. No one shall be held guilty of any criminal offence on account of any act or omission which did not constitute a criminal offence, under national or international law, at the time when it was committed. Nor shall a heavier penalty be imposed than the one that was applicable at

the time when the criminal offence was committed. If, subsequent to the commission of the offence, provision is made by law for the imposition of the lighter penalty, the offender shall benefit thereby.

2. Nothing in this Article shall prejudice the trial and punishment of any person for any act or omission which, at the time when it was committed, was criminal according to the general principles of law recognized by the community of nations.

Article 16

Everyone shall have the right to recognition everywhere as a person before the law.

Article 17

1. No one shall be subjected to arbitrary or unlawful interference with his privacy, family, home or correspondence, nor to unlawful attacks on his honour and reputation.

2. Everyone has the right to the protection of the law against such interference or attacks.

Article 18

1. Everyone shall have the right to freedom of thought, conscience and religion. This right shall include freedom to have or to adopt a religion or belief of his choice, and freedom, either individually or in community with others and in public or private, to manifest his religion or belief in worship, observance, practice and teaching.

2. No one shall be subject to coercion which would impair his freedom to have or to adopt a religion or belief of his choice.

3. Freedom to manifest one's religion or beliefs may be subject only to such limitations as are prescribed by law and are necessary to protect public safety, order, health, or morals or the fundamental rights and freedoms of others.

4. The States Parties to the present Covenant undertake to have respect for the liberty of parents and, when applicable, legal guardians to ensure the religious and moral education of their children in conformity with their own convictions.

Article 19

1. Everyone shall have the right to hold opinions without interference.

2. Everyone shall have the right to freedom of expression; this right shall include freedom to seek, receive and impart information and ideas of all kinds, regardless of frontiers, either orally, in writing or in print, in the form of art, or through any other media of his choice.

3. The exercise of the rights provided for in paragraph 2 of this Article carries with it special duties and responsibilities. It may therefore be subject to certain restrictions, but these shall only be such as are provided by law and are necessary:

a. for respect of the rights or reputations of others;
b. for the protection of national security or of public order *(ordre public)*, or of public health or morals.

Article 20

1. Any propaganda for war shall be prohibited by law.

2. Any advocacy of national, racial or religious hatred that constitutes incitement to discrimination, hostility or violence shall be prohibited by law.

Article 21

The right of peaceful assembly shall be recognized. No restrictions may be placed on the exercise of this right other than those imposed in conformity with the law and which are necessary in a democratic society in the interests of national security or public safety, public order *(ordre public)*, the protection of public health or morals or the protection of the rights and freedoms of others.

Article 22

1. Everyone shall have the right to freedom of association with others, including the right to form and join trade unions for the protection of his interests.

2. No restrictions may be placed on the exercise of this right other than those which are prescribed by law and which are necessary in a democratic society in the interests of national security or public safety, public order *(ordre public)*, the protection of public health or morals or the protection of the rights and freedoms of others. This Article shall not prevent the imposition of lawful restrictions on members of the armed forces and of the police in their exercise of this right.

3. Nothing in this Article shall authorize States Parties to the International Labour Organisation Convention of 1948 concerning Freedom of Association and Protection of the Right to Organize to take legislative measures which would prejudice, or to apply the law in such a manner as to prejudice the guarantees provided for in that Convention.

Article 23

1. The family is the natural and fundamental group unit of society and is entitled to protection by society and the State.

2. The right of men and women of marriageable age to marry and to found a family shall be recognized.

3. No marriage shall be entered into without the free and full consent of the intending spouses.

4. States Parties to the present Covenant shall take appropriate steps to ensure equality of rights and responsibilities of spouses as to marriage, during marriage and at its dissolution. In the case of dissolution, provision shall be made for the necessary protection of any children.

Article 24

1. Every child shall have, without any discrimination as to race, colour, sex, language, religion, national or social origin, property or birth, the right to such measures of protection as are required by his status as a minor, on the part of his family, society and the State.

2. Every child shall be registered immediately after birth and shall have a name.

3. Every child has the right to acquire a nationality.

Article 25

Every citizen shall have the right and the opportunity, without any of the distinctions mentioned in Article 2 and without unreasonable restrictions:

a. to take part in the conduct of public affairs, directly or through freely chosen representatives;

b. to vote and to be elected at genuine periodic elections which shall be by universal and equal suffrage and shall be held by secret ballot, guaranteeing the free expression of the will of the electors;

c. to have access, on general terms of equality, to public service in his country.

Article 26

All persons are equal before the law and are entitled without any discrimination to the equal protection of the law. In this respect, the law shall prohibit any discrimination and guarantee to all persons equal and effective protection against discrimination on any ground such as race, colour, sex, language, religion, political or other opinion, national or social origin, property, birth or other status.

Article 27

In those States in which ethnic, religious or linguistic minorities exist, persons belonging to such minorities shall not be denied the right, in community with the other members of their group, to enjoy their own culture, to profess and practise their own religion, or to use their own language.

Part IV

Article 28

1. There shall be established a Human Rights Committee (hereafter referred to in the present Covenant as the Committee). It shall consist of eighteen members and shall carry out the functions hereinafter provided.

2. The Committee shall be composed of nationals of the States Parties to the present Covenant who shall be persons of high moral character and recognized competence in the field of human rights, consideration being given to the usefulness of the participation of some persons having legal experience.

3. The members of the Committee shall be elected and shall serve in their personal capacity.

Article 29

1. The members of the Committee shall be elected by secret ballot from a list of persons possessing the qualifications prescribed in Article 28 and nominated for the purpose by the States Parties to the present Covenant.

2. Each State Party to the present Covenant may nominate not more than two persons. These persons shall be nationals of the nominating State.

3. A person shall be eligible for renomination.

Article 30

1. The initial election shall be held not later than six months after the date of the entry into force of the present Covenant.

2. At least four months before the date of each election to the Committee, other than an election to fill a vacancy declared in accordance with Article 34, the Secretary General of the United Nations shall address a written invitation to the States Parties to the present Covenant to submit their nominations for membership of the Committee within three months.

3. The Secretary General of the United Nations shall prepare a list in alphabetical order of all the persons thus nominated, with an indication of the States Parties which have nominated them, and shall submit it to the States Parties to the present Covenant no later than one month before the date of each election.

4. Elections of the members of the Committee shall be held at a meeting of the States Parties to the present Covenant convened by the Secretary General of the United Nations at the Headquarters of the United Nations. At that meeting, for which two-thirds of the States Parties to the present Covenant shall constitute a quorum, the persons elected to the Committee shall be those nominees who obtain the largest number of votes and an absolute majority of the votes of the representatives of States Parties present and voting.

Article 31

1. The Committee may not include more than one national of the same State.

2. In the election of the Committee, consideration shall be given to equitable geographical distribution of membership and to the representation of the different forms of civilization and of the principal legal systems.

Article 32

1. The members of the Committee shall be elected for a term of four years. They shall be eligible for re-election if renominated. However, the terms of nine of the members elected at the first election shall expire at the end of two years; immediately after the first election, the names of

these nine members shall be chosen by lot by the Chairman of the meeting referred to in Article 30, paragraph 4.

2. Elections at the expiry of office shall be held in accordance with the preceding Articles of this part of the present Covenant.

Article 33

1. If, in the unanimous opinion of the other members, a member of the Committee has ceased to carry out his functions for any cause other than absence of a temporary character, the Chairman of the Committee shall notify the Secretary General of the United Nations, who shall then declare the seat of that member to be vacant.

2. In the event of the death or the resignation of a member of the Committee, the Chairman shall immediately notify the Secretary General of the United Nations, who shall declare the seat vacant from the date of death or the date on which the resignation takes effect.

Article 34

1. When a vacancy is declared in accordance with Article 33 and if the term of office of the member to be replaced does not expire within six months of the declaration of the vacancy, the Secretary General of the United Nations shall notify each of the States Parties to the present Covenant, which may within two months submit nominations in accordance with Article 29 for the purpose of filling the vacancy.

2. The Secretary General of the United Nations shall prepare a list in alphabetical order of the persons thus nominated and shall submit it to the States Parties to the present Covenant. The election to fill the vacancy shall then take place in accordance with the relevant provisions of this part of the present Covenant.

3. A member of the Committee elected to fill a vacancy declared in accordance with Article 33 shall hold office for the remainder of the term of the member who vacated the seat on the Committee under the provisions of that Article.

Article 35

The members of the Committee shall, with the approval of the General Assembly of the United Nations, receive emoluments from United Nations resources on such terms and conditions as the General Assembly may decide, having regard to the importance of the Committee's responsibilities.

Article 36

The Secretary General of the United Nations shall provide the necessary staff and facilities for the effective performance of the functions of the Committee under the present Covenant.

Article 37

1. The Secretary General of the United Nations shall convene the initial meeting of the Committee at the Headquarters of the United Nations.

2. After its initial meeting, the Committee shall meet at such times as shall be provided in its rules of procedure.

3. The Committee shall normally meet at the Headquarters of the United Nations or at the United Nations Office at Geneva.

Article 38

Every member of the Committee shall, before taking up his duties, make a solemn declaration in open committee that he will perform his functions impartially and conscientiously.

Article 39

1. The Committee shall elect its officers for a term of two years. They may be re-elected.

2. The Committee shall establish its own rules of procedure, but these rules shall provide, *inter alia,* that:

a. twelve members shall constitute a quorum;

b. decisions of the Committee shall be made by a majority vote of the members present.

Article 40

1. The States Parties to the present Covenant undertake to submit reports on the measures they have adopted which give effect to the rights recognized herein and on the progress made in the enjoyment of those rights:

a. within one year of the entry into force of the present Covenant for the States Parties concerned;

b. thereafter whenever the Committee so requests.

2. All reports shall be submitted to the Secretary General of the United Nations, who shall transmit them to the Committee for consideration. Reports shall indicate the factors and difficulties, if any, affecting the implementation of the present Covenant.

3. The Secretary General of the United Nations may, after consultation with the Committee, transmit to the specialized agencies concerned copies of such parts of the reports as may fall within their field of competence.

4. The Committee shall study the reports submitted by the States Parties to the present Covenant. It shall transmit its reports, and such general comments as it may consider appropriate, to the States Parties. The Committee may also transmit to the Economic and Social Council these comments along with the copies of the reports it has received from States Parties to the present Covenant.

5. The States Parties to the present Covenant may submit to the Committee observations on any comments that may be made in accordance with paragraph 4 of this Article.

Article 41

1. A State Party to the present Covenant may at any time declare under this Article that it recognizes the competence of the Committee to receive and consider communications to the effect that a State Party claims that another State Party is not fulfilling its obligations under the present Covenant. Communications under this Article may be received and considered only if submitted by a State Party which has made a declaration recognizing in regard to itself the competence of the Committee. No communication shall be received by the Committee if it concerns a State Party which has not made such a declaration. Communications received under this Article shall be dealt with in accordance with the following procedure:

a. If a State Party to the present Covenant considers that another State Party is not giving effect to the provisions of the present Covenant, it may, by written communication, bring the matter to the attention of that State Party. Within three months after the receipt of the communication the receiving State shall afford the State which sent the communication an explanation, or any other statement in writing clarifying the matter which should include, to the extent possible and pertinent, reference to domestic procedures and remedies taken, pending, or available in the matter.

b. If the matter is not adjusted to the satisfaction of both States Parties concerned within six months after the receipt by the receiving State of the initial communication, either State shall have the right to refer the matter to the Committee, by notice given to the Committee and to the other State.

c. The Committee shall deal with a matter referred to it only after it has ascertained that all available domestic remedies have been invoked and exhausted in the matter, in conformity with the generally recognized principles of international law. This shall not be the rule where the application of the remedies is unreasonably prolonged.

d. The Committee shall hold closed meetings when examining communications under this Article.

e. Subject to the provisions of subparagraph *c*, the Committee shall make available its good offices to the States Parties concerned with a view to a friendly solution of the matter on the basis of respect for human rights and fundamental freedoms as recognized in the present Covenant.

f. In any matter referred to it, the Committee may call upon the States Parties concerned, referred to in subparagraph *b*, *to* supply any relevant information.

g. The States Parties concerned, referred to in subparagraph *b*, shall have the right to be represented when the matter is being considered in the Committee and to make submissions orally and/or in writing.

h. The Committee shall, within twelve months after the date of receipt of notice under subparagraph *b*, submit a report:

i. If a solution within the terms of subparagraph e is reached, the Committee shall confine its report to a brief statement of the facts and of the solution reached;

ii. If a solution within the terms of subparagraph e is not reached, the Committee shall confine its report to a brief statement of the facts; the written submissions and record of the oral submissions made by the States Parties concerned shall be attached to the report.

In every matter, the report shall be communicated to the States Parties concerned.

2. The provisions of this Article shall come into force when ten States Parties to the present Covenant have made declarations under paragraph 1 of this Article. Such declarations shall be deposited by the States Parties with the Secretary General of the United Nations, who shall transmit copies thereof to the other States Parties. A declaration may be withdrawn at any time by notification to the Secretary General. Such a withdrawal shall not prejudice the consideration of any matter which is the subject of a communication already transmitted under this Article; no further communication by any State Party shall be received after the notification of withdrawal of the declaration has been received by the Secretary General, unless the State Party concerned has made a new declaration.

Article 42

1.a. If a matter referred to the Committee in accordance with Article 41 is not resolved to the satisfaction of the States Parties concerned, the Committee may, with the prior consent of the States Parties concerned, appoint an *ad hoc* Conciliation Commission (hereafter referred to as the Commission). The good offices of the Commission shall be made available to the States Parties concerned with a view to an amicable solution of the matter on the basis of respect for the present Covenant.

b. The Commission shall consist of five persons acceptable to the States Parties concerned. If the States Parties concerned fail to reach agreement within three months on all or part of the composition of the Commission, the members of the Commission concerning whom no agreement has been reached shall be elected by secret ballot by a two-thirds majority vote of the Committee from among its members.

2. The members of the Commission shall serve in their personal capacity. They shall not be nationals of the States Parties concerned, or of a State not Party to the present Covenant, or of a State Party which has not made a declaration under Article 41.

3. The Commission shall elect its own Chairman and adopt its own rules of procedure.

4. The meetings of the Commission shall normally be held at the Headquarters of the United Nations or at the United Nations Office at Geneva. However, they may be held at such other convenient places as the Commission may determine in consultation with the Secretary General of the United Nations and the States Parties concerned.

5. The secretariat provided in accordance with Article 36 shall also service the commissions appointed under this Article.

6. The information received and collated by the Committee shall be made available to the Commission and the Commission may call upon the States Parties concerned to supply any other relevant information.

7. When the Commission has fully considered the matter, but in any event not later than twelve months after having been seized of the matter, it shall submit to the Chairman of the Committee a report for communication to the States Parties concerned:

a. If the Commission is unable to complete its consideration of the matter within twelve months, it shall confine its report to a brief statement of the status of its consideration of the matter;

b. If an amicable solution to the matter on the basis of respect for human rights as recognized in the present Covenant is reached, the Commission shall confine its report to a brief statement of the facts and of the solution reached;

c. If a solution within the terms of subparagraph *b* is not reached, the Commission's report shall embody its findings on all questions of fact relevant to the issues between the States Parties concerned, and its views on the possibilities of an amicable solution of the matter. This report shall also contain the written submissions and a record of the oral submissions made by the States Parties concerned;

d. If the Commission's report is submitted under subparagraph *c*, the States Parties concerned shall, within three months of the receipt of the report, notify the Chairman of the Committee whether or not they accept the contents of the report of the Commission.

8. The provisions of this Article are without prejudice to the responsibilities of the Committee under Article 41.

9. The States Parties concerned shall share equally all the expenses of the members of the Commission in accordance with estimates to be provided by the Secretary General of the United Nations.

10. The Secretary General of the United Nations shall be empowered to pay the expenses of the members of the Commission, if necessary, before reimbursement by the States Parties concerned, in accordance with paragraph 9 of this Article.

Article 43

The members of the Committee, and of the *ad hoc* conciliation commissions which may be appointed under Article 42, shall be entitled to the facilities, privileges and immunities of experts on mission for the United Nations as laid down in the relevant sections of the Convention on the Privileges and Immunities of the United Nations.

Article 44

The provisions for the implementation of the present Covenant shall apply without prejudice to the procedures prescribed in the field of human rights by or under the constituent instruments and the conventions of the United Nations and of the specialized agencies and shall not prevent the States Parties to the present Covenant from having recourse to other procedures for settling a dispute in accordance with general or special international agreements in force between them.

Article 45

The Committee shall submit to the General Assembly of the United Nations, through the Economic and Social Council, an annual report on its activities.

Part V

Article 46

Nothing in the present Covenant shall be interpreted as impairing the provisions of the Charter of the United Nations and of the constitutions of the specialized agencies which define the respective responsibilities of the various organs of the United Nations and of the specialized agencies in regard to the matters dealt with in the present Covenant.

Article 47

Nothing in the present Covenant shall be interpreted as impairing the inherent right of all peoples to enjoy and utilize fully and freely their natural wealth and resources.

Part VI

Article 48

1. The present Covenant is open for signature by any State Member of the United Nations or member of any of its specialized agencies, by any State Party to the Statute of the International Court of Justice, and by any other State which has been invited by the General Assembly of the United Nations to become a Party to the present Covenant.

2. The present Covenant is subject to ratification. Instruments of ratification shall be deposited with the Secretary General of the United Nations.

3. The present Covenant shall be open to accession by any State referred to in paragraph 1 of this Article.

4. Accession shall be effected by the deposit of an instrument of accession with the Secretary General of the United Nations.

5. The Secretary General of the United Nations shall inform all States which have signed this Covenant or acceded to it of the deposit of each instrument of ratification or accession.

Article 49

1. The present Covenant shall enter into force three months after the date of the deposit with the Secretary General of the United Nations of the thirty-fifth instrument of ratification or instrument of accession.

2. For each State ratifying the present Covenant or acceding to it after the deposit of the thirty-fifth instrument of ratification or instrument of accession, the present Covenant shall enter into force three months after the date of the deposit of its own instrument of ratification or instrument of accession.

Article 50

The provisions of the present Covenant shall extend to all parts of federal States without any limitations or exceptions.

Article 51

1. Any State Party to the present Covenant may propose an amendment and file it with the Secretary General of the United Nations. The Secretary General of the United Nations shall thereupon communicate any proposed amendments to the States Parties to the present Covenant with a request that they notify him whether they favour a conference of States Parties for the purpose of considering and voting upon the proposals. In the event that at least one-third of the States Parties favours such a conference, the Secretary General shall convene the conference under the auspices of the United Nations. Any amendment adopted by a majority of the States Parties present and voting at the conference shall be submitted to the General Assembly of the United Nations for approval.

2. Amendments shall come into force when they have been approved by the General Assembly of the United Nations and accepted by a two-thirds majority of the States Parties to the present Covenant in accordance with their respective constitutional processes.

3. When amendments come into force, they shall be binding on those States Parties which have accepted them, other States Parties still being bound by the provisions of the present Covenant and any earlier amendment which they have accepted.

Article 52

Irrespective of the notifications made under Article 48, paragraph 5, the Secretary General of the United Nations shall inform all States referred to in paragraph 1 of the same Article of the following particulars:

a. signatures, ratifications and accessions under Article 48;

b. the date of the entry into force of the present Covenant under Article 49 and the date of the entry into force of any amendments under Article 51.

Article 53

1. The present Covenant, of which the Chinese, English, French, Russian and Spanish texts are equally authentic, shall be deposited in the archives of the United Nations.

2. The Secretary General of the United Nations shall transmit certified copies of the present Covenant to all States referred to in Article 48.

4. **Optional Protocol to the International Covenant on Civil and Political Rights**

Adopted and opened for signature, ratification and accession by General Assembly Resolution 2200 A (XXI) of 16 December 1966

Entry into force: 23 March 1976, in accordance with Article 9

The States Parties to the present Protocol,

Considering that in order further to achieve the purposes of the International Covenant on Civil and Political Rights (hereinafter referred to as the Covenant) and the implementation of its provisions it would be appropriate to enable the Human Rights Committee set up in Part IV of the Covenant (hereinafter referred to as the Committee) to receive and consider, as provided in the present Protocol, communications from individuals claiming to be victims of violations of any of the rights set forth in the Covenant,

Have agreed as follows:

Article 1

A State Party to the Covenant that becomes a Party to the present Protocol recognizes the competence of the Committee to receive and consider communications from individuals subject to its jurisdiction who claim to be victims of a violation by that State Party of any of the rights set forth in the Covenant. No communication shall be received by the Committee if it concerns a State Party to the Covenant which is not a Party to the present Protocol.

Article 2

Subject to the provisions of Article 1, individuals who claim that any of their rights enumerated in the Covenant have been violated and who have exhausted all available domestic remedies may submit a written communication to the Committee for consideration.

Article 3

The Committee shall consider inadmissible any communication under the present Protocol which is anonymous, or which it considers to be an abuse of the right of submission of such communications or to be incompatible with the provisions of the Covenant.

Article 4

1. Subject to the provisions of Article 3, the Committee shall bring any communications submitted to it under the present Protocol to the attention of the State Party to the present Protocol alleged to be violating any provision of the Covenant.

2. Within six months, the receiving State shall submit to the Committee written explanations or statements clarifying the matter and the remedy, if any, that may have been taken by that State.

Article 5

1. The Committee shall consider communications received under the present Protocol in the light of all written information made available to it by the individual and by the State Party concerned.

2. The Committee shall not consider any communication from an individual unless it has ascertained that:

a. the same matter is not being examined under another procedure of international investigation or settlement;

b. the individual has exhausted all available domestic remedies. This shall not be the rule where the application of the remedies is unreasonably prolonged.

3. The Committee shall hold closed meetings when examining communications under the present Protocol.

4. The Committee shall forward its views to the State Party concerned and to the individual.

Article 6

The Committee shall include in its annual report under Article 45 of the Covenant a summary of its activities under the present Protocol.

Article 7

Pending the achievement of the objectives of Resolution 1514 (XV) adopted by the General Assembly of the United Nations on 14 December 1960 concerning the Declaration on the Granting of Independence to Colonial Countries and Peoples, the provisions of the present Protocol shall in no way limit the right of petition granted to these peoples by the Charter of the United Nations and other international conventions and instruments under the United Nations and its specialized agencies.

Article 8

1. The present Protocol is open for signature by any State which has signed the Covenant.

2. The present Protocol is subject to ratification by any State which has ratified or acceded to the Covenant. Instruments of ratification shall be deposited with the Secretary General of the United Nations.

3. The present Protocol shall be open to accession by any State which has ratified or acceded to the Covenant.

4. Accession shall be effected by the deposit of an instrument of accession with the Secretary General of the United Nations.

5. The Secretary General of the United Nations shall inform all States which have signed the present Protocol or acceded to it of the deposit of each instrument of ratification or accession.

Article 9

1. Subject to the entry into force of the Covenant, the present Protocol shall enter into force three months after the date of the deposit with the Secretary General of the United Nations of the tenth instrument of ratification or instrument of accession.

2. For each State ratifying the present Protocol or acceding to it after the deposit of the tenth instrument of ratification or instrument of accession, the present Protocol shall enter into force three months after the date of the deposit of its own instrument of ratification or instrument of accession.

Article 10

The provisions of the present Protocol shall extend to all parts of federal States without any limitations or exceptions.

Article 11

1. Any State Party to the present Protocol may propose an amendment and file it with the Secretary General of the United Nations. The Secretary General shall thereupon communicate any proposed amendments to the States Parties to the present Protocol with a request that they notify him whether they favour a conference of States Parties for the purpose of considering and voting upon the proposal. In the event that at least one third of the States Parties favours such a conference, the Secretary General shall convene the conference under the auspices of the United Nations. Any amendment adopted by a majority of the States Parties present and voting at the conference shall be submitted to the General Assembly of the United Nations for approval.

2. Amendments shall come into force when they have been approved by the General Assembly of the United Nations and accepted by a two-thirds majority of the States Parties to the present Protocol in accordance with their respective constitutional processes.

3. When amendments come into force, they shall be binding on those States Parties which have accepted them, other States Parties still being

bound by the provisions of the present Protocol and any earlier amendment which they have accepted.

Article 12

1. Any State Party may denounce the present Protocol at any time by written notification addressed to the Secretary General of the United Nations. Denunciation shall take effect three months after the date of receipt of the notification by the Secretary General.

2. Denunciation shall be without prejudice to the continued application of the provisions of the present Protocol to any communication submitted under Article 2 before the effective date of denunciation.

Article 13

Irrespective of the notifications made under Article 8, paragraph 5, of the present Protocol, the Secretary General of the United Nations shall inform all States referred to in Article 48, paragraph 1, of the Covenant of the following particulars:

a. signatures, ratifications and accessions under Article 8;

b. the date of the entry into force of the present Protocol under Article 9 and the date of the entry into force of any amendment under Article 11;

c. denunciations under Article 12.

Article 14

1. The present Protocol, of which the Chinese, English, French, Russian and Spanish texts are equally authentic, shall be deposited in the archives of the United Nations.

2. The Secretary General of the United Nations shall transmit certified copies of the present Protocol to all States referred to in Article 48 of the Covenant.

5. **Second Optional Protocol to the International Covenant on Civil and Political Rights, aiming at the abolition of the death penalty**

Adopted and opened for signature, ratification and acceptance by General Assembly Resolution 44/128 of 15 December 1989

The States Parties to the present Protocol,

Believing that abolition of the death penalty contributes to enhancement of human dignity and progressive development of human rights,

Recalling Article 3 of the Universal Declaration of Human Rights adopted on 10 December 1948 and Article 6 of the International Covenant on Civil and Political Rights adopted on 16 December 1966,

Noting that Article 6 of the International Covenant on Civil and Political Rights refers to abolition of the death penalty in terms that strongly suggest that abolition is desirable,

Convinced that all measures of abolition of the death penalty should be considered as progress in the enjoyment of the right to life,

Desirous to undertake hereby an international commitment to abolish the death penalty,

Have agreed as follows:

Article 1

1. No one within the jurisdiction of a State Party to the present Protocol shall be executed.

2. Each State Party shall take all necessary measures to abolish the death penalty within its jurisdiction.

Article 2

1. No reservation is admissible to the present Protocol, except for a reservation made at the time of ratification or accession that provides for the application of the death penalty in time of war pursuant to a conviction for a most serious crime of a military nature committed during wartime.

2. The State Party making such a reservation shall at the time of ratification or accession communicate to the Secretary General of the United Nations the relevant provisions of its national legislation applicable during wartime.

3. The State Party having made such a reservation shall notify the Secretary General of the United Nations of any beginning or ending of a state of war applicable to its territory.

Article 3

The States Parties to the present Protocol shall include in the reports they submit to the Human Rights Committee, in accordance with Article 40 of the Covenant, information on the measures that they have adopted to give effect to the present Protocol.

Article 4

With respect to the States Parties to the Covenant that have made a declaration under Article 41, the competence of the Human Rights Committee to receive and consider communications when a State Party claims that another State Party is not fulfilling its obligations shall extend to the provisions of the present Protocol, unless the State Party concerned has made a statement to the contrary at the moment of ratification or accession.

Article 5

With respect to the States Parties to the first Optional Protocol to the International Covenant on Civil and Political Rights adopted on 16 December 1966, the competence of the Human Rights Committee to receive and consider communications from individuals subject to its jurisdiction shall extend to the provisions of the present Protocol, unless the State Party concerned has made a statement to the contrary at the moment of ratification or accession.

Article 6

1. The provisions of the present Protocol shall apply as additional provisions to the Covenant.

2. Without prejudice to the possibility of a reservation under Article 2 of the present Protocol, the right guaranteed in Article 1, paragraph 1, of the present Protocol shall not be subject to any derogation under Article 4 of the Covenant.

Article 7

1. The present Protocol is open for signature by any State that has signed the Covenant.

2. The present Protocol is subject to ratification by any State that has ratified the Covenant or acceded to it. Instruments of ratification shall be deposited with the Secretary General of the United Nations.

3. The present Protocol shall be open to accession by any State that has ratified the Covenant or acceded to it.

4. Accession shall be effected by the deposit of an instrument of accession with the Secretary General of the United Nations.

5. The Secretary General of the United Nations shall inform all States that have signed the present Protocol or acceded to it of the deposit of each instrument of ratification or accession.

Article 8

1. The present Protocol shall enter into force three months after the date of the deposit with the Secretary General of the United Nations of the tenth instrument of ratification or accession.

2. For each State ratifying the present Protocol or acceding to it after the deposit of the tenth instrument of ratification or accession, the present Protocol shall enter into force three months after the date of the deposit of its own instrument of ratification or accession.

Article 9

The provisions of the present Protocol shall extend to all parts of federal States without any limitations or exceptions.

Article 10

The Secretary General of the United Nations shall inform all States referred to in Article 48, paragraph 1, of the Covenant of the following particulars:

a. reservations, communications and notifications under Article 2 of the present Protocol;

b. statements made under Articles 4 or 5 of the present Protocol;

c. signatures, ratifications and accessions under Article 7 of the present Protocol;

d. the date of the entry into force of the present Protocol under Article 8 thereof.

Article 11

1. The present Protocol, of which the Arabic, Chinese, English, French, Russian and Spanish texts are equally authentic, shall be deposited in the archives of the United Nations.

2. The Secretary General of the United Nations shall transmit certified copies of the present Protocol to all States referred to in Article 48 of the Covenant.

6. International Convention on the Elimination of All Forms of Racial Discrimination

Adopted and opened for signature and ratification by General Assembly Resolution 2106 A (XX) of 21 December 1965

Entry into force: 4 January 1969, in accordance with Article 19

The States Parties to this Convention,

Considering that the Charter of the United Nations is based on the principles of the dignity and equality inherent in all human beings, and that all Member States have pledged themselves to take joint and separate action, in co-operation with the Organization, for the achievement of one of the purposes of the United Nations which is to promote and encourage universal respect for and observance of human rights and fundamental freedoms for all, without distinction as to race, sex, language or religion,

Considering that the Universal Declaration of Human Rights proclaims that all human beings are born free and equal in dignity and rights and that everyone is entitled to all the rights and freedoms set out therein, without distinction of any kind, in particular as to race, colour or national origin,

Considering that all human beings are equal before the law and are entitled to equal protection of the law against any discrimination and against any incitement to discrimination,

Considering that the United Nations has condemned colonialism and all practices of segregation and discrimination associated therewith, in whatever form and wherever they exist, and that the Declaration on the Granting of Independence to Colonial Countries and Peoples of

14 December 1960 (General Assembly Resolution 1514 (XV)) has affirmed and solemnly proclaimed the necessity of bringing them to a speedy and unconditional end,

Considering that the United Nations Declaration on the Elimination of All Forms of Racial Discrimination of 20 November 1963 (General Assembly Resolution 1904 (XVIII)) solemnly affirms the necessity of speedily eliminating racial discrimination throughout the world in all its forms and manifestations and of securing understanding of and respect for the dignity of the human person,

Convinced that any doctrine of superiority based on racial differentiation is scientifically false, morally condemnable, socially unjust and dangerous, and that there is no justification for racial discrimination, in theory or in practice, anywhere,

Reaffirming that discrimination between human beings on the grounds of race, colour or ethnic origin is an obstacle to friendly and peaceful relations among nations and is capable of disturbing peace and security among peoples and the harmony of persons living side by side even within one and the same State,

Convinced that the existence of racial barriers is repugnant to the ideals of any human society,

Alarmed by manifestations of racial discrimination still in evidence in some areas of the world and by governmental policies based on racial superiority or hatred, such as policies of *apartheid*, segregation or separation,

Resolved to adopt all necessary measures for speedily eliminating racial discrimination in all its forms and manifestations, and to prevent and combat racist doctrines and practices in order to promote understanding between races and to build an international community free from all forms of racial segregation and racial discrimination,

Bearing in mind the Convention concerning Discrimination in respect of Employment and Occupation adopted by the International Labour Organisation in 1958, and the Convention against Discrimination in Education adopted by the United Nations Educational, Scientific and Cultural Organisation in 1960,

Desiring to implement the principles embodied in the United Nations Declaration on the Elimination of All Forms of Racial Discrimination and to secure the earliest adoption of practical measures to that end,

Have agreed as follows:

Part I

Article 1

1. In this Convention, the term 'racial discrimination' shall mean any distinction, exclusion, restriction or preference based on race, colour, descent, or national or ethnic origin which has the purpose or effect of nullifying or impairing the recognition, enjoyment or exercise, on an equal footing, of human rights and fundamental freedoms in the political, economic, social, cultural or any other field of public life.

2. This Convention shall not apply to distinctions, exclusions, restrictions or preferences made by a State Party to this Convention between citizens and non-citizens.

3. Nothing in this Convention may be interpreted as affecting in any way the legal provisions of States Parties concerning nationality, citizenship or naturalization, provided that such provisions do not discriminate against any particular nationality.

4. Special measures taken for the sole purpose of securing adequate advancement of certain racial or ethnic groups or individuals requiring such protection as may be necessary in order to ensure such groups or individuals equal enjoyment or exercise of human rights and fundamental

freedoms shall not be deemed racial discrimination, provided, however, that such measures do not, as a consequence, lead to the maintenance of separate rights for different racial groups and that they shall not be continued after the objectives for which they were taken have been achieved.

Article 2

1. States Parties condemn racial discrimination and undertake to pursue by all appropriate means and without delay a policy of eliminating racial discrimination in all its forms and promoting understanding among all races, and, to this end:

a. Each State Party undertakes to engage in no act or practice of racial discrimination against persons, groups of persons or institutions and to ensure that all public authorities and public institutions, national and local, shall act in conformity with this obligation;

b. Each State Party undertakes not to sponsor, defend or support racial discrimination by any persons or organizations;

c. Each State Party shall take effective measures to review governmental, national and local policies, and to amend, rescind or nullify any laws and regulations which have the effect of creating or perpetuating racial discrimination wherever it exists;

d. Each State Party shall prohibit and bring to an end, by all appropriate means, including legislation as required by circumstances, racial discrimination by any persons, group or organization;

e. Each State Party undertakes to encourage, where appropriate, integrationalist multiracial organizations and movements and other means of eliminating barriers between races, and to discourage anything which tends to strengthen racial division.

2. States Parties shall, when the circumstances so warrant, take, in the social, economic, cultural and other fields, special and concrete measures to ensure the adequate development and protection of certain racial groups or individuals belonging to them, for the purpose of guaranteeing them the full and equal enjoyment of human rights and fundamental

freedoms. These measures shall in no case entail as a consequence the maintenance of unequal or separate rights for different racial groups after the objectives for which they were taken have been achieved.

Article 3

States Parties particularly condemn racial segregation and *apartheid* and undertake to prevent, prohibit and eradicate all practices of this nature in territories under their jurisdiction.

Article 4

States Parties condemn all propaganda and all organizations which are based on ideas or theories of superiority of one race or group of persons of one colour or ethnic origin, or which attempt to justify or promote racial hatred and discrimination in any form, and undertake to adopt immediate and positive measures designed to eradicate all incitement to, or acts of, such discrimination and, to this end, with due regard to the principles embodied in the Universal Declaration of Human Rights and the rights expressly set forth in Article 5 of this Convention, *inter alia*:

a. shall declare an offence punishable by law all dissemination of ideas based on racial superiority or hatred, incitement to racial discrimination, as well as all acts of violence or incitement to such acts against any race or group of persons of another colour or ethnic origin, and also the provision of any assistance to racist activities, including the financing thereof;

b. shall declare illegal and prohibit organizations, and also organized and all other propaganda activities, which promote and incite racial discrimination, and shall recognize participation in such organizations or activities as an offence punishable by law;

c. shall not permit public authorities or public institutions, national or local, to promote or incite racial discrimination.

Article 5

In compliance with the fundamental obligations laid down in Article 2 of this Convention, States Parties undertake to prohibit and to eliminate racial discrimination in all its forms and to guarantee the right of everyone, without distinction as to race, colour, or national or ethnic origin, to equality before the law, notably in the enjoyment of the following rights:

a. the right to equal treatment before the tribunals and all other organs administering justice;

b. the right to security of person and protection by the State against violence or bodily harm, whether inflicted by government officials or by any individual group or institution;

c. political rights, in particular the rights to participate in elections – to vote and to stand for election – on the basis of universal and equal suffrage, to take part in the Government as well as in the conduct of public affairs at any level and to have equal access to public service;

d. other civil rights, in particular:

   i. the right to freedom of movement and residence within the border of the State;

   ii. the right to leave any country, including one's own, and to return to one's country;

   iii. the right to nationality;

   iv. the right to marriage and choice of spouse;

   v. the right to own property alone as well as in association with others;

   vi. the right to inherit;

   vii. the right to freedom of thought, conscience and religion;

   viii. the right to freedom of opinion and expression;

   ix. the right to freedom of peaceful assembly and association;

e. economic, social and cultural rights, in particular:

   i. the rights to work, to free choice of employment, to just and favourable conditions of work, to protection against unemployment, to equal pay for equal work, to just and favourable remuneration;

   ii. the right to form and join trade unions;

   iii. the right to housing;

   iv. the right to public health, medical care, social security and social services;

   v. the right to education and training;

vi. the right to equal participation in cultural activities;

f. the right of access to any place or service intended for use by the general public, such as transport, hotels, restaurants, cafés, theatres and parks.

Article 6

States Parties shall assure to everyone within their jurisdiction effective protection and remedies, through the competent national tribunals and other State institutions, against any acts of racial discrimination which violate his human rights and fundamental freedoms contrary to this Convention, as well as the right to seek from such tribunals just and adequate reparation or satisfaction for any damage suffered as a result of such discrimination.

Article 7

States Parties undertake to adopt immediate and effective measures, particularly in the fields of teaching, education, culture and information, with a view to combating prejudices which lead to racial discrimination and to promoting understanding, tolerance and friendship among nations and racial or ethnical groups, as well as to propagating the purposes and principles of the Charter of the United Nations, the Universal Declaration of Human Rights, the United Nations Declaration on the Elimination of All Forms of Racial Discrimination, and this Convention.

Part II

Article 8

1. There shall be established a Committee on the Elimination of Racial Discrimination (hereinafter referred to as the Committee) consisting of eighteen experts of high moral standing and acknowledged impartiality elected by States Parties from among their nationals, who shall serve in their personal capacity, consideration being given to equitable geographical distribution and to the representation of the different forms of civilization as well as of the principal legal systems.

2. The members of the Committee shall be elected by secret ballot from a list of persons nominated by the States Parties. Each State Party may nominate one person from among its own nationals.

3. The initial election shall be held six months after the date of the entry into force of this Convention. At least three months before the date of each election the Secretary General of the United Nations shall address a letter to the States Parties inviting them to submit their nominations within two months. The Secretary General shall prepare a list in alphabetical order of all persons thus nominated, indicating the States Parties which have nominated them, and shall submit it to the States Parties.

4. Elections of the members of the Committee shall be held at a meeting of States Parties convened by the Secretary General at United Nations Headquarters. At that meeting, for which two thirds of the States Parties shall constitute a quorum, the persons elected to the Committee shall be nominees who obtain the largest number of votes and an absolute majority of the votes of the representatives of States Parties present and voting.

5.a. The members of the Committee shall be elected for a term of four years. However, the terms of nine of the members elected at the first election shall expire at the end of two years; immediately after the first election the names of these nine members shall be chosen by lot by the Chairman of the Committee;

b. For the filling of casual vacancies, the State Party whose expert has ceased to function as a member of the Committee shall appoint another expert from among its nationals, subject to the approval of the Committee.

6. States Parties shall be responsible for the expenses of the members of the Committee while they are in performance of Committee duties.

Article 9

1. States Parties undertake to submit to the Secretary General of the United Nations, for consideration by the Committee, a report on the

legislative, judicial, administrative or other measures which they have adopted and which give effect to the provisions of this Convention: *a.* within one year after the entry into force of the Convention for the State concerned; and *b.* thereafter every two years and whenever the Committee so requests. The Committee may request further information from the States Parties.

2. The Committee shall report annually, through the Secretary General, to the General Assembly of the United Nations on its activities and may make suggestions and general recommendations based on the examination of the reports and information received from the States Parties. Such suggestions and general recommendations shall be reported to the General Assembly together with comments, if any, from States Parties.

Article 10

1. The Committee shall adopt its own rules of procedure.

2. The Committee shall elect its officers for a term of two years.

3. The Secretariat of the Committee shall be provided by the Secretary General of the United Nations.

4. The meetings of the Committee shall normally be held at United Nations Headquarters.

Article 11

1. If a State Party considers that another State Party is not giving effect to the provisions of this Convention, it may bring the matter to the attention of the Committee. The Committee shall then transmit the communication to the State Party concerned. Within three months, the receiving State shall submit to the Committee written explanations or statements clarifying the matter and the remedy, if any, that may have been taken by that State.

2. If the matter is not adjusted to the satisfaction of both parties, either by bilateral negotiations or by any other procedure open to them, within

six months after the receipt by the receiving State of the initial communication, either State shall have the right to refer the matter again to the Committee by notifying the Committee and also the other State.

3. The Committee shall deal with a matter referred to it in accordance with paragraph 2 of this Article after it has ascertained that all available domestic remedies have been invoked and exhausted in the case, in conformity with the generally recognized principles of international law. This shall not be the rule where the application of the remedies is unreasonably prolonged.

4. In any matter referred to it, the Committee may call upon the States Parties concerned to supply any other relevant information.

5. When any matter arising out of this Article is being considered by the Committee, the States Parties concerned shall be entitled to send a representative to take part in the proceedings of the Committee, without voting rights, while the matter is under consideration.

Article 12

1.a. After the Committee has obtained and collated all the information it deems necessary, the Chairman shall appoint an *ad hoc* Conciliation Commission (hereinafter referred to as the Commission) comprising five persons who may or may not be members of the Committee. The members of the Commission shall be appointed with the unanimous consent of the parties to the dispute, and its good offices shall be made available to the States concerned with a view to an amicable solution of the matter on the basis of respect for this Convention.

b. If the States Parties to the dispute fail to reach agreement within three months on all or part of the composition of the Commission, the members of the Commission not agreed upon by the States Parties to the dispute shall be elected by secret ballot by a two-thirds majority vote of the Committee from among its own members.

2. The members of the Commission shall serve in their personal capacity. They shall not be nationals of the States Parties to the dispute or of a State not Party to this Convention.

3. The Commission shall elect its own Chairman and adopt its own rules of procedure.

4. The meetings of the Commission shall normally be held at United Nations Headquarters or at any other convenient place as determined by the Commission.

5. The secretariat provided in accordance with Article 10, paragraph 3, of this Convention shall also service the Commission whenever a dispute among States Parties brings the Commission into being.

6. The States Parties to the dispute shall share equally all the expenses of the members of the Commission in accordance with estimates to be provided by the Secretary General of the United Nations.

7. The Secretary General shall be empowered to pay the expenses of the members of the Commission, if necessary, before reimbursement by the States Parties to the dispute in accordance with paragraph 6 of this Article.

8. The information obtained and collated by the Committee shall be made available to the Commission, and the Commission may call upon the States concerned to supply any other relevant information.

Article 13

1. When the Commission has fully considered the matter, it shall prepare and submit to the Chairman of the Committee a report embodying its findings on all questions of fact relevant to the issue between the parties and containing such recommendations as it may think proper for the amicable solution of the dispute.

2. The Chairman of the Committee shall communicate the report of the Commission to each of the States Parties to the dispute. These States shall, within three months, inform the Chairman of the Committee whether or not they accept the recommendations contained in the report of the Commission.

3. After the period provided for in paragraph 2 of this Article, the Chairman of the Committee shall communicate the report of the Commission and the declarations of the States Parties concerned to the other States Parties to this Convention.

Article 14

1. A State Party may at any time declare that it recognizes the competence of the Committee to receive and consider communications from individuals or groups of individuals within its jurisdiction claiming to be victims of a violation by that State Party of any of the rights set forth in this Convention. No communication shall be received by the Committee if it concerns a State Party which has not made such a declaration.

2. Any State Party which makes a declaration as provided for in paragraph 1 of this Article may establish or indicate a body within its national legal order which shall be competent to receive and consider petitions from individuals and groups of individuals within its jurisdiction who claim to be victims of a violation of any of the rights set forth in this Convention and who have exhausted other available local remedies.

3. A declaration made in accordance with paragraph 1 of this Article and the name of any body established or indicated in accordance with paragraph 2 of this Article shall be deposited by the State Party concerned with the Secretary General of the United Nations, who shall transmit copies thereof to the other States Parties. A declaration may be withdrawn at any time by notification to the Secretary General, but such a withdrawal shall not affect communications pending before the Committee.

4. A register of petitions shall be kept by the body established or indicated in accordance with paragraph 2 of this Article, and certified copies of the register shall be filed annually through appropriate channels with the Secretary General on the understanding that the contents shall not be publicly disclosed.

5. In the event of failure to obtain satisfaction from the body established or indicated in accordance with paragraph 2 of this Article, the petitioner

shall have the right to communicate the matter to the Committee within six months.

6.a. The Committee shall confidentially bring any communication referred to it to the attention of the State Party alleged to be violating any provision of this Convention, but the identity of the individual or groups of individuals concerned shall not be revealed without his or their express consent. The Committee shall not receive anonymous communications.

b. Within three months, the receiving State shall submit to the Committee written explanations or statements clarifying the matter and the remedy, if any, that may have been taken by that State.

7.a. The Committee shall consider communications in the light of all information made available to it by the State Party concerned and by the petitioner. The committee shall not consider any communication from a petitioner unless it has ascertained that the petitioner has exhausted all available domestic remedies. However, this shall not be the rule where the application of the remedies is unreasonably prolonged.

b. The Committee shall forward its suggestions and recommendations if any, to the State Party concerned and to the petitioner.

8. The Committee shall include in its annual report a summary of such communications and, where appropriate, a summary of the explanations and statements of the States Parties concerned and of its own suggestions and recommendations.

9. The Committee shall be competent to exercise the functions provided for in this Article only when at least ten States Parties to this Convention are bound by declarations in accordance with paragraph 1 of this Article.

Article 15

1. Pending the achievement of the objectives of the Declaration on the Granting of Independence to Colonial Countries and Peoples, contained in General Assembly Resolution 1514 (XV) of 14 December 1960, the provisions of this Convention shall in no way limit the right of petition

granted to these peoples by other international instruments or by the United Nations and its specialized agencies.

2.a. The Committee established under Article 8, paragraph 1, of this Convention shall receive copies of the petitions from, and submit expressions of opinion and recommendations on these petitions to, the bodies of the United Nations which deal with matters directly related to the principles and objectives of this Convention in their consideration of petitions from the inhabitants of Trust and Non-Self-Governing Territories and all other territories to which General Assembly Resolution 1514 (XV) applies, relating to matters covered by this Convention which are before these bodies.

b. The Committee shall receive from the competent bodies of the United Nations copies of the reports concerning the legislative, judicial, administrative or other measures directly related to the principles and objectives of this Convention applied by the administering Powers within the Territories mentioned in sub-paragraph *a* of this paragraph, and shall express opinions and make recommendations to these bodies.

3. The Committee shall include in its report to the General Assembly a summary of the petitions and reports it has received from United Nations bodies, and the expressions of opinion and recommendations of the Committee relating to the said petitions and reports.

4. The Committee shall request from the Secretary General of the United Nations all information relevant to the objectives of this Convention and available to him regarding the Territories mentioned in paragraph 2.*a* of this article.

Article 16

The provisions of this Convention concerning the settlement of disputes or complaints shall be applied without prejudice to other procedures for settling disputes or complaints in the field of discrimination laid down in the constituent instruments of, or conventions adopted by, the United Nations and its specialized agencies, and shall not prevent the States Parties from having recourse to other procedures for settling a dispute in accordance with general or special international agreements in force between them.

Part III

Article 17

1. This Convention is open for signature by any State Member of the United Nations or member of any of its specialized agencies, by any State Party to the Statute of the International Court of Justice, and by any other State which has been invited by the General Assembly of the United Nations to become a party to this Convention.

2. This Convention is subject to ratification. Instruments of ratification shall be deposited with the Secretary General of the United Nations.

Article 18

1. This Convention shall be open to accession by any State referred to in Article 17, paragraph 1, of the Convention.

2. Accession shall be effected by the deposit of an instrument of accession with the Secretary General of the United Nations.

Article 19

1. This Convention shall enter into force on the thirtieth day after the date of the deposit with the Secretary General of the United Nations of the twenty-seventh instrument of ratification or instrument of accession.

2. For each State ratifying this Convention or acceding to it after the deposit of the twenty-seventh instrument of ratification or instrument of accession, the Convention shall enter into force on the thirtieth day after the date of the deposit of its own instrument of ratification or instrument of accession.

Article 20

1. The Secretary General of the United Nations shall receive and circulate to all States which are or may become Parties to this Convention reservations made by States at the time of ratification or accession. Any State which objects to the reservation shall, within a period of ninety days from the date of the said communication, notify the Secretary General that it does not accept it.

2. A reservation incompatible with the object and purpose of this Convention shall not be permitted, nor shall a reservation the effect of which would inhibit the operation of any of the bodies established by this Convention be allowed. A reservation shall be considered incompatible or inhibitive if at least two-thirds of the States Parties to this Convention object to it.

3. Reservations may be withdrawn at any time by notification to this effect addressed to the Secretary General. Such notification shall take effect on the date on which it is received.

Article 21

A State Party may denounce this Convention by written notification to the Secretary General of the United Nations. Denunciation shall take effect one year after the date of receipt of the notification by the Secretary General.

Article 22

Any dispute between two or more States Parties with respect to the interpretation or application of this Convention, which is not settled by negotiation or by the procedures expressly provided for in this Convention, shall, at the request of any of the parties to the dispute, be referred to the International Court of Justice for decision, unless the disputants agree to another mode of settlement.

Article 23

1. A request for the revision of this Convention may be made at any time by any State Party by means of a notification in writing addressed to the Secretary General of the United Nations.

2. The General Assembly of the United Nations shall decide upon the steps, if any, to be taken in respect of such a request.

Article 24

The Secretary General of the United Nations shall inform all States referred to in Article 17, paragraph 1, of this Convention of the following particulars:

a. signatures, ratifications and accessions under Articles 17 and 18;
b. the date of entry into force of this Convention under Article 19;
c. communications and declarations received under Articles 14, 20 and 23;
d. denunciations under Article 21.

Article 25

1. This Convention, of which the Chinese, English, French, Russian and Spanish texts are equally authentic, shall be deposited in the archives of the United Nations.

2. The Secretary General of the United Nations shall transmit certified copies of the Convention to all States belonging to any of the categories mentioned in Article 17, paragraph 1, of the Convention.

7. Convention on the Elimination of All Forms of Discrimination against Women

Adopted and opened for signature, ratification and accession by General Assembly Resolution 34/180 of 18 December 1979

Entry into force: 3 September 1981, in accordance with Article 27

The States Parties to the present Convention,

Noting that the Charter of the United Nations reaffirms faith in fundamental human rights, in the dignity and worth of the human person and in the equal rights of men and women,

Noting that the Universal Declaration of Human Rights affirms the principle of the inadmissibility of discrimination and proclaims that all human beings are born free and equal in dignity and rights and that everyone is entitled to all the rights and freedoms set forth therein, without distinction of any kind, including distinction based on sex,

Noting that the States Parties to the International Covenants on Human Rights have the obligation to ensure the equal rights of men and women to enjoy all economic, social, cultural, civil and political rights,

Considering the international conventions concluded under the auspices of the United Nations and the specialized agencies promoting equality of rights of men and women,

Noting also the resolutions, declarations and recommendations adopted by the United Nations and the specialized agencies promoting equality of rights of men and women,

Concerned, however, that despite these various instruments extensive discrimination against women continues to exist,

Recalling that discrimination against women violates the principles of equality of rights and respect for human dignity, is an obstacle to the participation of women, on equal terms with men, in the political, social, economic and cultural life of their countries, hampers the growth of the prosperity of society and the family and makes more difficult the full development of the potentialities of women in the service of their countries and of humanity,

Concerned that in situations of poverty women have the least access to food, health, education, training and opportunities for employment and other needs,

Convinced that the establishment of the new international economic order based on equity and justice will contribute significantly towards the promotion of equality between men and women,

Emphasising that the eradication of *apartheid*, all forms of racism, racial discrimination, colonialism, neo-colonialism, aggression, foreign occupation and domination and interference in the internal affairs of States is essential to the full enjoyment of the rights of men and women,

Affirming that the strengthening of international peace and security, the relaxation of international tension, mutual co-operation among all States irrespective of their social and economic systems, general and complete disarmament, in particular nuclear disarmament under strict and effective international control, the affirmation of the principles of justice, equality and mutual benefit in relations among countries and the realization of the right of peoples under alien and colonial domination and foreign occupation to self-determination and independence, as well as respect for national sovereignty and territorial integrity, will promote social progress and development and as a consequence will contribute to the attainment of full equality between men and women,

Convinced that the full and complete development of a country, the welfare of the world and the cause of peace require the maximum participation of women on equal terms with men in all fields,

Bearing in mind the great contribution of women to the welfare of the family and to the development of society, so far not fully recognised, the social significance of maternity and the role of both parents in the family and in the upbringing of children, and aware that the role of women in procreation should not be a basis for discrimination but that the upbringing of children requires a sharing of responsibility between men and women and society as a whole,

Aware that a change in the traditional role of men as well as the role of women in society and in the family is needed to achieve full equality between men and women,

Determined to implement the principles set forth in the Declaration on the Elimination of Discrimination against Women and, for that purpose, to adopt the measures required for the elimination of such discrimination in all its forms and manifestations,

Have agreed on the following:

Part I

Article 1

For the purposes of the present Convention, the term 'discrimination against women' shall mean any distinction, exclusion or restriction made on the basis of sex which has the effect or purpose of impairing or nullifying the recognition, enjoyment or exercise by women, irrespective of their marital status, on a basis of equality of men and women, of human rights and fundamental freedoms in the political, economic, social, cultural, civil or any other field.

Article 2

States Parties condemn discrimination against women in all its forms, agree to pursue by all appropriate means and without delay a policy of eliminating discrimination against women and, to this end, undertake:

a. to embody the principle of the equality of men and women in their national constitutions or other appropriate legislation if not yet incorporated therein and to ensure, through law and other appropriate means, the practical realization of this principle;

b. to adopt appropriate legislative and other measures, including sanctions where appropriate, prohibiting all discrimination against women;

c. to establish legal protection of the rights of women on an equal basis with men and to ensure through competent national tribunals and other public institutions the effective protection of women against any act of discrimination;

d. to refrain from engaging in any act or practice of discrimination against women and to ensure that public authorities and institutions shall act in conformity with this obligation;

e. to take all appropriate measures to eliminate discrimination against women by any person, organization or enterprise;

f. to take all appropriate measures, including legislation, to modify or abolish existing laws, regulations, customs and practices which constitute discrimination against women;

g. to repeal all national penal provisions which constitute discrimination against women.

Article 3

States Parties shall take in all fields, in particular in the political, social, economic and cultural fields, all appropriate measures, including legislation, to ensure the full development and advancement of women, for the purpose of guaranteeing them the exercise and enjoyment of human rights and fundamental freedoms on a basis of equality with men.

Article 4

1. Adoption by States Parties of temporary special measures aimed at accelerating *de facto* equality between men and women shall not be considered discrimination as defined in the present Convention, but shall in no way entail as a consequence the maintenance of unequal or separate standards; these measures shall be discontinued when the objectives of equality of opportunity and treatment have been achieved.

2. Adoption by States Parties of special measures, including those measures contained in the present Convention, aimed at protecting maternity shall not be considered discriminatory.

Article 5

States Parties shall take all appropriate measures:

a. to modify the social and cultural patterns of conduct of men and women, with a view to achieving the elimination of prejudices and customary and all other practices which are based on the idea of the inferiority or the superiority of either of the sexes or on stereotyped roles for men and women;

b. to ensure that family education includes a proper understanding of maternity as a social function and the recognition of the common responsibility of men and women in the upbringing and development of their children, it being understood that the interest of the children is the primordial consideration in all cases.

Article 6

States Parties shall take all appropriate measures, including legislation, to suppress all forms of traffic in women and exploitation of prostitution of women.

Part II

Article 7

States Parties shall take all appropriate measures to eliminate discrimination against women in the political and public life of the country and, in particular, shall ensure to women, on equal terms with men, the right:

a. to vote in all elections and public referenda and to be eligible for election to all publicly elected bodies;

b. to participate in the formulation of government policy and the implementation thereof and to hold public office and perform all public functions at all levels of government;

c. to participate in non-governmental organizations and associations concerned with the public and political life of the country.

Article 8

States Parties shall take all appropriate measures to ensure to women, on equal terms with men and without any discrimination, the opportunity to represent their Governments at the international level and to participate in the work of international organizations.

Article 9

1. States Parties shall grant women equal rights with men to acquire, change or retain their nationality. They shall ensure in particular that neither marriage to an alien nor change of nationality by the husband during marriage shall automatically change the nationality of the wife, render her stateless or force upon her the nationality of the husband.

2. States Parties shall grant women equal rights with men with respect to the nationality of their children.

Part III

Article 10

States Parties shall take all appropriate measures to eliminate discrimination against women in order to ensure to them equal rights with men in the field of education and in particular to ensure, on a basis of equality of men and women:

a. the same conditions for career and vocational guidance, for access to studies and for the achievement of diplomas in educational establishments of all categories in rural as well as in urban areas; this equality shall be ensured in pre-school, general, technical, professional and higher technical education, as well as in all types of vocational training;

b. access to the same curricula, the same examinations, teaching staff with qualifications of the same standard and school premises and equipment of the same quality;

c. the elimination of any stereotyped concept of the roles of men and women at all levels and in all forms of education by encouraging coeducation and other types of education which will help to achieve this aim and, in particular, by the revision of textbooks and school programmes and the adaptation of teaching methods;

d. the same opportunities to benefit from scholarships and other study grants;

e. the same opportunities for access to programmes of continuing education, including adult and functional literacy programmes, particularly those aimed at reducing, at the earliest possible time, any gap in education existing between men and women;

f. the reduction of female student drop-out rates and the organisation of programmes for girls and women who have left school prematurely;

g. the same opportunities to participate actively in sports and physical education;

h. access to specific educational information to help to ensure the health and well-being of families, including information and advice on family planning.

Article 11

1. States Parties shall take all appropriate measures to eliminate discrimination against women in the field of employment in order to ensure, on a basis of equality of men and women, the same rights, in particular:

a. the right to work as an inalienable right of all human beings;

b. the right to the same employment opportunities, including the application of the same criteria for selection in matters of employment;

c. the right to free choice of profession and employment, the right to promotion, job security and all benefits and conditions of service and the right to receive vocational training and retraining, including apprenticeships, advanced vocational training and recurrent training;

d. the right to equal remuneration, including benefits, and to equal treatment in respect of work of equal value, as well as equality of treatment in the evaluation of the quality of work;

e. the right to social security, particularly in cases of retirement, unemployment, sickness, invalidity and old age and other incapacity to work, as well as the right to paid leave;

f. the right to protection of health and to safety in working conditions, including the safeguarding of the function of reproduction.

2. In order to prevent discrimination against women on the grounds of marriage or maternity and to ensure their effective right to work, States Parties shall take appropriate measures:

a. to prohibit, subject to the imposition of sanctions, dismissal on the grounds of pregnancy or of maternity leave and discrimination in dismissals on the basis of marital status;

b. to introduce maternity leave with pay or with comparable social benefits without loss of former employment, seniority or social allowances;

c. to encourage the provision of the necessary supporting social services to enable parents to combine family obligations with work responsibilities and participation in public life, in particular through promoting the establishment and development of a network of child-care facilities;

d. to provide special protection to women during pregnancy in types of work proved to be harmful to them.

3. Protective legislation relating to matters covered in this Article shall be reviewed periodically in the light of scientific and technological knowledge and shall be revised, repealed or extended as necessary.

Article 12

1. States Parties shall take all appropriate measures to eliminate discrimination against women in the field of health care in order to ensure, on a basis of equality of men and women, access to health care services, including those related to family planning.

2. Notwithstanding the provisions of paragraph 1 of this Article, States Parties shall ensure to women appropriate services in connection with pregnancy, confinement and the post-natal period, granting free services where necessary, as well as adequate nutrition during pregnancy and lactation.

Article 13

States Parties shall take all appropriate measures to eliminate discrimination against women in other areas of economic and social life in order to ensure, on a basis of equality of men and women, the same rights, in particular:

a. the right to family benefits;
b. the right to bank loans, mortgages and other forms of financial credit;
c. the right to participate in recreational activities, sports and all aspects of cultural life.

Article 14

1. States Parties shall take into account the particular problems faced by rural women and the significant roles which rural women play in the economic survival of their families, including their work in the non-monetised sectors of the economy, and shall take all appropriate measures to ensure the application of the provisions of the present Convention to women in rural areas.

2. States Parties shall take all appropriate measures to eliminate discrimination against women in rural areas in order to ensure, on a basis of equality of men and women, that they participate in and benefit from rural development and, in particular, shall ensure to such women the right:

a. to participate in the elaboration and implementation of development planning at all levels;
b. to have access to adequate health care facilities, including information, counselling and services in family planning;

c. to benefit directly from social security programmes;

d. to obtain all types of training and education, formal and non-formal, including that relating to functional literacy, as well as, *inter alia*, the benefit of all community and extension services, in order to increase their technical proficiency;

e. to organise self-help groups and co-operatives in order to obtain equal access to economic opportunities through employment or self-employment;

f. to participate in all community activities;

g. to have access to agricultural credit and loans, marketing facilities, appropriate technology and equal treatment in land and agrarian reform as well as in land resettlement schemes;

h. to enjoy adequate living conditions, particularly in relation to housing, sanitation, electricity and water supply, transport and communications.

Part IV

Article 15

1. States Parties shall accord to women equality with men before the law.

2. States Parties shall accord to women, in civil matters, a legal capacity identical to that of men and the same opportunities to exercise that capacity. In particular, they shall give women equal rights to conclude contracts and to administer property and shall treat them equally in all stages of procedure in courts and tribunals.

3. States Parties agree that all contracts and all other private instruments of any kind with a legal effect which is directed at restricting the legal capacity of women shall be deemed null and void.

4. States Parties shall accord to men and women the same rights with regard to the law relating to the movement of persons and the freedom to choose their residence and domicile.

Article 16

1. States Parties shall take all appropriate measures to eliminate discrimination against women in all matters relating to marriage and family relations and in particular shall ensure, on a basis of equality of men and women:

a. the same right to enter into marriage;
b. the same right freely to choose a spouse and to enter into marriage only with their free and full consent;
c. the same rights and responsibilities during marriage and at its dissolution;
d. the same rights and responsibilities as parents, irrespective of their marital status, in matters relating to their children; in all cases the interests of the children shall be paramount;
e. the same rights to decide freely and responsibly on the number and spacing of their children and to have access to the information, education and means to enable them to exercise these rights;
f. the same rights and responsibilities with regard to guardianship, wardship, trusteeship and adoption of children, or similar institutions where these concepts exist in national legislation; in all cases the interests of the children shall be paramount;
g. the same personal rights as husband and wife, including the right to choose a family name, a profession and an occupation;
h. the same rights for both spouses in respect of the ownership, acquisition, management, administration, enjoyment and disposition of property, whether free of charge or for a valuable consideration.

2. The betrothal and the marriage of a child shall have no legal effect, and all necessary action, including legislation, shall be taken to specify a minimum age for marriage and to make the registration of marriages in an official registry compulsory.

Part V

Article 17

1. For the purpose of considering the progress made in the implementation of the present Convention, there shall be established a Committee on the Elimination of Discrimination against Women (hereinafter referred to as the Committee) consisting, at the time of entry into force of the Convention, of eighteen and, after ratification of or accession to the Convention by the thirty-fifth State Party, of twenty-three experts of high moral standing and competence in the field covered by the Convention. The experts shall be elected by States Parties from among their nationals and shall serve in their personal capacity, consideration being given to equitable geographical distribution and to the representation of the different forms of civilisation as well as the principal legal systems.

2. The members of the Committee shall be elected by secret ballot from a list of persons nominated by States Parties. Each State Party may nominate one person from among its own nationals.

3. The initial election shall be held six months after the date of the entry into force of the present Convention. At least three months before the date of each election the Secretary General of the United Nations shall address a letter to the States Parties inviting them to submit their nominations within two months. The Secretary General shall prepare a list in alphabetical order of all persons thus nominated, indicating the States Parties which have nominated them, and shall submit it to the States Parties.

4. Elections of the members of the Committee shall be held at a meeting of States Parties convened by the Secretary General at United Nations Headquarters. At that meeting, for which two-thirds of the States Parties shall constitute a quorum, the persons elected to the Committee shall be those nominees who obtain the largest number of votes and an absolute majority of the votes of the representatives of States Parties present and voting.

5. The members of the Committee shall be elected for a term of four years. However, the terms of nine of the members elected at the first election shall expire at the end of two years; immediately after the first election the names of these nine members shall be chosen by lot by the Chairman of the Committee.

6. The election of the five additional members of the Committee shall be held in accordance with the provisions of paragraphs 2, 3 and 4 of this Article, following the thirty-fifth ratification or accession. The terms of two of the additional members elected on this occasion shall expire at the end of two years, the names of these two members having been chosen by lot by the Chairman of the Committee.

7. For the filling of casual vacancies, the State Party whose expert has ceased to function as a member of the Committee shall appoint another expert from among its nationals, subject to the approval of the Committee.

8. The members of the Committee shall, with the approval of the General Assembly, receive emoluments from United Nations resources on such terms and conditions as the Assembly may decide, having regard to the importance of the Committee's responsibilities.

9. The Secretary General of the United Nations shall provide the necessary staff and facilities for the effective performance of the functions of the Committee under the present Convention.

Article 18

1. States Parties undertake to submit to the Secretary General of the United Nations, for consideration by the Committee, a report on the legislative, judicial, administrative or other measures which they have adopted to give effect to the provisions of the present Convention and on the progress made in this respect:

a. within one year after the entry into force for the State concerned;
b. thereafter at least every four years and further whenever the Committee so requests.

2. Reports may indicate factors and difficulties affecting the degree of fulfilment of obligations under the present Convention.

Article 19

1. The Committee shall adopt its own rules of procedure.

2. The Committee shall elect its officers for a term of two years.

Article 20

1. The Committee shall normally meet for a period of not more than two weeks annually in order to consider the reports submitted in accordance with Article 18 of the present Convention.

2. The meetings of the Committee shall normally be held at United Nations Headquarters or at any other convenient place as determined by the Committee.

Article 21

1. The Committee shall, through the Economic and Social Council, report annually to the General Assembly of the United Nations on its activities and may make suggestions and general recommendations based on the examination of reports and information received from the States Parties. Such suggestions and general recommendations shall be included in the report of the Committee together with comments, if any, from States Parties.

2. The Secretary General of the United Nations shall transmit the reports of the Committee to the Commission on the Status of Women for its information.

Article 22

The specialized agencies shall be entitled to be represented at the consideration of the implementation of such provisions of the present Convention as fall within the scope of their activities. The Committee may invite the specialized agencies to submit reports on the implementation of the Convention in areas falling within the scope of their activities.

Part VI

Article 23

Nothing in the present Convention shall affect any provisions that are more conducive to the achievement of equality between men and women which may be contained:

a. in the legislation of a State Party; or
b. in any other international convention, treaty or agreement in force for that State.

Article 24

States Parties undertake to adopt all necessary measures at the national level aimed at achieving the full realization of the rights recognized in the present Convention.

Article 25

1. The present Convention shall be open for signature by all States.

2. The Secretary General of the United Nations is designated as the depositary of the present Convention.

3. The present Convention is subject to ratification. Instruments of ratification shall be deposited with the Secretary General of the United Nations.

4. The present Convention shall be open to accession by all States. Accession shall be effected by the deposit of an instrument of accession with the Secretary General of the United Nations.

Article 26

1. A request for the revision of the present Convention may be made at any time by any State Party by means of a notification in writing addressed to the Secretary General of the United Nations.

2. The General Assembly of the United Nations shall decide upon the steps, if any, to be taken in respect of such a request.

Article 27

1. The present Convention shall enter into force on the thirtieth day after the date of deposit with the Secretary General of the United Nations of the twentieth instrument of ratification or accession.

2. For each State ratifying the present Convention or acceding to it after the deposit of the twentieth instrument of ratification or accession, the Convention shall enter into force on the thirtieth day after the date of the deposit of its own instrument of ratification or accession.

Article 28

1. The Secretary General of the United Nations shall receive and circulate to all States the text of reservations made by States at the time of ratification or accession.

2. A reservation incompatible with the object and purpose of the present Convention shall not be permitted.

3. Reservations may be withdrawn at any time by notification to this effect addressed to the Secretary General of the United Nations, who shall then inform all States thereof. Such notification shall take effect on the date on which it is received.

Article 29

1. Any dispute between two or more States Parties concerning the interpretation or application of the present Convention which is not settled

by negotiation shall, at the request of one of them, be submitted to arbitration. If within six months from the date of the request for arbitration the parties are unable to agree on the organisation of the arbitration, any one of those parties may refer the dispute to the International Court of Justice by request in conformity with the Statute of the Court.

2. Each State Party may at the time of signature or ratification of the present Convention or accession thereto declare that it does not consider itself bound by paragraph 1 of this Article. The other States Parties shall not be bound by that paragraph with respect to any State Party which has made such a reservation.

3. Any State Party which has made a reservation in accordance with paragraph 2 of this Article may at any time withdraw that reservation by notification to the Secretary General of the United Nations.

Article 30

The present Convention, the Arabic, Chinese, English, French, Russian and Spanish texts of which are equally authentic, shall be deposited with the Secretary General of the United Nations.

8. **Convention against Torture and Other Cruel, Inhuman or Degrading Treatment or Punishment**

Adopted and opened for signature, ratification and accession by General Assembly Resolution 39/46 of 10 December 1984

Entry into force: 26 June 1987, in accordance with Article 27

The States Parties to this Convention,

Considering that, in accordance with the principles proclaimed in the Charter of the United Nations, recognition of the equal and inalienable rights of all members of the human family is the foundation of freedom, justice and peace in the world,

Recognizing that those rights derive from the inherent dignity of the human person,

Considering the obligation of States under the Charter, in particular Article 55, to promote universal respect for, and observance of, human rights and fundamental freedoms,

Having regard to Article 5 of the Universal Declaration of Human Rights and Article 7 of the International Covenant on Civil and Political Rights, both of which provide that no one shall be subjected to torture or to cruel, inhuman or degrading treatment or punishment,

Having regard also to the Declaration on the Protection of All Persons from Being Subjected to Torture and Other Cruel, Inhuman or Degrading Treatment or Punishment, adopted by the General Assembly on 9 December 1975,

Desiring to make more effective the struggle against torture and other cruel, inhuman or degrading treatment or punishment throughout the world,

Have agreed as follows:

Part I

Article 1

1. For the purposes of this Convention, the term 'torture' means any act by which severe pain or suffering, whether physical or mental, is intentionally inflicted on a person for such purposes as obtaining from him or a third person information or a confession, punishing him for an act he or a third person has committed or is suspected of having committed, or intimidating or coercing him or a third person, or for any reason based on discrimination of any kind, when such pain or suffering is inflicted by or at the instigation of or with the consent or acquiescence of a public official or other person acting in an official capacity. It does not include pain or suffering arising only from, inherent in or incidental to lawful sanctions.

2. This Article is without prejudice to any international instrument or national legislation which does or may contain provisions of wider application.

Article 2

1. Each State Party shall take effective legislative, administrative, judicial or other measures to prevent acts of torture in any territory under its jurisdiction.

2. No exceptional circumstances whatsoever, whether a state of war or a threat of war, internal political instability or any other public emergency, may be invoked as a justification of torture.

3. An order from a superior officer or a public authority may not be invoked as a justification of torture.

Article 3

1. No State Party shall expel, return (*refouler*) or extradite a person to another State where there are substantial grounds for believing that he would be in danger of being subjected to torture.

2. For the purpose of determining whether there are such grounds, the competent authorities shall take into account all relevant considerations including, where applicable, the existence in the State concerned of a consistent pattern of gross, flagrant or mass violations of human rights.

Article 4

1. Each State Party shall ensure that all acts of torture are offences under its criminal law. The same shall apply to an attempt to commit torture and to an act by any person which constitutes complicity or participation in torture.

2. Each State Party shall make these offences punishable by appropriate penalties which take into account their grave nature.

Article 5

1. Each State Party shall take such measures as may be necessary to establish its jurisdiction over the offences referred to in Article 4 in the following cases:

a. when the offences are committed in any territory under its jurisdiction or on board a ship or aircraft registered in that State;
b. when the alleged offender is a national of that State;
c. when the victim is a national of that State if that State considers it appropriate.

2. Each State Party shall likewise take such measures as may be necessary to establish its jurisdiction over such offences in cases where the alleged offender is present in any territory under its jurisdiction and it does not extradite him pursuant to Article 8 to any of the States mentioned in paragraph 1 of this Article.

3. This Convention does not exclude any criminal jurisdiction exercised in accordance with internal law.

Article 6

1. Upon being satisfied, after an examination of information available to it, that the circumstances so warrant, any State Party in whose territory a person alleged to have committed any offence referred to in Article 4 is present shall take him into custody or take other legal measures to ensure his presence. The custody and other legal measures shall be as provided in the law of that State but may be continued only for such time as is necessary to enable any criminal or extradition proceedings to be instituted.

2. Such State shall immediately make a preliminary inquiry into the facts.

3. Any person in custody pursuant to paragraph 1 of this Article shall be assisted in communicating immediately with the nearest appropriate representative of the State of which he is a national, or, if he is a stateless person, with the representative of the State where he usually resides.

4. When a State, pursuant to this Article, has taken a person into custody, it shall immediately notify the States referred to in Article 5, paragraph 1, of the fact that such person is in custody and of the circumstances which warrant his detention. The State which makes the preliminary inquiry contemplated in paragraph 2 of this Article shall promptly report its findings to the said States and shall indicate whether it intends to exercise jurisdiction.

Article 7

1. The State Party in the territory under whose jurisdiction a person alleged to have committed any offence referred to in Article 4 is found shall in the cases contemplated in Article 5, if it does not extradite him, submit the case to its competent authorities for the purpose of prosecution.

2. These authorities shall take their decision in the same manner as in the case of any ordinary offence of a serious nature under the law of that

State. In the cases referred to in Article 5, paragraph 2, the standards of evidence required for prosecution and conviction shall in no way be less stringent than those which apply in the cases referred to in Article 5, paragraph 1.

3. Any person regarding whom proceedings are brought in connection with any of the offences referred to in Article 4 shall be guaranteed fair treatment at all stages of the proceedings.

Article 8

1. The offences referred to in Article 4 shall be deemed to be included as extraditable offences in any extradition treaty existing between States Parties. States Parties undertake to include such offences as extraditable offences in every extradition treaty to be concluded between them.

2. If a State Party which makes extradition conditional on the existence of a treaty receives a request for extradition from another State Party with which it has no extradition treaty, it may consider this Convention as the legal basis for extradition in respect of such offences. Extradition shall be subject to the other conditions provided by the law of the requested State.

3. States Parties which do not make extradition conditional on the existence of a treaty shall recognize such offences as extraditable offences between themselves subject to the conditions provided by the law of the requested State.

4. Such offences shall be treated, for the purpose of extradition between States Parties, as if they had been committed not only in the place in which they occurred but also in the territories of the States required to establish their jurisdiction in accordance with Article 5, paragraph 1.

Article 9

1. States Parties shall afford one another the greatest measure of assistance in connection with criminal proceedings brought in respect of

any of the offences referred to in Article 4, including the supply of all evidence at their disposal necessary for the proceedings.

2. States Parties shall carry out their obligations under paragraph 1 of this Article in conformity with any treaties on mutual judicial assistance that may exist between them.

Article 10

1. Each State Party shall ensure that education and information regarding the prohibition against torture are fully included in the training of law enforcement personnel, civil or military, medical personnel, public officials and other persons who may be involved in the custody, interrogation or treatment of any individual subjected to any form of arrest, detention or imprisonment.

2. Each State Party shall include this prohibition in the rules or instructions issued in regard to the duties and functions of any such person.

Article 11

Each State Party shall keep under systematic review interrogation rules, instructions, methods and practices as well as arrangements for the custody and treatment of persons subjected to any form of arrest, detention or imprisonment in any territory under its jurisdiction, with a view to preventing any cases of torture.

Article 12

Each State Party shall ensure that its competent authorities proceed to a prompt and impartial investigation, wherever there is reasonable ground to believe that an act of torture has been committed in any territory under its jurisdiction.

Article 13

Each State Party shall ensure that any individual who alleges he has been subjected to torture in any territory under its jurisdiction has the right to complain to, and to have his case promptly and impartially examined by, its competent authorities. Steps shall be taken to ensure that the complainant and witnesses are protected against all ill-treatment or intimidation as a consequence of his complaint or any evidence given.

Article 14

1. Each State Party shall ensure in its legal system that the victim of an act of torture obtains redress and has an enforceable right to fair and adequate compensation, including the means for as full rehabilitation as possible. In the event of the death of the victim as a result of an act of torture, his dependants shall be entitled to compensation.

2. Nothing in this Article shall affect any right of the victim or other persons to compensation which may exist under national law.

Article 15

Each State Party shall ensure that any statement which is established to have been made as a result of torture shall not be invoked as evidence in any proceedings, except against a person accused of torture as evidence that the statement was made.

Article 16

1. Each State Party shall undertake to prevent in any territory under its jurisdiction other acts of cruel, inhuman or degrading treatment or punishment which do not amount to torture as defined in Article 1, when such acts are committed by or at the instigation of or with the consent or acquiescence of a public official or other person acting in an official capacity. In particular, the obligations contained in Articles 10, 11, 12 and 13 shall apply with the substitution for references to torture of references to other forms of cruel, inhuman or degrading treatment or punishment.

2. The provisions of this Convention are without prejudice to the provisions of any other international instrument or national law which prohibits cruel, inhuman or degrading treatment or punishment or which relates to extradition or expulsion.

Part II

Article 17

1. There shall be established a Committee against Torture (hereinafter referred to as the Committee) which shall carry out the functions hereinafter provided. The Committee shall consist of ten experts of high moral standing and recognized competence in the field of human rights, who shall serve in their personal capacity. The experts shall be elected by the States Parties, consideration being given to equitable geographical distribution and to the usefulness of the participation of some persons having legal experience.

2. The members of the Committee shall be elected by secret ballot from a list of persons nominated by States Parties. Each State Party may nominate one person from among its own nationals. States Parties shall bear in mind the usefulness of nominating persons who are also members of the Human Rights Committee established under the International Covenant on Civil and Political Rights and who are willing to serve on the Committee against Torture.

3. Elections of the members of the Committee shall be held at biennial meetings of States Parties convened by the Secretary General of the United Nations. At those meetings, for which two thirds of the States Parties shall constitute a quorum, the persons elected to the Committee shall be those who obtain the largest number of votes and an absolute majority of the votes of the representatives of States Parties present and voting.

4. The initial election shall be held no later than six months after the date of the entry into force of this Convention. At least four months before the date of each election, the Secretary General of the United Nations shall address a letter to the States Parties inviting them to submit their nominations within three months. The Secretary General shall prepare a list in alphabetical order of all persons thus nominated, indicating the States Parties which have nominated them, and shall submit it to the States Parties.

5. The members of the Committee shall be elected for a term of four years. They shall be eligible for re-election if renominated. However, the term of five of the members elected at the first election shall expire at the end of two years; immediately after the first election the names of these five members shall be chosen by lot by the chairman of the meeting referred to in paragraph 3 of this Article.

6. If a member of the Committee dies or resigns or for any other cause can no longer perform his Committee duties, the State Party which nominated him shall appoint another expert from among its nationals to serve for the remainder of his term, subject to the approval of the majority of the States Parties. The approval shall be considered given unless half or more of the States Parties respond negatively within six weeks after having been informed by the Secretary General of the United Nations of the proposed appointment.

7. States Parties shall be responsible for the expenses of the members of the Committee while they are in performance of Committee duties.

Article 18

1. The Committee shall elect its officers for a term of two years. They may be re-elected.

2. The Committee shall establish its own rules of procedure, but these rules shall provide, *inter alia*, that:

a. six members shall constitute a quorum;
b. decisions of the Committee shall be made by a majority vote of the members present.

3. The Secretary General of the United Nations shall provide the necessary staff and facilities for the effective performance of the functions of the Committee under this Convention.

4. The Secretary General of the United Nations shall convene the initial meeting of the Committee. After its initial meeting, the Committee

shall meet at such times as shall be provided in its rules of procedure.

5. The States Parties shall be responsible for expenses incurred in connection with the holding of meetings of the States Parties and of the Committee, including reimbursement to the United Nations for any expenses, such as the cost of staff and facilities, incurred by the United Nations pursuant to paragraph 3 of this Article.

Article 19

1. The States Parties shall submit to the Committee, through the Secretary General of the United Nations, reports on the measures they have taken to give effect to their undertakings under this Convention, within one year after the entry into force of the Convention for the State Party concerned. Thereafter the States Parties shall submit supplementary reports every four years on any new measures taken and such other reports as the Committee may request.

2. The Secretary General of the United Nations shall transmit the reports to all States Parties.

3. Each report shall be considered by the Committee which may make such general comments on the report as it may consider appropriate, and shall forward these to the State Party concerned. That State Party may respond with any observations it chooses to the Committee.

4. The Committee may, at its discretion, decide to include any comments made by it in accordance with paragraph 3 of this Article, together with the observations thereon received from the State Party concerned, in its annual report made in accordance with Article 24. If so requested by the State Party concerned, the Committee may also include a copy of the report submitted under paragraph 1 of this Article.

Article 20

1. If the Committee receives reliable information which appears to it to contain well-founded indications that torture is being systematically

practised in the territory of a State Party, the Committee shall invite that State Party to co-operate in the examination of the information and to this end to submit observations with regard to the information concerned.

2. Taking into account any observations which may have been submitted by the State Party concerned, as well as any other relevant information available to it, the Committee may, if it decides that this is warranted, designate one or more of its members to make a confidential inquiry and to report to the Committee urgently.

3. If an inquiry is made in accordance with paragraph 2 of this Article, the Committee shall seek the co-operation of the State Party concerned. In agreement with that State Party, such an inquiry may include a visit to its territory.

4. After examining the findings of its member or members submitted in accordance with paragraph 2 of this Article, the Committee shall transmit these findings to the State Party concerned together with any comments or suggestions which seem appropriate in view of the situation.

5. All the proceedings of the Committee referred to in paragraphs 1 to 4 of this Article shall be confidential, and at all stages of the proceedings the co-operation of the State Party shall be sought. After such proceedings have been completed with regard to an inquiry made in accordance with paragraph 2, the Committee may, after consultations with the State Party concerned, decide to include a summary account of the results of the proceedings in its annual report made in accordance with Article 24.

Article 21

1. A State Party to this Convention may at any time declare under this Article that it recognizes the competence of the Committee to receive and consider communications to the effect that a State Party claims that another State Party is not fulfilling its obligations under this Convention. Such communications may be received and considered according to the

procedures laid down in this Article only if submitted by a State Party which has made a declaration recognizing in regard to itself the competence of the Committee. No communication shall be dealt with by the Committee under this Article if it concerns a State Party which has not made such a declaration. Communications received under this Article shall be dealt with in accordance with the following procedure:

a. If a State Party considers that another State Party is not giving effect to the provisions of this Convention, it may, by written communication, bring the matter to the attention of that State Party. Within three months after the receipt of the communication the receiving State shall afford the State which sent the communication an explanation or any other statement in writing clarifying the matter which should include, to the extent possible and pertinent, reference to domestic procedures and remedies taken, pending or available in the matter;

b. If the matter is not adjusted to the satisfaction of both States Parties concerned within six months after the receipt by the receiving State of the initial communication, either State shall have the right to refer the matter to the Committee, by notice given to the Committee and to the other State;

c. The Committee shall deal with a matter referred to it under this Article only after it has ascertained that all domestic remedies have been invoked and exhausted in the matter, in conformity with the generally recognized principles of international law. This shall not be the rule where the application of the remedies is unreasonably prolonged or is unlikely to bring effective relief to the person who is the victim of the violation of this Convention;

d. The Committee shall hold closed meetings when examining communications under this Article;

e. Subject to the provisions of subparagraph *c*, the Committee shall make available its good offices to the States Parties concerned with a view to a friendly solution of the matter on the basis of respect for the obligations provided for in this Convention. For this purpose, the Committee may, when appropriate, set up an *ad hoc* conciliation commission;

f. In any matter referred to it under this Article, the Committee may call upon the States Parties concerned, referred to in subparagraph *b*, to supply any relevant information;

g. The States Parties concerned, referred to in subparagraph *b*, shall have the right to be represented when the matter is being considered by the Committee and to make submissions orally and/or in writing;

h. The Committee shall, within twelve months after the date of receipt of notice under subparagraph *b*, submit a report:

   i. If a solution within the terms of subparagraph *e* is reached, the Committee shall confine its report to a brief statement of the facts and of the solution reached;

   ii. If a solution within the terms of subparagraph *e* is not reached, the Committee shall confine its report to a brief statement of the facts; the written submissions and record of the oral submissions made by the States Parties concerned shall be attached to the report. In every matter, the report shall be communicated to the States Parties concerned.

2. The provisions of this Article shall come into force when five States Parties to this Convention have made declarations under paragraph 1 of this Article. Such declarations shall be deposited by the States Parties with the Secretary General of the United Nations, who shall transmit copies thereof to the other States Parties. A declaration may be withdrawn at any time by notification to the Secretary General. Such a withdrawal shall not prejudice the consideration of any matter which is the subject of a communication already transmitted under this Article; no further communication by any State Party shall be received under this Article after the notification of withdrawal of the declaration has been received by the Secretary General, unless the State Party concerned has made a new declaration.

Article 22

1. A State Party to this Convention may at any time declare under this Article that it recognizes the competence of the Committee to receive and consider communications from or on behalf of individuals subject to its jurisdiction who claim to be victims of a violation by a State Party of

the provisions of the Convention. No communication shall be received by the Committee if it concerns a State Party which has not made such a declaration.

2. The Committee shall consider inadmissible any communication under this Article which is anonymous or which it considers to be an abuse of the right of submission of such communications or to be incompatible with the provisions of this Convention.

3. Subject to the provisions of paragraph 2, the Committee shall bring any communications submitted to it under this Article to the attention of the State Party to this Convention which has made a declaration under paragraph 1 and is alleged to be violating any provisions of the Convention. Within six months, the receiving State shall submit to the Committee written explanations or statements clarifying the matter and the remedy, if any, that may have been taken by that State.

4. The Committee shall consider communications received under this Article in the light of all information made available to it by or on behalf of the individual and by the State Party concerned.

5. The Committee shall not consider any communications from an individual under this Article unless it has ascertained that:

a. The same matter has not been, and is not being, examined under another procedure of international investigation or settlement;

b. The individual has exhausted all available domestic remedies; this shall not be the rule where the application of the remedies is unreasonably prolonged or is unlikely to bring effective relief to the person who is the victim of the violation of this Convention.

6. The Committee shall hold closed meetings when examining communications under this Article.

7. The Committee shall forward its views to the State Party concerned and to the individual.

8. The provisions of this Article shall come into force when five States Parties to this Convention have made declarations under paragraph 1 of this Article. Such declarations shall be deposited by the States Parties with the Secretary General of the United Nations, who shall transmit copies thereof to the other States Parties. A declaration may be withdrawn at any time by notification to the Secretary General. Such a withdrawal shall not prejudice the consideration of any matter which is the subject of a communication already transmitted under this Article; no further communication by or on behalf of an individual shall be received under this Article after the notification of withdrawal of the declaration has been received by the Secretary General, unless the State Party has made a new declaration.

Article 23

The members of the Committee and of the *ad hoc* conciliation commissions which may be appointed under Article 21, paragraph 1.*e*, shall be entitled to the facilities, privileges and immunities of experts on mission for the United Nations as laid down in the relevant sections of the Convention on the Privileges and Immunities of the United Nations.

Article 24

The Committee shall submit an annual report on its activities under this Convention to the States Parties and to the General Assembly of the United Nations.

Part III

Article 25

1. This Convention is open for signature by all States.

2. This Convention is subject to ratification. Instruments of ratification shall be deposited with the Secretary General of the United Nations.

Article 26

This Convention is open to accession by all States. Accession shall be effected by the deposit of an instrument of accession with the Secretary General of the United Nations.

Article 27

1. This Convention shall enter into force on the thirtieth day after the date of the deposit with the Secretary General of the United Nations of the twentieth instrument of ratification or accession.

2. For each State ratifying this Convention or acceding to it after the deposit of the twentieth instrument of ratification or accession, the Convention shall enter into force on the thirtieth day after the date of the deposit of its own instrument of ratification or accession.

Article 28

1. Each State may, at the time of signature or ratification of this Convention or accession thereto, declare that it does not recognize the competence of the Committee provided for in Article 20.

2. Any State Party having made a reservation in accordance with paragraph 1 of this Article may, at any time, withdraw this reservation by notification to the Secretary General of the United Nations.

Article 29

1. Any State Party to this Convention may propose an amendment and file it with the Secretary General of the United Nations. The Secretary General shall thereupon communicate the proposed amendment to the States Parties with a request that they notify him whether they favour a conference of States Parties for the purpose of considering and voting upon the proposal. In the event that within four months from the date of such communication at least one third of the States Parties favours such a conference, the Secretary General shall convene the conference under the auspices of the United Nations. Any amendment adopted by

a majority of the States Parties present and voting at the conference shall be submitted by the Secretary General to all the States Parties for acceptance.

2. An amendment adopted in accordance with paragraph 1 of this Article shall enter into force when two thirds of the States Parties to this Convention have notified the Secretary General of the United Nations that they have accepted it in accordance with their respective constitutional processes.

3. When amendments enter into force, they shall be binding on those States Parties which have accepted them, other States Parties still being bound by the provisions of this Convention and any earlier amendments which they have accepted.

Article 30

1. Any dispute between two or more States Parties concerning the interpretation or application of this Convention which cannot be settled through negotiation shall, at the request of one of them, be submitted to arbitration. If within six months from the date of the request for arbitration the Parties are unable to agree on the organization of the arbitration, any one of those Parties may refer the dispute to the International Court of Justice by request in conformity with the Statute of the Court.

2. Each State may, at the time of signature or ratification of this Convention or accession thereto, declare that it does not consider itself bound by paragraph 1 of this Article. The other States Parties shall not be bound by paragraph 1 of this Article with respect to any State Party having made such a reservation.

3. Any State Party having made a reservation in accordance with paragraph 2 of this Article may at any time withdraw this reservation by notification to the Secretary General of the United Nations.

Article 31

1. A State Party may denounce this Convention by written notification to the Secretary General of the United Nations. Denunciation becomes effective one year after the date of receipt of the notification by the Secretary General.

2. Such a denunciation shall not have the effect of releasing the State Party from its obligations under this Convention in regard to any act or omission which occurs prior to the date at which the denunciation becomes effective, nor shall denunciation prejudice in any way the continued consideration of any matter which is already under consideration by the Committee prior to the date at which the denunciation becomes effective.

3. Following the date at which the denunciation of a State Party becomes effective, the Committee shall not commence consideration of any new matter regarding that State.

Article 32

The Secretary General of the United Nations shall inform all States Members of the United Nations and all States which have signed this Convention or acceded to it of the following:

a. signatures, ratifications and accessions under Articles 25 and 26;
b. the date of entry into force of this Convention under Article 27 and the date of the entry into force of any amendments under Article 29;
c. denunciations under Article 31.

Article 33

1. This Convention, of which the Arabic, Chinese, English, French, Russian and Spanish texts are equally authentic, shall be deposited with the Secretary General of the United Nations.

2. The Secretary General of the United Nations shall transmit certified copies of this Convention to all States.

9. **Convention on the Rights of the Child**

Adopted and opened for signature, ratification and accession by General Assembly Resolution 44/25 of 20 November 1989

Entry into force: 2 September 1990,
in accordance with Article 49

Preamble

The States Parties to the present Convention,

Considering that, in accordance with the principles proclaimed in the Charter of the United Nations, recognition of the inherent dignity and of the equal and inalienable rights of all members of the human family is the foundation of freedom, justice and peace in the world,

Bearing in mind that the peoples of the United Nations have, in the Charter, reaffirmed their faith in fundamental human rights and in the dignity and worth of the human person, and have determined to promote social progress and better standards of life in larger freedom,

Recognising that the United Nations has, in the Universal Declaration of Human Rights and in the International Covenants on Human Rights, proclaimed and agreed that everyone is entitled to all the rights and freedoms set forth therein, without distinction of any kind, such as race, colour, sex, language, religion, political or other opinion, national or social origin, property, birth or other status,

Recalling that, in the Universal Declaration of Human Rights, the United Nations has proclaimed that childhood is entitled to special care and assistance,

Convinced that the family, as the fundamental group of society and the natural environment for the growth and well-being of all its members and particularly children, should be afforded the necessary protection and assistance so that it can fully assume its responsibilities within the community,

Recognising that the child, for the full and harmonious development of his or her personality, should grow up in a family environment, in an atmosphere of happiness, love and understanding,

Considering that the child should be fully prepared to live an individual life in society, and brought up in the spirit of the ideals proclaimed in the Charter of the United Nations, and in particular in the spirit of peace, dignity, tolerance, freedom, equality and solidarity,

Bearing in mind that the need to extend particular care to the child has been stated in the Geneva Declaration of the Rights of the Child of 1924 and in the Declaration of the Rights of the Child adopted by the General Assembly on 20 November 1959 and recognised in the Universal Declaration of Human Rights, in the International Covenant on Civil and Political Rights (in particular in Articles 23 and 24), in the International Covenant on Economic, Social and Cultural Rights (in particular in Article 10) and in the statutes and relevant instruments of specialised agencies and international organisations concerned with the welfare of children,

Bearing in mind that, as indicated in the Declaration of the Rights of the Child, "the child, by reason of his physical and mental immaturity, needs special safeguards and care, including appropriate legal protection, before as well as after birth",

Recalling the provisions of the Declaration on Social and Legal Principles relating to the Protection and Welfare of Children, with Special Reference to Foster Placement and Adoption Nationally and Internationally, the United Nations Standard Minimum Rules for the Administration of Juvenile Justice (The Beijing Rules), and the Declaration on the Protection of Women and Children in Emergency and Armed Conflict,

Recognising that, in all countries in the world, there are children living in exceptionally difficult conditions, and that such children need special consideration,

Taking due account of the importance of the traditions and cultural values of each people for the protection and harmonious development of the child,

Recognising the importance of international co-operation for improving the living conditions of children in every country, in particular in the developing countries,

Have agreed as follows:

Part I

Article 1

For the purposes of the present Convention, a child means every human being below the age of eighteen years unless, under the law applicable to the child, majority is attained earlier.

Article 2

1. States Parties shall respect and ensure the rights set forth in the present Convention to each child within their jurisdiction without discrimination of any kind, irrespective of the child's or his or her parent's or legal guardian's race, colour, sex, language, religion, political or other opinion, national, ethnic or social origin, property, disability, birth or other status.

2. States Parties shall take all appropriate measures to ensure that the child is protected against all forms of discrimination or punishment on the basis of the status, activities, expressed opinions, or beliefs of the child's parents, legal guardians, or family members.

Article 3

1. In all actions concerning children, whether undertaken by public or private social welfare institutions, courts of law, administrative authorities or legislative bodies, the best interests of the child shall be a primary consideration.

2. States Parties undertake to ensure the child such protection and care as is necessary for his or her well-being, taking into account the rights and duties of his or her parents, legal guardians, or other individuals legally responsible for him or her, and, to this end, shall take all appropriate legislative and administrative measures.

3. States Parties shall ensure that the institutions, services and facilities responsible for the care or protection of children shall conform with the standards established by competent authorities, particularly in the areas of safety, health, in the number and suitability of their staff, as well as competent supervision.

Article 4

States Parties shall undertake all appropriate legislative, administrative, and other measures for the implementation of the rights recognised in the present Convention. With regard to economic, social and cultural rights, States Parties shall undertake such measures to the maximum extent of their available resources and, where needed, within the framework of international co-operation.

Article 5

States Parties shall respect the responsibilities, rights and duties of parents or, where applicable, the members of the extended family or community as provided for by local custom, legal guardians or other persons legally responsible for the child, to provide, in a manner consistent with the evolving capacities of the child, appropriate direction and guidance in the exercise by the child of the rights recognised in the present Convention.

Article 6

1. States Parties recognise that every child has the inherent right to life.

2. States Parties shall ensure to the maximum extent possible the survival and development of the child.

Article 7

1. The child shall be registered immediately after birth and shall have the right from birth to a name, the right to acquire a nationality and, as far as possible, the right to know and be cared for by his or her parents.

2. States Parties shall ensure the implementation of these rights in accordance with their national law and their obligations under the relevant international instruments in this field, in particular where the child would otherwise be stateless.

Article 8

1. States Parties undertake to respect the right of the child to preserve his or her identity, including nationality, name and family relations as recognised by law without unlawful interference.

2. Where a child is illegally deprived of some or all of the elements of his or her identity, States Parties shall provide appropriate assistance and protection, with a view to speedily re-establishing his or her identity.

Article 9

1. States Parties shall ensure that a child shall not be separated from his or her parents against their will, except when competent authorities subject to judicial review determine, in accordance with applicable law and procedures, that such separation is necessary for the best interests of the child. Such determination may be necessary in a particular case such as one involving abuse or neglect of the child by the parents, or one where the parents are living separately and a decision must be made as to the child's place of residence.

2. In any proceedings pursuant to paragraph 1 of the present Article, all interested parties shall be given an opportunity to participate in the proceedings and make their views known.

3. States Parties shall respect the right of the child who is separated from one or both parents to maintain personal relations and direct contact with both parents on a regular basis, except if it is contrary to the child's best interests.

4. Where such separation results from any action initiated by a State Party, such as the detention, imprisonment, exile, deportation or death (including death arising from any cause while the person is in the custody of the State) of one or both parents or of the child, that State Party shall, upon request, provide the parents, the child or, if appropriate, another member of the family with the essential information concerning the whereabouts of the absent member(s) of the family unless the provision of the information would be detrimental to the well-being of the child. States Parties shall further ensure that the submission of such a request shall of itself entail no adverse consequences for the person(s) concerned.

Article 10

1. In accordance with the obligation of States Parties under Article 9, paragraph 1, applications by a child or his or her parents to enter or leave a State Party for the purpose of family reunification shall be dealt with by States Parties in a positive, humane and expeditious manner. States Parties shall further ensure that the submission of such a request shall entail no adverse consequences for the applicants and for the members of their family.

2. A child whose parents reside in different States shall have the right to maintain on a regular basis, save in exceptional circumstances, personal relations and direct contacts with both parents. Towards that end and in accordance with the obligation of States Parties under Article 9, paragraph 2, States Parties shall respect the right of the child and his or her parents to leave any country, including their own, and to enter their own country. The right to leave any country shall be subject only to such

restrictions as are prescribed by law and which are necessary to protect the national security, public order *(ordre public)*, public health or morals or the rights and freedoms of others and are consistent with the other rights recognised in the present Convention.

Article 11

1. States Parties shall take measures to combat the illicit transfer and non-return of children abroad.

2. To this end, States Parties shall promote the conclusion of bilateral or multilateral agreements or accession to existing agreements.

Article 12

1. States Parties shall assure to the child who is capable of forming his or her own views the right to express those views freely in all matters affecting the child, the views of the child being given due weight in accordance with the age and maturity of the child.

2. For this purpose, the child shall in particular be provided the opportunity to be heard in any judicial and administrative proceedings affecting the child, either directly, or through a representative or an appropriate body, in a manner consistent with the procedural rules of national law.

Article 13

1. The child shall have the right to freedom of expression; this right shall include freedom to seek, receive and impart information and ideas of all kinds, regardless of frontiers, either orally, in writing or in print, in the form of art, or through any other media of the child's choice.

2. The exercise of this right may be subject to certain restrictions, but these shall only be such as are provided by law and are necessary:

a. for respect of the rights or reputations of others; or
b. for the protection of national security or of public order *(ordre public)*, or of public health or morals.

Article 14

1. States Parties shall respect the right of the child to freedom of thought, conscience and religion.

2. States Parties shall respect the rights and duties of the parents and, when applicable, legal guardians, to provide direction to the child in the exercise of his or her right in a manner consistent with the evolving capacities of the child.

3. Freedom to manifest one's religion or beliefs may be subject only to such limitations as are prescribed by law and are necessary to protect public safety, order, health or morals, or the fundamental rights and freedoms of others.

Article 15

1. States Parties recognise the rights of the child to freedom of association and to freedom of peaceful assembly.

2. No restrictions may be placed on the exercise of these rights other than those imposed in conformity with the law and which are necessary in a democratic society in the interests of national security or public safety, public order *(ordre public)*, the protection of public health or morals or the protection of the rights and freedoms of others.

Article 16

1. No child shall be subjected to arbitrary or unlawful interference with his or her privacy, family, home or correspondence, nor to unlawful attacks on his or her honour and reputation.

2. The child has the right to the protection of the law against such interference or attacks.

Article 17

States Parties recognise the important function performed by the mass media and shall ensure that the child has access to information and material from a diversity of national and international sources, especially those aimed at the promotion of his or her social, spiritual and moral well-being and physical and mental health. To this end, States Parties shall:

a. encourage the mass media to disseminate information and material of social and cultural benefit to the child and in accordance with the spirit of Article 29;

b. encourage international co-operation in the production, exchange and dissemination of such information and material from a diversity of cultural, national and international sources;

c. encourage the production and dissemination of children's books;

d. encourage the mass media to have particular regard to the linguistic needs of the child who belongs to a minority group or who is indigenous;

e. encourage the development of appropriate guidelines for the protection of the child from information and material injurious to his or her well-being, bearing in mind the provisions of Articles 13 and 18.

Article 18

1. States Parties shall use their best efforts to ensure recognition of the principle that both parents have common responsibilities for the upbringing and development of the child. Parents or, as the case may be, legal guardians, have the primary responsibility for the upbringing and development of the child. The best interests of the child will be their basic concern.

2. For the purpose of guaranteeing and promoting the rights set forth in the present Convention, States Parties shall render appropriate assistance to parents and legal guardians in the performance of their child-rearing responsibilities and shall ensure the development of institutions, facilities and services for the care of children.

3. States Parties shall take all appropriate measures to ensure that children of working parents have the right to benefit from child-care services and facilities for which they are eligible.

Article 19

1. States Parties shall take all appropriate legislative, administrative, social and educational measures to protect the child from all forms of physical or mental violence, injury or abuse, neglect or negligent treatment, maltreatment or exploitation, including sexual abuse, while in the care of parent(s), legal guardian(s) or any other person who has the care of the child.

2. Such protective measures should, as appropriate, include effective procedures for the establishment of social programmes to provide necessary support for the child and for those who have the care of the child, as well as for other forms of prevention and for identification, reporting, referral, investigation, treatment and follow-up of instances of child maltreatment described heretofore, and, as appropriate, for judicial involvement.

Article 20

1. A child temporarily or permanently deprived of his or her family environment, or in whose own best interests cannot be allowed to remain in that environment, shall be entitled to special protection and assistance provided by the State.

2. States Parties shall in accordance with their national laws ensure alternative care for such a child.

3. Such care could include, *inter alia*, foster placement, *kafalah* of Islamic law, adoption or if necessary placement in suitable institutions for the care of children. When considering solutions, due regard shall be paid to the desirability of continuity in a child's upbringing and to the child's ethnic, religious, cultural and linguistic background.

Article 21

States Parties that recognise and/or permit the system of adoption shall ensure that the best interests of the child shall be the paramount consideration and they shall:

a. ensure that the adoption of a child is authorised only by competent authorities who determine, in accordance with applicable law and procedures and on the basis of all pertinent and reliable information, that the adoption is permissible in view of the child's status concerning parents, relatives and legal guardians and that, if required, the persons concerned have given their informed consent to the adoption on the basis of such counselling as may be necessary;

b. recognise that inter-country adoption may be considered as an alternative means of child's care, if the child cannot be placed in a foster or an adoptive family or cannot in any suitable manner be cared for in the child's country of origin;

c. ensure that the child concerned by inter-country adoption enjoys safeguards and standards equivalent to those existing in the case of national adoption;

d. take all appropriate measures to ensure that, in inter-country adoption, the placement does not result in improper financial gain for those involved in it;

e. promote, where appropriate, the objectives of the present Article by concluding bilateral or multilateral arrangements or agreements, and endeavour, within this framework, to ensure that the placement of the child in another country is carried out by competent authorities or organs.

Article 22

1. States Parties shall take appropriate measures to ensure that a child who is seeking refugee status or who is considered a refugee in accordance with applicable international or domestic law and procedures shall, whether unaccompanied or accompanied by his or her parents or by any other person, receive appropriate protection and humanitarian assistance in the enjoyment of applicable rights set forth in the present Convention and in other international human rights or humanitarian instruments to which the said States are Parties.

2. For this purpose, States Parties shall provide, as they consider appropriate, co-operation in any efforts by the United Nations and other competent intergovernmental organisations or non-governmental organisations co-operating with the United Nations to protect and assist

such a child and to trace the parents or other members of the family of any refugee child in order to obtain information necessary for reunification with his or her family. In cases where no parents or other members of the family can be found, the child shall be accorded the same protection as any other child permanently or temporarily deprived of his or her family environment for any reason, as set forth in the present Convention.

Article 23

1. States Parties recognise that a mentally or physically disabled child should enjoy a full and decent life, in conditions which ensure dignity, promote self-reliance and facilitate the child's active participation in the community.

2. States Parties recognise the right of the disabled child to special care and shall encourage and ensure the extension, subject to available resources, to the eligible child and those responsible for his or her care, of assistance for which application is made and which is appropriate to the child's condition and to the circumstances of the parents or others caring for the child.

3. Recognising the special needs of a disabled child, assistance extended in accordance with paragraph 2 of the present Article shall be provided free of charge, whenever possible, taking into account the financial resources of the parents or others caring for the child, and shall be designed to ensure that the disabled child has effective access to and receives education, training, health care services, rehabilitation services, preparation for employment and recreation opportunities in a manner conducive to the child's achieving the fullest possible social integration and individual development, including his or her cultural and spiritual development.

4. States Parties shall promote, in the spirit of international co-operation, the exchange of appropriate information in the field of preventive health care and of medical, psychological and functional treatment of disabled children, including dissemination of and access to information concerning methods of rehabilitation, education and vocational services, with the

aim of enabling States Parties to improve their capabilities and skills and to widen their experience in these areas. In this regard, particular account shall be taken of the needs of developing countries.

Article 24

1. States Parties recognise the right of the child to the enjoyment of the highest attainable standard of health and to facilities for the treatment of illness and rehabilitation of health. States Parties shall strive to ensure that no child is deprived of his or her right of access to such health care services.

2. States Parties shall pursue full implementation of this right and, in particular, shall take appropriate measures:

a. to diminish infant and child mortality;

b. to ensure the provision of necessary medical assistance and health care to all children with emphasis on the development of primary health care;

c. to combat disease and malnutrition, including within the framework of primary health care, through, *inter alia*, the application of readily available technology and through the provision of adequate nutritious foods and clean drinking-water, taking into consideration the dangers and risks of environmental pollution;

d. to ensure appropriate pre-natal and post-natal health care for mothers;

e. to ensure that all segments of society, in particular parents and children, are informed, have access to education and are supported in the use of basic knowledge of child health and nutrition, the advantages of breast-feeding, hygiene and environmental sanitation and the prevention of accidents;

f. to develop preventive health care, guidance for parents and family planning education and services.

3. States Parties shall take all effective and appropriate measures with a view to abolishing traditional practices prejudicial to the health of children.

4. States Parties undertake to promote and encourage international co-operation with a view to achieving progressively the full realisation of the right recognised in the present Article. In this regard, particular account shall be taken of the needs of developing countries.

Article 25

States Parties recognise the right of a child who has been placed by the competent authorities for the purposes of care, protection or treatment of his or her physical or mental health, to a periodic review of the treatment provided to the child and all other circumstances relevant to his or her placement.

Article 26

1. States Parties shall recognise for every child the right to benefit from social security, including social insurance, and shall take the necessary measures to achieve the full realisation of this right in accordance with their national law.

2. The benefits should, where appropriate, be granted, taking into account the resources and the circumstances of the child and persons having responsibility for the maintenance of the child, as well as any other consideration relevant to an application for benefits made by or on behalf of the child.

Article 27

1. States Parties recognise the right of every child to a standard of living adequate for the child's physical, mental, spiritual, moral and social development.

2. The parent(s) or others responsible for the child have the primary responsibility to secure, within their abilities and financial capacities, the conditions of living necessary for the child's development.

3. States Parties, in accordance with national conditions and within their means, shall take appropriate measures to assist parents and others

responsible for the child to implement this right and shall in case of need provide material assistance and support programmes, particularly with regard to nutrition, clothing and housing.

4. States Parties shall take all appropriate measures to secure the recovery of maintenance for the child from the parents or other persons having financial responsibility for the child, both within the State Party and from abroad. In particular, where the person having financial responsibility for the child lives in a State different from that of the child, States Parties shall promote the accession to international agreements or the conclusion of such agreements, as well as the making of other appropriate arrangements.

Article 28

1. States Parties recognise the right of the child to education, and with a view to achieving this right progressively and on the basis of equal opportunity, they shall, in particular:

a. make primary education compulsory and available free to all;
b. encourage the development of different forms of secondary education, including general and vocational education, make them available and accessible to every child, and take appropriate measures such as the introduction of free education and offering financial assistance in case of need;
c. make higher education accessible to all on the basis of capacity by every appropriate means;
d. make educational and vocational information and guidance available and accessible to all children;
e. take measures to encourage regular attendance at schools and the reduction of drop-out rates.

2. States Parties shall take all appropriate measures to ensure that school discipline is administered in a manner consistent with the child's human dignity and in conformity with the present Convention.

3. States Parties shall promote and encourage international co-operation in matters relating to education, in particular with a view to contributing

to the elimination of ignorance and illiteracy throughout the world and facilitating access to scientific and technical knowledge and modern teaching methods. In this regard, particular account shall be taken of the needs of developing countries.

Article 29

1. States Parties agree that the education of the child shall be directed to:

a. the development of the child's personality, talents and mental and physical abilities to their fullest potential;
b. the development of respect for human rights and fundamental freedoms, and for the principles enshrined in the Charter of the United Nations;
c. the development of respect for the child's parents, his or her own cultural identity, language and values, for the national values of the country in which the child is living, the country from which he or she may originate, and for civilisations different from his or her own;
d. the preparation of the child for responsible life in a free society, in the spirit of understanding, peace, tolerance, equality of sexes, and friendship among all peoples, ethnic, national and religious groups and persons of indigenous origin;
e. the development of respect for the natural environment.

2. No part of the present Article or Article 28 shall be construed so as to interfere with the liberty of individuals and bodies to establish and direct educational institutions, subject always to the observance of the principles set forth in paragraph 1 of the present Article and to the requirements that the education given in such institutions shall conform to such minimum standards as may be laid down by the State.

Article 30

In those States in which ethnic, religious or linguistic minorities or persons of indigenous origin exist, a child belonging to such a minority or who is indigenous shall not be denied the right, in community with other members of his or her group, to enjoy his or her own culture, to profess and practise his or her own religion, or to use his or her own language.

Article 31

1. States Parties recognise the right of the child to rest and leisure, to engage in play and recreational activities appropriate to the age of the child and to participate freely in cultural life and the arts.

2. States Parties shall respect and promote the right of the child to participate fully in cultural and artistic life and shall encourage the provision of appropriate and equal opportunities for cultural, artistic, recreational and leisure activity.

Article 32

1. States Parties recognise the right of the child to be protected from economic exploitation and from performing any work that is likely to be hazardous or to interfere with the child's education, or to be harmful to the child's health or physical, mental, spiritual, moral or social development.

2. States Parties shall take legislative, administrative, social and educational measures to ensure the implementation of the present Article. To this end, and having regard to the relevant provisions of other international instruments, States Parties shall in particular:

a. provide for a minimum age or minimum ages for admission to employment;

b. provide for appropriate regulation of the hours and conditions of employment;

c. provide for appropriate penalties or other sanctions to ensure the effective enforcement of the present Article.

Article 33

States Parties shall take all appropriate measures, including legislative, administrative, social and educational measures, to protect children from the illicit use of narcotic drugs and psychotropic substances as defined in the relevant international treaties, and to prevent the use of children in the illicit production and trafficking of such substances.

Article 34

States Parties undertake to protect the child from all forms of sexual exploitation and sexual abuse. For these purposes, States Parties shall in particular take all appropriate national, bilateral and multilateral measures to prevent:

a. the inducement or coercion of a child to engage in any unlawful sexual activity;
b. the exploitative use of children in prostitution or other unlawful sexual practices;
c. the exploitative use of children in pornographic performances and materials.

Article 35

States Parties shall take all appropriate national, bilateral and multilateral measures to prevent the abduction of, the sale of or traffic in children for any purpose or in any form.

Article 36

States Parties shall protect the child against all other forms of exploitation prejudicial to any aspects of the child's welfare.

Article 37

States Parties shall ensure that:

a. no child shall be subjected to torture or other cruel, inhuman or degrading treatment or punishment. Neither capital punishment nor life imprisonment without possibility of release shall be imposed for offences committed by persons below eighteen years of age;
b. no child shall be deprived of his or her liberty unlawfully or arbitrarily. The arrest, detention or imprisonment of a child shall be in conformity with the law and shall be used only as a measure of last resort and for the shortest appropriate period of time;
c. every child deprived of liberty shall be treated with humanity and respect for the inherent dignity of the human person, and in a manner

which takes into account the needs of persons of his or her age. In particular, every child deprived of liberty shall be separated from adults unless it is considered in the child's best interest not to do so and shall have the right to maintain contact with his or her family through correspondence and visits, save in exceptional circumstances;

d. every child deprived of his or her liberty shall have the right to prompt access to legal and other appropriate assistance, as well as the right to challenge the legality of the deprivation of his or her liberty before a court or other competent, independent and impartial authority, and to a prompt decision on any such action.

Article 38

1. States Parties undertake to respect and to ensure respect for rules of international humanitarian law applicable to them in armed conflicts which are relevant to the child.

2. States Parties shall take all feasible measures to ensure that persons who have not attained the age of fifteen years do not take a direct part in hostilities.

3. States Parties shall refrain from recruiting any person who has not attained the age of fifteen years into their armed forces. In recruiting among those persons who have attained the age of fifteen years but who have not attained the age of eighteen years, States Parties shall endeavour to give priority to those who are oldest.

4. In accordance with their obligations under international humanitarian law to protect the civilian population in armed conflicts, States Parties shall take all feasible measures to ensure protection and care of children who are affected by an armed conflict.

Article 39

States Parties shall take all appropriate measures to promote physical and psychological recovery and social reintegration of a child victim of: any form of neglect, exploitation, or abuse; torture or any other form of cruel, inhuman or degrading treatment or punishment; or armed conflicts. Such recovery and reintegration shall take place in an environment which fosters the health, self-respect and dignity of the child.

Article 40

1. States Parties recognise the right of every child alleged as, accused of, or recognised as having infringed the penal law to be treated in a manner consistent with the promotion of the child's sense of dignity and worth, which reinforces the child's respect for the human rights and fundamental freedoms of others and which takes into account the child's age and the desirability of promoting the child's reintegration and the child's assuming a constructive role in society.

2. To this end, and having regard to the relevant provisions of international instruments, States Parties shall, in particular, ensure that:

a. no child shall be alleged as, be accused of, or recognised as having infringed the penal law by reason of acts or omissions that were not prohibited by national or international law at the time they were committed;

b. every child alleged as or accused of having infringed the penal law has at least the following guarantees:

i. to be presumed innocent until proven guilty according to law;

ii. to be informed promptly and directly of the charges against him or her, and, if appropriate, through his or her parents or legal guardians, and to have legal or other appropriate assistance in the preparation and presentation of his or her defence;

iii. to have the matter determined without delay by a competent, independent and impartial authority or judicial body in a fair hearing according to law, in the presence of legal or other appropriate assistance and, unless it is considered not to be in the best interest of the child, in particular, taking into account his or her age or situation, his or her parents or legal guardians;

iv. not to be compelled to give testimony or to confess guilt; to examine or have examined adverse witnesses and to obtain the participation and examination of witnesses on his or her behalf under conditions of equality;

v. if considered to have infringed the penal law, to have this decision and any measures imposed in consequence thereof reviewed by a higher competent, independent and impartial authority or judicial body according to law;

vi. to have the free assistance of an interpreter if the child cannot understand or speak the language used;

vii. to have his or her privacy fully respected at all stages of the proceedings.

3. States Parties shall seek to promote the establishment of laws, procedures, authorities and institutions specifically applicable to children alleged as, accused of, or recognised as having infringed the penal law, and, in particular:

a. the establishment of a minimum age below which children shall be presumed not to have the capacity to infringe the penal law;

b. whenever appropriate and desirable, measures for dealing with such children without resorting to judicial proceedings, providing that human rights and legal safeguards are fully respected.

4. A variety of dispositions, such as care, guidance and supervision orders; counselling; probation; foster care; education and vocational training programmes and other alternatives to institutional care shall be available to ensure that children are dealt with in a manner appropriate to their well-being and proportionate both to their circumstances and the offence.

Article 41

Nothing in the present Convention shall affect any provisions which are more conducive to the realisation of the rights of the child and which may be contained in:

a. the law of a State Party; or
b. international law in force for that State.

Part II

Article 42

States Parties undertake to make the principles and provisions of the Convention widely known, by appropriate and active means, to adults and children alike.

Article 43

1. For the purpose of examining the progress made by States Parties in achieving the realisation of the obligations undertaken in the present Convention, there shall be established a Committee on the Rights of the Child, which shall carry out the functions hereinafter provided.

2. The Committee shall consist of ten experts of high moral standing and recognised competence in the field covered by this Convention. The members of the Committee shall be elected by States Parties from among their nationals and shall serve in their personal capacity, consideration being given to equitable geographical distribution, as well as to the principal legal systems.

3. The members of the Committee shall be elected by secret ballot from a list of persons nominated by States Parties. Each State Party may nominate one person from among its own nationals.

4. The initial election to the Committee shall be held no later than six months after the date of the entry into force of the present Convention and thereafter every second year. At least four months before the date of each election, the Secretary General of the United Nations shall address a letter to States Parties inviting them to submit their nominations within two months. The Secretary General shall subsequently prepare a list in alphabetical order of all persons thus nominated, indicating States Parties which have nominated them, and shall submit it to the States Parties to the present Convention.

5. The elections shall be held at meetings of States Parties convened by the Secretary General at United Nations Headquarters. At those

meetings, for which two-thirds of States Parties shall constitute a quorum, the persons elected to the Committee shall be those who obtain the largest number of votes and an absolute majority of the votes of the representatives of States Parties present and voting.

6. The members of the Committee shall be elected for a term of four years. They shall be eligible for re-election if renominated. The term of five of the members elected at the first election shall expire at the end of two years; immediately after the first election, the names of these five members shall be chosen by lot by the Chairman of the meeting.

7. If a member of the Committee dies or resigns or declares that for any other cause he or she can no longer perform the duties of the Committee, the State Party which nominated the member shall appoint another expert from among its nationals to serve for the remainder of the term, subject to the approval of the Committee.

8. The Committee shall establish its own rules of procedure.

9. The Committee shall elect its officers for a period of two years.

10. The meetings of the Committee shall normally be held at United Nations Headquarters or at any other convenient place as determined by the Committee. The Committee shall normally meet annually. The duration of the meetings of the Committee shall be determined, and reviewed, if necessary, by a meeting of the States Parties to the present Convention, subject to the approval of the General Assembly.

11. The Secretary General of the United Nations shall provide the necessary staff and facilities for the effective performance of the functions of the Committee under the present Convention.

12. With the approval of the General Assembly, the members of the Committee established under the present Convention shall receive emoluments from United Nations resources on such terms and conditions as the Assembly may decide.

Article 44

1. States Parties undertake to submit to the Committee, through the Secretary General of the United Nations, reports on the measures they have adopted which give effect to the rights recognised herein and on the progress made on the enjoyment of those rights:

a. within two years of the entry into force of the Convention for the State Party concerned;
b. thereafter every five years.

2. Reports made under the present Article shall indicate factors and difficulties, if any, affecting the degree of fulfilment of the obligations under the present Convention. Reports shall also contain sufficient information to provide the Committee with a comprehensive understanding of the implementation of the Convention in the country concerned.

3. A State Party which has submitted a comprehensive initial report to the Committee need not, in its subsequent reports submitted in accordance with paragraph 1.*b* of the present Article, repeat basic information previously provided.

4. The Committee may request from States Parties further information relevant to the implementation of the Convention.

5. The Committee shall submit to the General Assembly, through the Economic and Social Council, every two years, reports on its activities.

6. States Parties shall make their reports widely available to the public in their own countries.

Article 45

In order to foster the effective implementation of the Convention and to encourage international co-operation in the field covered by the Convention:

a. the specialised agencies, the United Nations Children's Fund, and other United Nations organs shall be entitled to be represented at the consideration of the implementation of such provisions of the present Convention as fall within the scope of their mandate. The Committee may invite the specialised agencies, the United Nations Children's Fund and other competent bodies as it may consider appropriate to provide expert advice on the implementation of the Convention in areas falling within the scope of their respective mandates. The Committee may invite the specialised agencies, the United Nations Children's Fund, and other United Nations organs to submit reports on the implementation of the Convention in areas falling within the scope of their activities;

b. the Committee shall transmit, as it may consider appropriate, to the specialised agencies, the United Nations Children's Fund and other competent bodies, any reports from States Parties that contain a request, or indicate a need, for technical advice or assistance, along with the Committee's observations and suggestions, if any, on these requests or indications;

c. the Committee may recommend to the General Assembly to request the Secretary General to undertake on its behalf studies on specific issues relating to the rights of the child;

d. the Committee may make suggestions and general recommendations based on information received pursuant to Articles 44 and 45 of the present Convention. Such suggestions and general recommendations shall be transmitted to any State Party concerned and reported to the General Assembly, together with comments, if any, from States Parties.

Part III

Article 46

The present Convention shall be open for signature by all States.

Article 47

The present Convention is subject to ratification. Instruments of ratification shall be deposited with the Secretary General of the United Nations.

Article 48

The present Convention shall remain open for accession by any State. The instruments of accession shall be deposited with the Secretary General of the United Nations.

Article 49

1. The present Convention shall enter into force on the thirtieth day following the date of deposit with the Secretary General of the United Nations of the twentieth instrument of ratification or accession.

2. For each State ratifying or acceding to the Convention after the deposit of the twentieth instrument of ratification or accession, the Convention shall enter into force on the thirtieth day after the deposit by such State of its instrument of ratification or accession.

Article 50

1. Any State Party may propose an amendment and file it with the Secretary General of the United Nations. The Secretary General shall thereupon communicate the proposed amendment to States Parties, with a request that they indicate whether they favour a conference of States Parties for the purpose of considering and voting upon the proposals. In the event that, within four months from the date of such communication, at least one-third of the States Parties favour such a conference, the Secretary General shall convene the conference under the auspices of the United Nations. Any amendment adopted by a majority of States Parties present and voting at the conference shall be submitted to the General Assembly for approval.

2. An amendment adopted in accordance with paragraph 1 of the present Article shall enter into force when it has been approved by the General Assembly of the United Nations and accepted by a two-thirds majority of States Parties.

3. When an amendment enters into force, it shall be binding on those States Parties which have accepted it, other States Parties still being

bound by the provisions of the present Convention and any earlier amendments which they have accepted.

Article 51

1. The Secretary General of the United Nations shall receive and circulate to all States the text of reservations made by States at the time of ratification or accession.

2. A reservation incompatible with the object and purpose of the present Convention shall not be permitted.

3. Reservations may be withdrawn at any time by notification to that effect addressed to the Secretary General of the United Nations, who shall then inform all States. Such notification shall take effect on the date on which it is received by the Secretary General.

Article 52

A State Party may denounce the present Convention by written notification to the Secretary General of the United Nations. Denunciation becomes effective one year after the date of receipt of the notification by the Secretary General.

Article 53

The Secretary General of the United Nations is designated as the depositary of the present Convention.

Article 54

The original of the present Convention, of which the Arabic, Chinese, English, French, Russian and Spanish texts are equally authentic, shall be deposited with the Secretary General of the United Nations.

10. **Resolution 728 F (XXVIII)**

Communications concerning human rights

Adopted by the Economic and Social Council on 30 July 1959

The Economic and Social Council,

Having considered chapter V of the report of the Commission on Human Rights on its first session, concerning communications, and chapter IX of the report of the Commission on its fifteenth session,

1. Approves the statement that the Commission on Human Rights recognizes that it has no power to take any action in regard to any complaints concerning human rights;

2. Requests the Secretary General:

a. to compile and distribute to members of the Commission on Human Rights before each session a non-confidential list containing a brief indication of the substance of each communication, however addressed, which deals with the principles involved in the promotion of universal respect for, and observance of, human rights and to divulge the identity of the authors of such communications unless they indicate that they wish their names to remain confidential;

b. to compile before each session of the Commission a confidential list containing a brief indication of the substance of other communications concerning human rights, however addressed, and to furnish this list to members of the Commission, in private meeting, without divulging the identity of the authors of communications except in cases where the authors state that they have already divulged or intend to divulge their names or that they have no objection to their names being divulged;

c. to enable the members of the Commission, upon request, to consult the originals of communications dealing with the principles involved in the promotion of universal respect for, and observance of, human rights;

d. to inform the writers of all communications concerning human rights, however addressed, that their communications will be handled in accordance with this resolution, indicating that the Commission has no power to take any action in regard to any complaint concerning human rights;

e. to furnish each Member State concerned with a copy of any communication concerning human rights which refers explicitly to that State or to territories under its jurisdiction, without divulging the identity of the author, except as provided for in sub-paragraph *b* above;

f. to ask Governments sending replies to communications brought to their attention in accordance with sub-paragraph *e* whether they wish their replies to be presented to the Commission in summary form or in full;

3. Resolves to give members of the Sub-Commission on Prevention of Discrimination and Protection of Minorities, with respect to communications dealing with discrimination and minorities, the same facilities as are enjoyed by members of the Commission on Human Rights under the present resolution;

4. Suggests to the Commission on Human Rights that it should at each session appoint an *ad hoc* committee to meet shortly before its next session for the purpose of reviewing the list of communications prepared by the Secretary General under paragraph 2.*a* above and of recommending which of these communications, in original, should, in accordance with paragraph 2.*c* above, be made available to members of the Commission on request.

11. **Resolution 1235 (XLII)**

Question of the violation of human rights and fundamental freedoms, including policies of racial discrimination and segregation and of *apartheid*, in all countries, with particular reference to colonial and other dependent countries and territories

Adopted by the Economic and Social Council on 6 June 1967

The Economic and Social Council,

Noting Resolutions 8 (XXIII) and 9 (XXIII) of the Commission on Human Rights,

1. Welcomes the decision of the Commission on Human Rights to give annual consideration to the item entitled "Question of the violation of human rights and fundamental freedoms, including policies of racial discrimination and segregation and of *apartheid*, in all countries, with particular reference to colonial and other dependent countries and territories", without prejudice to the functions and powers of organs already in existence or which may be established within the framework of measures of implementation included in international covenants and conventions on the protection of human rights and fundamental freedoms; and concurs with the requests for assistance addressed to the Sub-Commission on Prevention of Discrimination and Protection of Minorities and to the Secretary General;

2. Authorizes the Commission on Human Rights and the Sub-Commission on Prevention of Discrimination and Protection of Minorities, in conformity with the provisions of paragraph 1 of the Commission's Resolution 8 (XXIII), to examine information relevant to gross violations of human rights and fundamental freedoms, as exemplified by the policy of *apartheid* as practised in the Republic of South Africa and in the Territory of South West Africa under the direct responsibility of the United Nations and now illegally occupied by the Government of the

Republic of South Africa, and to racial discrimination as practised notably in Southern Rhodesia, contained in the communications listed by the Secretary General pursuant to Economic and Social Council Resolution 728 F (XXVIII) of 30 July 1959;

3. Decides that the Commission on Human Rights may, in appropriate cases, and after careful consideration of the information thus made available to it, in conformity with the provisions of paragraph 1 above, make a thorough study of situations which reveal a consistent pattern of violations of human rights, as exemplified by the policy of *apartheid* as practised in the Republic of South Africa and in the Territory of South West Africa under the direct responsibility of the United Nations and now illegally occupied by the Government of the Republic of South Africa, and racial discrimination as practised notably in Southern Rhodesia, and report, with recommendations thereon, to the Economic and Social Council;

4. Decides to review the provisions of paragraphs 2 and 3 of the present resolution after the entry into force of the International Covenants on Human Rights;

5. Takes note of the fact that the Commission on Human Rights, in its Resolution 6 (XXIII), has instructed an *ad hoc* study group to study in all its aspects the question of the ways and means by which the Commission might be enabled or assisted to discharge functions in relation to violations of human rights and fundamental freedoms, whilst maintaining and fulfilling its other functions;

6. Requests the Commission on Human Rights to report to it on the result of this study after having given consideration to the conclusions of the *ad hoc* study group referred to in paragraph 5 above.

12. **Resolution 1503 (XLVIII)**

Procedure for dealing with communications relating to violations of human rights and fundamental freedoms

Adopted by the Economic and Social Council on 27 May 1970

The Economic and Social Council,

Noting Resolutions 7 (XXVI) and 17 (XXV) of the Commission on Human Rights and Resolution 2 (XXI) of the Sub-Commission on Prevention of Discrimination and Protection of Minorities,

1. Authorizes the Sub-Commission on Prevention of Discrimination and Protection of Minorities to appoint a working group consisting of not more than five of its members, with due regard to geographical distribution, to meet once a year in private meetings for a period not exceeding ten days immediately before the sessions of the Sub-Commission to consider all communications, including replies of Governments thereon, received by the Secretary General under Council Resolution 728 F (XXVIII) of 30 July 1959 with a view to bringing to the attention of the Sub-Commission those communications, together with replies of Governments, if any, which appear to reveal a consistent pattern of gross and reliably attested violations of human rights and fundamental freedoms within the terms of reference of the Sub-Commission;

2. Decides that the Sub-Commission on Prevention of Discrimination and Protection of Minorities should, as the first stage in the implementation of the present resolution, devise at its twenty-third session appropriate procedures for dealing with the question of admissibility of communications received by the Secretary General under Council Resolution 728 F (XXVIII) and in accordance with Council Resolution 1235 (XLII) of 6 June 1967;

3. Requests the Secretary General to prepare a document on the question of admissibility of communications for the Sub-Commission's consideration at its twenty-third session;

4. Further requests the Secretary General:

a. to furnish to the members of the Sub-Commission every month a list of communications prepared by him in accordance with Council Resolution 728 F (XXVIII) and a brief description of them, together with the text of any replies received from Governments;
b. to make available to the members of the working group at their meetings the originals of such communications listed as they may request, having due regard to the provisions of paragraph 2.*b* of Council Resolution 728 F (XXVIII) concerning the divulging of the identity of the authors of communications;
c. to circulate to the members of the Sub-Commission, in the working languages, the originals of such communications as are referred to the Sub-Commission by the working group;

5. Requests the Sub-Commission on Prevention of Discrimination and Protection of Minorities to consider in private meetings, in accordance with paragraph 1 above, the communications brought before it in accordance with the decision of a majority of the members of the working group and any replies of Governments relating thereto and other relevant information, with a view to determining whether to refer to the Commission on Human Rights particular situations which appear to reveal a consistent pattern of gross and reliably attested violations of human rights requiring consideration by the Commission;

6. Requests the Commission on Human Rights after it has examined any situation referred to it by the Sub-Commission to determine:

a. whether it requires a thorough study by the Commission and a report and recommendations thereon to the Council in accordance with paragraph 3 of Council Resolution 1235 (XLII);
b. whether it may be a subject of an investigation by an *ad hoc* committee to be appointed by the Commission which shall be undertaken

only with the express consent of the State concerned and shall be conducted in constant co-operation with that State and under conditions determined by agreement with it. In any event, the investigation may be undertaken only if:

i. all available means at the national level have been resorted to and exhausted;

ii. the situation does not relate to a matter which is being dealt with under other procedures prescribed in the constituent instruments of, or conventions adopted by, the United Nations and the specialized agencies, or in regional conventions, or which the State concerned wishes to submit to other procedures in accordance with general or special international agreements to which it is a party;

7. Decides that if the Commission on Human Rights appoints an *ad hoc* committee to carry on an investigation with the consent of the State concerned:

a. the composition of the committee shall be determined by the Commission. The members of the committee shall be independent persons whose competence and impartiality is beyond question. Their appointment shall be subject to the consent of the Government concerned;

b. the committee shall establish its own rules of procedure. It shall be subject to the quorum rule. It shall have authority to receive communications and hear witnesses, as necessary. The investigation shall be conducted in co-operation with the Government concerned;

c. the committee's procedure shall be confidential, its proceedings shall be conducted in private meetings and its communications shall not be publicized in any way;

d. the committee shall strive for friendly solutions before, during and even after the investigation;

e. the committee shall report to the Commission on Human Rights with such observations and suggestions as it may deem appropriate;

8. Decides that all actions envisaged in the implementation of the present resolution by the Sub-Commission on Prevention of Discrimination and Protection of Minorities or the Commission on Human Rights shall re-

main confidential until such time as the Commission may decide to make recommendations to the Economic and Social Council;

9. Decides to authorize the Secretary General to provide all facilities which may be required to carry out the present resolution, making use of the existing staff of the Division of Human Rights of the United Nations Secretariat;

10. Decides that the procedure set out in the present resolution for dealing with communications relating to violations of human rights and fundamental freedoms should be reviewed if any new organ entitled to deal with such communications should be established within the United Nations or by international agreement.

13. **Resolution 1 (XXIV)**

Question of the violation of human rights and fundamental freedoms, including policies of racial discrimination and segregation and of *apartheid* in all countries, with particular reference to colonial and other dependent countries and territories

Adopted by the Sub-Commission on Prevention of Discrimination and Protection of Minorities on 13 August 1971

The Sub-Commission on Prevention of Discrimination and Protection of Minorities,

Considering that the Economic and Social Council, by its Resolution 1503 (XLVIII), decided that the Sub-Commission should devise appropriate procedures for dealing with the question of admissibility of communications received by the Secretary General under Council Resolution 728 F (XXVIII) of 30 July 1959 and in accordance with Council Resolution 1235 (XLII) of 6 June 1967,

Adopts the following provisional procedures for dealing with the question of admissibility of communications referred to above:

1. *Standards and criteria*

a. The object of the communication must not be inconsistent with the relevant principles of the Charter, of the Universal Declaration of Human Rights and of the other applicable instruments in the field of human rights.

b. Communications shall be admissible only if, after consideration thereof, together with the replies if any of the Governments concerned, there are reasonable grounds to believe that they may reveal a consistent pattern of gross and reliably attested violations of human rights and fundamental freedoms, including policies of racial discrimination and segregation and of *apartheid* in any country, including colonial and other dependent countries and peoples.

2. *Source of communications*

a. Admissible communications may originate from a person or group of persons who, it can be reasonably presumed, are victims of the violations referred to in sub-paragraph 1.*b* above, any person or group of persons who have direct and reliable knowledge of those violations, or non-governmental organizations acting in good faith in accordance with recognized principles of human rights, not resorting to politically motivated stands contrary to the provisions of the Charter of the United Nations and having direct and reliable knowledge of such violations.

b. Anonymous communications shall be inadmissible; subject to the requirements of sub-paragraph 2.*b* of Resolution 728 F (XXVIII) of the Economic and Social Council, the author of a communication, whether an individual, a group of individuals or an organization, must be clearly identified.

c. Communications shall not be inadmissible solely because the knowledge of the individual authors is second-hand, provided that they are accompanied by clear evidence.

3. *Contents of communications and nature of allegations*

a. The communication must contain a description of the facts and must indicate the purpose of the petition and the rights that have been violated.

b. Communications shall be inadmissible if their language is essentially abusive and in particular if they contain insulting references to the State against which the complaint is directed. Such communications may be considered if they meet the other criteria for admissibility after deletion of the abusive language.

c. A communication shall be inadmissible if it has manifestly political motivations and its subject is contrary to the provisions of the Charter of the United Nations.

d. A communication shall be inadmissible if it appears that it is based exclusively on reports disseminated by mass media.

4. *Existence of other remedies*

a. Communications shall be inadmissible if their admission would prejudice the functions of the specialized agencies of the United Nations system.

b. Communications shall be inadmissible if domestic remedies have not been exhausted, unless it appears that such remedies would be ineffective or unreasonably prolonged. Any failure to exhaust remedies should be satisfactorily established.

c. Communications relating to cases which have been settled by the State concerned in accordance with the principles set forth in the Universal Declaration of Human Rights and other applicable documents in the field of human rights will not be considered.

5. *Timeliness*

A communication shall be inadmissible if it is not submitted to the United Nations within a reasonable time after the exhaustion of the domestic remedies as provided above.

B. Regional protection of human rights

I. Texts prepared within the Council of Europe

Treaties

1. Statute of the Council of Europe

(Extracts)

London, 5 May 1949

The Governments of the Kingdom of Belgium, the Kingdom of Denmark, the French Republic, the Irish Republic, the Italian Republic, the Grand Duchy of Luxembourg, the Kingdom of the Netherlands, the Kingdom of Norway, the Kingdom of Sweden and the United Kingdom of Great Britain and Northern Ireland,

Convinced that the pursuit of peace based upon justice and international co-operation is vital for the preservation of human society and civilisation;

Reaffirming their devotion to the spiritual and moral values which are the common heritage of their peoples and the true source of individual freedom, political liberty and the rule of law, principles which form the basis of all genuine democracy;

Believing that, for the maintenance and further realisation of these ideals and in the interests of economic and social progress, there is need of a closer unity between all like-minded countries of Europe;

Considering that, to respond to this need and to the expressed aspirations of their peoples in this regard, it is necessary forthwith to create an organisation which will bring European States into closer association,

Have in consequence decided to set up a Council of Europe consisting of a Committee of representatives of Governments and of a Consultative Assembly, and have for this purpose adopted the following Statute.

(...)

Article 1

a. The aim of the Council of Europe is to achieve a greater unity between its Members for the purpose of safeguarding and realising the ideals and principles which are their common heritage and facilitating their economic and social progress.
b. This aim shall be pursued through the organs of the Council by discussion of questions of common concern and by agreements and common action in economic, social, cultural, scientific, legal and administrative matters and in the maintenance and further realisation of human rights and fundamental freedoms.
c. Participation in the Council of Europe shall not affect the collaboration of its Members in the work of the United Nations and of other international organisations or unions to which they are parties.
d. Matters relating to National Defence do not fall within the scope of the Council of Europe.

(...)

Article 3

Every Member of the Council of Europe must accept the principles of the rule of law and of the enjoyment by all persons within its jurisdiction of human rights and fundamental freedoms, and collaborate sincerely and effectively in the realisation of the aim of the Council as specified in Chapter I.

Article 4

Any European State which is deemed to be able and willing to fulfil the provisions of Article 3 may be invited to become a Member of the Council of Europe by the Committee of Ministers. Any State so invited shall become a Member on the deposit on its behalf with the Secretary General of an instrument of accession to the present Statute.

Article 5

a. In special circumstances, a European country which is deemed to be able and willing to fulfil the provisions of Article 3 may be invited by the Committee of Ministers to become an Associate Member of the Council of Europe. Any country so invited shall become an Associate Member on the deposit on its behalf with the Secretary General of an instrument accepting the present Statute. An associate Member shall be entitled to be represented in the Consultative Assembly only.

b. The expression "Member" in this Statute includes an Associate Member except when used in connexion with representation on the Committee of Ministers.

(...)

Article 8

Any Member of the Council of Europe which has seriously violated Article 3 may be suspended from its rights of representation and requested by the Committee of Ministers to withdraw under Article 7. If such Member does not comply with this request, the Committee may decide that it has ceased to be a Member of the Council as from such date as the Committee may determine.

(...)

2. Convention for the Protection of Human Rights and Fundamental Freedoms

Rome, 4 November 1950

Entry into force: 3 September 1953,
in accordance with Article 66

Text amended according to the provisions
of Protocol No. 3, which entered into force on 21 September 1970,
of Protocol No. 5, which entered into force on 20 December 1971
and of Protocol No. 8, which entered into force on 1 January 1990,
and comprising also the text of Protocol No. 2 which, in accordance with Article 5, paragraph 3, thereof, has been an integral part of the Convention since its entry into force on 21 September 1970

The governments signatory hereto, being members of the Council of Europe,

Considering the Universal Declaration of Human Rights proclaimed by the General Assembly of the United Nations on 10th December 1948;

Considering that this declaration aims at securing the universal and effective recognition and observance of the rights therein declared;

Considering that the aim of the Council of Europe is the achievement of greater unity between its members and that one of the methods by which that aim is to be pursued is the maintenance and further realisation of human rights and fundamental freedoms;

Reaffirming their profound belief in those fundamental freedoms which are the foundation of justice and peace in the world and are best maintained on the one hand by an effective political democracy and on the other by a common understanding and observance of the human rights upon which they depend;

Being resolved, as the governments of European countries which are like-minded and have a common heritage of political traditions, ideals, freedom and the rule of law, to take the first steps for the collective enforcement of certain of the rights stated in the Universal Declaration,

Have agreed as follows:

Article 1

The High Contracting Parties shall secure to everyone within their jurisdiction the rights and freedoms defined in Section I of this Convention.

Section I

Article 2

1. Everyone's right to life shall be protected by law. No one shall be deprived of his life intentionally save in the execution of a sentence of a court following his conviction of a crime for which this penalty is provided by law.

2. Deprivation of life shall not be regarded as inflicted in contravention of this article when it results from the use of force which is no more than absolutely necessary:

a. in defence of any person from unlawful violence;
b. in order to effect a lawful arrest or to prevent the escape of a person lawfully detained;
c. in action lawfully taken for the purpose of quelling a riot or insurrection.

Article 3

No one shall be subjected to torture or to inhuman or degrading treatment or punishment.

Article 4

1. No one shall be held in slavery or servitude.

2. No one shall be required to perform forced or compulsory labour.

3. For the purpose of this article the term "forced or compulsory labour" shall not include:

a. any work required to be done in the ordinary course of detention imposed according to the provisions of Article 5 of this Convention or during conditional release from such detention;
b. any service of a military character or, in case of conscientious objectors in countries where they are recognised, service exacted instead of compulsory military service;
c. any service exacted in case of an emergency or calamity threatening the life or well-being of the community;
d. any work or service which forms part of normal civic obligations.

Article 5

1. Everyone has the right to liberty and security of person. No one shall be deprived of his liberty save in the following cases and in accordance with a procedure prescribed by law:

a. the lawful detention of a person after conviction by a competent court;
b. the lawful arrest or detention of a person for non-compliance with the lawful order of a court or in order to secure the fulfilment of any obligation prescribed by law;
c. the lawful arrest or detention of a person effected for the purpose of a bringing him before the competent legal authority on reasonable suspicion of having committed an offence or when it is reasonably considered necessary to prevent his committing an offence or fleeing after having done so;
d. the detention of a minor by lawful order for the purpose of educational supervision or his lawful detention for the purpose of bringing him before the competent legal authority;

e. the lawful detention of persons for the prevention of the spreading of infectious diseases, of persons of unsound mind, alcoholics or drug addicts or vagrants;

f. the lawful arrest or detention of a person to prevent his effecting an unauthorised entry into the country or of a person against whom action is being taken with a view to deportation or extradition.

2. Everyone who is arrested shall be informed promptly, in a language which he understands, of the reasons for his arrest and of any charge against him.

3. Everyone arrested or detained in accordance with the provisions of paragraph 1.*c* of this article shall be brought promptly before a judge or other officer authorised by law to exercise judicial power and shall be entitled to trial within a reasonable time or to release pending trial. Release may be conditioned by guarantees to appear for trial.

4. Everyone who is deprived of his liberty by arrest or detention shall be entitled to take proceedings by which the lawfulness of his detention shall be decided speedily by a court and his release ordered if the detention is not lawful.

5. Everyone who has been the victim of arrest or detention in contravention of the provisions of this article shall have an enforceable right to compensation.

Article 6

1. In the determination of his civil rights and obligations or of any criminal charge against him, everyone is entitled to a fair and public hearing within a reasonable time by an independent and impartial tribunal established by law. Judgment shall be pronounced publicly but the press and public may be excluded from all or part of the trial in the interest of morals, public order or national security in a democratic society, where the interests of juveniles or the protection of the private life of the parties so require, or to the extent strictly necessary in the opinion of the court in special circumstances wherd publicity would prejudice the interests of justice.

2. Everyone charged with a criminal offence shall be presumed innocent until proved guilty according to law.

3. Everyone charged with a criminal offence has the following minimum rights:

a. to be informed promptly, in a language which he understands and in detail, of the nature and cause of the accusation against him;
b. to have adequate time and facilities for the preparation of his defence;
c. to defend himself in person or through legal assistance of his own choosing or, if he has not sufficient means to pay for legal assistance, to be given it free when the interests of justice so require;
d. to examine or have examined witnesses against him and to obtain the attendance and examination of witnesses on his behalf under the same conditions as witnesses against him
e. to have the free assistance of an interpreter if he cannot understand or speak the language used in court.

Article 7

1. No one shall be held guilty of any criminal offence on account of any act or omission which did not constitute a criminal offence under national or international law at the time when it was committed. Nor shall a heavier penalty be imposed than the one that was applicable at the time the criminal offence was committed.

2. This article shall not prejudice the trial and punishment of any person for any act or omission which, at the time when it was committed, was criminal according to the general principles of law recognised by civilised nations.

Article 8

1. Everyone has the right to respect for his private and family life, his home and his correspondence.

2. There shall be no interference by a public authority with the exercise of this right except such as is in accordance with the law and is necessary in a democratic society in the interests of national security, public safety or the economic well-being of the country, for the prevention of disorder or crime, for the protection of health or morals, or for the protection of the rights and freedoms of others.

Article 9

1. Everyone has the right to freedom of thought, conscience and religion; this right includes freedom to change his religion or belief and freedom, either alone or in community with others and in public or in private, to manifest his religion or belief, in worship, teaching, practice and observance.

2. Freedom to manifest one's religion or beliefs shall be subject only to such limitations as are prescribed by law and are necessary in a democratic society in the interests of public safety, for the protection of public order, health or morals, or for the protection of the rights and freedoms of others.

Article 10

1. Everyone has the right to freedom of expression. This right shall include freedom to hold opinions and to receive and impart information and ideas without interference by public authority and regardless of frontiers. This article shall not prevent States from requiring the licensing of broadcasting, television or cinema enterprises.

2. The exercise of these freedoms, since it carries with it duties and responsibilities, may be subject to such formalities, conditions, restrictions or penalties as are prescribed by law and are necessary in a democratic society, in the interests of national security, territorial integrity or public safety, for the prevention of disorder or crime, for the protection of health or morals, for the protection of the reputation or rights of others, for preventing the disclosure of information received in confidence, or for maintaining the authority and impartiality of the judiciary.

Article 11

1. Everyone has the right to freedom of peaceful assembly and to freedom of association with others, including the right to form and to join trade unions for the protection of his interests.

2. No restrictions shall be placed on the exercise of these rights other than such as are prescribed by law and are necessary in a democratic society in the interests of national security or public safety, for the prevention of disorder or crime, for the protection of health or morals or for the protection of the rights and freedoms of others. This article shall not prevent the imposition of lawful restrictions on the exercise of these rights by members of the armed forces, of the police or of the administration of the State.

Article 12

Men and women of marriageable age have the right to marry and to found a family, according to the national laws governing the exercise of this right.

Article 13

Everyone whose rights and freedoms as set forth in this Convention are violated shall have an effective remedy before a national authority notwithstanding that the violation has been committed by persons acting in an official capacity.

Article 14

The enjoyment of the rights and freedoms set forth in this Convention shall be secured without discrimination on any ground such as sex, race, colour, language, religion, political or other opinion, national or social origin, association with a national minority, property, birth or other status.

Article 15

1. In time of war or other public emergency threatening the life of the nation any High Contracting Party may take measures derogating from

its obligations under this Convention to the extent strictly required by the exigencies of the situation, provided that such measures are not inconsistent with its other obligations under international law.

2. No derogation from Article 2, except in respect of deaths resulting from lawful acts of war, or from Articles 3, 4 (paragraph 1) and 7 shall be made under this provision.

3. Any High Contracting Party availing itself of this right of derogation shall keep the Secretary General of the Council of Europe fully informed of the measures which it has taken and the reasons therefor. It shall also inform the Secretary General of the Council of Europe when such measures have ceased to operate and the provisions of the Convention are again being fully executed.

Article 16

Nothing in Articles 10, 11 and 14 shall be regarded as preventing the High Contracting Parties from imposing restrictions on the political activity of aliens.

Article 17

Nothing in this Convention may be interpreted as implying for any State, group or person any right to engage in any activity or perform any act aimed at the destruction of any of the rights and freedoms set forth herein or at their limitation to a greater extent than is provided for in the Convention.

Article 18

The restrictions permitted under this Convention to the said rights and freedoms shall not be applied for any purpose other than those for which they have been prescribed.

Section II

Article 19

To ensure the observance of the engagements undertaken by the High Contracting Parties in the present Convention, there shall be set up:

a. a European Commission of Human Rights, hereinafter referred to as "the Commission";
b. a European Court of Human Rights, hereinafter referred to as "the Court".

Section III

Article 20

1. The Commission shall consist of a number of members equal to that of the High Contracting Parties. No two members of the Commission may be nationals of the same State.

2. The Commission shall sit in plenary session. It may, however, set up chambers, each composed of at least seven members. The chambers may examine petitions submitted under Article 25 of this Convention which can be dealt with on the basis of established case-law or which raise no serious question affecting the interpretation or application of the Convention. Subject to this restriction and to the provisions of paragraph 5 of this article, the chambers shall exercise all the powers conferred on the Commission by the Convention.

The member of the Commission elected in respect of a High Contracting Party against which a petition has been lodged shall have the right to sit on a chamber to which that petition has been referred.

3. The Commission may set up committees, each composed of at least three members, with the power, exercisable by a unanimous vote, to declare inadmissible or strike from its list of cases a petition submitted

under Article 25, when such a decision can be taken without further examination.

4. A chamber or committee may at any time relinquish jurisdiction in favour of the plenary Commission, which may also order the transfer to it of any petition referred to a chamber or committee.

5. Only the plenary Commission can exercise the following powers:

a. the examination of applications submitted under Article 24;
b. the bringing of a case before the Court in accordance with Article 48.*a*.
c. the drawing up of rules of procedure in accordance with Article 36.

Article 21

1. The members of the Commission shall be elected by the Committee of Ministers by an absolute majority of votes, from a list of names drawn up by the Bureau of the Consultative Assembly; each group of the representatives of the High Contracting Parties in the Consultative Assembly shall put forward three candidates, of whom two at least shall be its nationals.

2. As far as applicable, the same procedure shall be followed to complete the Commission in the event of other States subsequently becoming Parties to this Convention, and in filling casual vacancies.

3. The candidates shall be of high moral character and must either possess the qualifications required for appointment to high judicial office or be persons of recognised competence in national or international law.

Article 22

1. The members of the Commission shall be elected for a period of six years. They may be re-elected. However, of the members elected at the first election, the terms of seven members shall expire at the end of three years.

2. The members whose terms are to expire at the end of the initial period of three years shall be chosen by lot by the Secretary General of the Council of Europe immediately after the first election has been completed.

3. In order to ensure that, as far as possible, one half of the membership of the Commission shall be renewed every three years, the Committee of Ministers may decide, before proceeding to any subsequent election, that the term or terms of office of one or more members to be elected shall be for a period other than six years but not more than nine and not less than three years.

4. In cases where more than one term of office is involved and the Committee of Ministers applies the preceding paragraph, the allocation of the terms of office shall be effected by the drawing of lots by the Secretary General, immediately after the election.

5. A member of the Commission elected to replace a member whose term of office has not expired shall hold office for the remainder of his predecessor's term.

6. The members of the Commission shall hold office until replaced. After having been replaced, they shall continue to deal with such cases as they already have under consideration.

Article 23

The members of the Commission shall sit on the Commission in their individual capacity. During their term of office they shall not hold any position which is incompatible with their independence and impartiality as members of the Commission or the demands of this office.

Article 24

Any High Contracting Party may refer to the Commission, through the Secretary General of the Council of Europe, any alleged breach of the provisions of the Convention by another High Contracting Party.

Article 25

1. The Commission may receive petitions addressed to the Secretary General of the Council of Europe from any person, non-governmental organisation or group of individuals claiming to be the victim of a violation by one of the High Contracting Parties of the rights set forth in this Convention, provided that the High Contracting Party against which the complaint has been lodged has declared that it recognises the competence of the Commission to receive such petitions. Those of the High Contracting Parties who have made such a declaration undertake not to hinder in any way the effective exercise of this right.

2. Such declarations may be made for a specific period.

3. The declarations shall be deposited with the Secretary General of the Council of Europe who shall transmit copies thereof to the High Contracting Parties and publish them.

4. The Commission shall only exercise the powers provided for in this article when at least six High Contracting Parties are bound by declarations made in accordance with the preceding paragraphs.

Article 26

The Commission may only deal with the matter after all domestic remedies have been exhausted, according to the generally recognised rules of international law, and within a period of six months from the date on which the final decision was taken.

Article 27

1. The Commission shall not deal with any petition submitted under Article 25 which:

a. is anonymous, or

b. is substantially the same as a matter which has already been examined by the Commission or has already been submitted to another procedure of international investigation or settlement and if it contains no relevant new information.

2. The Commission shall consider inadmissible any petition submitted under Article 25 which it considers incompatible with the provisions of the present Convention, manifestly ill-founded, or an abuse of the right of petition.

3. The Commission shall reject any petition referred to it which it considers inadmissible under Article 26.

Article 28

1. In the event of the Commission accepting a petition referred to it:

a. it shall, with a view to ascertaining the facts, undertake together with the representatives of the parties an examination of the petition and, if need be, an investigation, for the effective conduct of which the States concerned shall furnish all necessary facilities, after an exchange of views with the Commission;

b. it shall at the same time place itself at the disposal of the parties concerned with a view to securing a friendly settlement of the matter on the basis of respect for human rights as defined in this Convention.

2. If the Commission succeeds in effecting a friendly settlement, it shall draw up a report which shall be sent to the States concerned, to the Committee of Ministers and to the Secretary General of the Council of Europe for publication. This report shall be confined to a brief statement of the facts and of the solution reached.

Article 29

After it has accepted a petition submitted under Article 25, the Commission may nevertheless decide by a majority of two-thirds of its members to reject the petition if, in the course of its examination, it finds that the existence of one of the grounds for non-acceptance provided for in Article 27 has been established. In such a case, the decision shall be communicated to the parties.

Article 30

1. The Commission may at any stage of the proceedings decide to strike a petition out of its list of cases where the circumstances lead to the conclusion that:

a. the applicant does not intend to pursue his petition, or
b. the matter has been resolved, or
c. for any other reason established by the Commission, it is no longer justified to continue the examination of the petition.

However, the Commission shall continue the examination of a petition if respect for human rights as defined in this Convention so requires.

2. If the Commission decides to strike a petition out of its list after having accepted it, it shall draw up a report which shall contain a statement of the facts and the decision striking out the petition together with the reasons therefor. The report shall be transmitted to the parties, as well as to the Committee of Ministers for information. The Commission may publish it.

3. The Commission may decide to restore a petition to its list of cases if it considers that the circumstances justify such a course.

Article 31

1. If the examination of a petition has not been completed in accordance with Article 28 (paragraph 2), 29 or 30, the Commission shall draw up a report on the facts and state its opinion as to whether the facts found disclose a breach by the State concerned of its obligations under the Convention. The individual opinions of members of the Commission on this point may be stated in the report.

2. The report shall be transmitted to the Committee of Ministers. It shall also be transmitted to the States concerned, who shall not be at liberty to publish it.

3. In transmitting the report to the Committee of Ministers the Commission may make such proposals as it thinks fit.

Article 32

1. If the question is not referred to the Court in accordance with Article 48 of this Convention within a period of three months from the date of the transmission of the report to the Committee of Ministers, the Committee of Ministers shall decide by a majority of two-thirds of the members entitled to sit on the Committee whether there has been a violation of the Convention.

2. In the affirmative case the Committee of Ministers shall prescribe a period during which the High Contracting Party concerned must take the measures required by the decision of the Committee of Ministers.

3. If the High Contracting Party concerned has not taken satisfactory measures within the prescribed period, the Committee of Ministers shall decide by the majority provided for in paragraph 1 above what effect shall be given to its original decision and shall publish the report.

4. The High Contracting Parties undertake to regard as binding on them any decision which the Committee of Ministers may take in application of the preceding paragraphs.

Article 33

The Commission shall meet in camera.

Article 34

Subject to the provisions of Articles 20 (paragraph 3) and 29, the Commission shall take its decisions by a majority of the members present and voting.

Article 35

The Commission shall meet as the circumstances require. The meetings shall be convened by the Secretary General of the Council of Europe.

Article 36

The Commission shall draw up its own rules of procedure.

Article 37

The secretariat of the Commission shall be provided by the Secretary General of the Council of Europe.

Section IV

Article 38

The European Court of Human Rights shall consist of a number of judges equal to that of the members of the Council of Europe. No two judges may be nationals of the same State.

Article 39

1. The members of the Court shall be elected by the Consultative Assembly by a majority of the votes cast from a list of persons nominated by the members of the Council of Europe; each member shall nominate three candidates, of whom two at least shall be its nationals.

2. As far as applicable, the same procedure shall be followed to complete the Court in the event of the admission of new members of the Council of Europe, and in filling casual vacancies.

3. The candidates shall be of high moral character and must either possess the qualifications required for appointment to high judicial office or be jurisconsults of recognised competence.

Article 40

1. The members of the Court shall be elected for a period of nine years. They may be re-elected. However, of the members elected at the first election the terms of four members shall expire at the end of three years, and the terms of four more members shall expire at the end of six years.

2. The members whose terms are to expire at the end of the initial periods of three and six years shall be chosen by lot by the Secretary General immediately after the first election has been completed.

3. In order to ensure that, as far as possible, one third of the membership of the Court shall be renewed every three years, the Consultative Assembly may decide, before proceeding to any subsequent election, that the term or terms of office of one or more members to be elected shall be for a period other than nine years but not more than twelve and not less than six years.

4. In cases where more than one term of office is involved and the Consultative Assembly applies the preceding paragraph, the allocation of the terms of office shall be effected by the drawing of lots by the Secretary General immediately after the election.

5. A member of the Court elected to replace a member whose term of office has not expired shall hold office for the remainder of his predecessor's term.

6. The members of the Court shall hold office until replaced. After having been replaced, they shall continue to deal with such cases as they already have under consideration.

7. The members of the Court shall sit on the Court in their individual capacity. During their term of office they shall not hold any position which is incompatible with their independence and impartiality as members of the Court or the demands of this office.

Article 41

The Court shall elect its President and one or two Vice-Presidents for a period of three years. They may be re-elected.

Article 42

The members of the Court shall receive for each day of duty a compensation to be determined by the Committee of Ministers.

Article 43

For the consideration of each case brought before it the Court shall consist of a chamber composed of nine judges. There shall sit as an *ex officio* member of the chamber the judge who is a national of any State Party concerned, or, if there is none, a person of its choice who shall sit in the capacity of judge; the names of the other judges shall be chosen by lot by the President before the opening of the case.

Article 44

Only the High Contracting Parties and the Commission shall have the right to bring a case before the Court.

Article 45

The jurisdiction of the Court shall extend to all cases concerning the interpretation and application of the present Convention which the High Contracting Parties or the Commission shall refer to it in accordance with Article 48.

Article 46

1. Any of the High Contracting Parties may at any time declare that it recognises as compulsory *ipso facto* and without special agreement the jurisdiction of the Court in all matters concerning the interpretation and application of the present Convention.

2. The declarations referred to above may be made unconditionally or on condition of reciprocity on the part of several or certain other High Contracting Parties or for a specified period.

3. These declarations shall be deposited with the Secretary General of the Council of Europe who shall transmit copies thereof to the High Contracting Parties.

Article 47

The Court may only deal with a case after the Commission has acknowledged the failure of efforts for a friendly settlement and within the period of three months provided for in Article 32.

Article 48

The following may bring a case before the Court, provided that the High Contracting Party concerned, if there is only one, or the High Contracting Parties concerned, if there is more than one, are subject to the compulsory jurisdiction of the Court or, failing that, with the consent of the High Contracting Party concerned, if there is only one, or of the High Contracting Parties concerned if there is more than one:

a. the Commission;
b. a High Contracting Party whose national is alleged to be a victim;
c. a High Contracting Party which referred the case to the Commission;
d. a High Contracting Party against which the complaint has been lodged.

Article 49

In the event of dispute as to whether the Court has jurisdiction, the matter shall be settled by the decision of the Court.

Article 50

If the Court finds that a decision or a measure taken by a legal authority or any other authority of a High Contracting Party is completely or partially in conflict with the obligations arising from the present Convention, and if the internal law of the said Party allows only partial reparation to be made for the consequences of this decision or measure, the decision of the Court shall, if necessary, afford just satisfaction to the injured party.

Article 51

1. Reasons shall be given for the judgment of the Court.

2. If the judgment does not represent in whole or in part the unanimous opinion of the judges, any judge shall be entitled to deliver a separate opinion.

Article 52

The judgment of the Court shall be final.

Article 53

The High Contracting Parties undertake to abide by the decision of the Court in any case to which they are parties.

Article 54

The judgment of the Court shall be transmitted to the Committee of Ministers which shall supervise its execution.

Article 55

The Court shall draw up its own rules and shall determine its own procedure.

Article 56

1. The first election of the members of the Court shall take place after the declarations by the High Contracting Parties mentioned in Article 46 have reached a total of eight.

2. No case can be brought before the Court before this election.

Section V

Article 57

On receipt of a request from the Secretary General of the Council of Europe any High Contracting Party shall furnish an explanation of the manner in which its internal law ensures the effective implementation of any of the provisions of this Convention.

Article 58

The expenses of the Commission and the Court shall be borne by the Council of Europe.

Article 59

The members of the Commission and of the Court shall be entitled, during the discharge of their functions, to the privileges and immunities provided for in Article 40 of the Statute of the Council of Europe and in the agreements made thereunder.

Article 60

Nothing in this Convention shall be construed as limiting or derogating from any of the human rights and fundamental freedoms which may be ensured under the laws of any High Contracting Party or under any other agreement to which it is a Party.

Article 61

Nothing in this Convention shall prejudice the powers conferred on the Committee of Ministers by the Statute of the Council of Europe.

Article 62

The High Contracting Parties agree that, except by special agreement, they will not avail themselves of treaties, conventions or declarations in force between them for the purpose of submitting, by way of petition, a dispute arising out of the interpretation or application of this Convention to a means of settlement other than those provided for in this Convention.

Article 63

1. Any State may at the time of its ratification or at any time thereafter declare by notification addressed to the Secretary General of the Council of Europe that the present Convention shall extend to all or any of the territories for whose international relations it is responsible.

2. The Convention shall extend to the territory or territories named in the notification as from the thirtieth day after the receipt of this notification by the Secretary General of the Council of Europe.

3. The provisions of this Convention shall be applied in such territories with due regard, however, to local requirements.

4. Any State which has made a declaration in accordance with paragraph 1 of this Article may at any time thereafter declare on behalf of one or more of the territories to which the declaration relates that it accepts the competence of the Commission to receive petitions from individuals, non-governmental organisations or groups of individuals in accordance with Article 25 of the present Convention.

Article 64

1. Any State may, when signing this Convention or when depositing its instrument of ratification, make a reservation in respect of any particular provision of the Convention to the extent that any law then in force in its territory is not in conformity with the provision. Reservations of a general character shall not be permitted under this article.

2. Any reservation made under this article shall contain a brief statement of the law concerned.

Article 65

1. A High Contracting Party may denounce the present Convention only after the expiry of five years from the date on which it became a Party to it and after six months' notice contained in a notification addressed to the Secretary General of the Council of Europe, who shall inform the other High Contracting Parties.

2. Such a denunciation shall not have the effect of releasing the High Contracting Party concerned from its obligations under this Convention in respect of any act which, being capable of constituting a violation of such obligations, may have been performed by it before the date at which the denunciation became effective.

3. Any High Contracting Party which shall cease to be a member of the Council of Europe shall cease to be a Party to this Convention under the same conditions.

4. The Convention may be denounced in accordance with the provisions of the preceding paragraphs in respect of any territory to which it has been declared to extend under the terms of Article 63.

Article 66

1. This Convention shall be open to the signature of the members of the Council of Europe. It shall be ratified. Ratifications shall be deposited with the Secretary General of the Council of Europe.

2. The present Convention shall come into force after the deposit of ten instruments of ratification.

3. As regards any signatory ratifying subsequently, the Convention shall come into force at the date of the deposit of its instrument of ratification.

4. The Secretary General of the Council of Europe shall notify all the members of the Council of Europe of the entry into force of the Convention, the names of the High Contracting Parties who have ratified it, and the deposit of all instruments of ratification which may be effected subsequently.

Done at Rome this 4th day of November 1950, in English and French, both texts being equally authentic, in a single copy which shall remain deposited in the archives of the Council of Europe. The Secretary General shall transmit certified copies to each of the signatories.

Protocol No. 2

to the Convention for the Protection of Human Rights and Fundamental Freedoms, conferring upon the European Court of Human Rights competence to give advisory opinions

Strasbourg, 6 May 1963

Entry into force: 21 September 1970,
in accordance with Article 5

The member States of the Council of Europe signatory hereto,

Having regard to the provisions of the Convention for the Protection of Human Rights and Fundamental Freedoms signed at Rome on 4 November 1950 (hereinafter referred to as "the Convention") and, in particular, Article 19 instituting, among other bodies, a European Court of Human Rights (hereinafter referred to as "the Court");

Considering that it is expedient to confer upon the Court competence to give advisory opinions subject to certain conditions,

Have agreed as follows:

Article 1

1. The Court may, at the request of the Committee of Ministers, give advisory opinions on legal questions concerning the interpretation of the Convention and the Protocols thereto.

2. Such opinions shall not deal with any question relating to the content or scope of the rights or freedoms defined in Section I of the Convention and in the Protocols thereto, or with any other question which the Commission, the Court or the Committee of Ministers might have to consider in consequence of any such proceedings as could be instituted in accordance with the Convention.

3. Decisions of the Committee of Ministers to request an advisory opinion of the Court shall require a two-thirds majority vote of the representatives entitled to sit on the Committee.

Article 2

The Court shall decide whether a request for an advisory opinion submitted by the Committee of Ministers is within its consultative competence as defined in Article 1 of this Protocol.

Article 3

1. For the consideration of requests for an advisory opinion, the Court shall sit in plenary session.

2. Reasons shall be given for advisory opinions of the Court.

3. If the advisory opinion does not represent in whole or in part the unanimous opinion of the judges, any judge shall be entitled to deliver a separate opinion.

4. Advisory opinions of the Court shall be communicated to the Committee of Ministers.

Article 4

The powers of the Court under Article 55 of the Convention shall extend to the drawing up of such rules and the determination of such procedure as the Court may think necessary for the purposes of this Protocol.

Article 5

1. This Protocol shall be open to signature by member States of the Council of Europe, signatories to the Convention, who may become Parties to it by:

a. signature without reservation in respect of ratification or acceptance;

b. signature with reservation in respect of ratification or acceptance, followed by ratification or acceptance.

Instruments of ratification or acceptance shall be deposited with the Secretary General of the Council of Europe.

2. This Protocol shall enter into force as soon as all States Parties to the Convention shall have become Parties to the Protocol, in accordance with the provisions of paragraph 1 of this article.

3. From the date of the entry into force of this Protocol, Articles 1 to 4 shall be considered an integral part of the Convention.

4. The Secretary General of the Council of Europe shall notify the member States of the Council of:

a. any signature without reservation in respect of ratification or acceptance;
b. any signature with reservation in respect of ratification or acceptance;
c. the deposit of any instrument of ratification or acceptance;
d. the date of entry into force of this Protocol in accordance with paragraph 2 of this article.

In witness whereof, the undersigned, being duly authorised thereto, have signed this Protocol.

Done at Strasbourg, this 6th day of May 1963, in English and French, both texts being equally authoritative, in a single copy which shall remain deposited in the archives of the Council of Europe. The Secretary General shall transmit certified copies to each of the signatory States.

3. Protocols to the Convention for the Protection of Human Rights and Fundamental Freedoms

Protocol No. 1

to the Convention for the Protection of Human Rights and Fundamental Freedoms, securing certain rights and freedoms other than those already included in the Convention

Paris, 20 March 1952

Entry into force: 18 May 1954,
in accordance with Article 6

The governments signatory hereto, being members of the Council of Europe,

Being resolved to take steps to ensure the collective enforcement of certain rights and freedoms other than those already included in Section I of the Convention for the Protection of Human Rights and Fundamental Freedoms signed at Rome on 4 November, 1950 (hereinafter referred to as "the Convention"),

Have agreed as follows:

Article 1

Every natural or legal person is entitled to the peaceful enjoyment of his possessions. No one shall be deprived of his possessions except in the public interest and subject to the conditions provided for by law and by the general principles of international law.
The preceding provisions shall not, however, in any way impair the right of a State to enforce such laws as it deems necessary to control the use of property in accordance with the general interest or to secure the payment of taxes or other contributions or penalties.

Article 2

No person shall be denied the right to education. In the exercise of any functions which it assumes in relation to education and to teaching, the State shall respect the right of parents to ensure such education and teaching in conformity with their own religious and philosophical convictions.

Article 3

The High Contracting Parties undertake to hold free elections at reasonable intervals by secret ballot, under conditions which will ensure the free expression of the opinion of the people in the choice of the legislature.

Article 4

Any High Contracting Party may at the time of signature or ratification or at any time thereafter communicate to the Secretary General of the Council of Europe a declaration stating the extent to which it undertakes that the provisions of the present Protocol shall apply to such of the territories for the international relations of which it is responsible as are named therein.

Any High Contracting Party which has communicated a declaration in virtue of the preceding paragraph may from time to time communicate a further declaration modifying the terms of any former declaration or terminating the application of the provisions of this Protocol in respect of any territory.

A declaration made in accordance with this Article shall be deemed to have been made in accordance with paragraph 1 of Article 63 of the Convention.

Article 5

As between the High Contracting Parties the provisions of articles 1, 2, 3 and 4 of this Protocol shall be regarded as additional articles to the Convention and all the provisions of the Convention shall apply accordingly.

Article 6

This Protocol shall be open for signature by the members of the Council of Europe, who are the signatories of the Convention; it shall be ratified at the same time as or after the ratification of the Convention. It shall enter into force after the deposit of ten instruments of ratification. As regards any signatory ratifying subsequently, the Protocol shall enter into force at the date of the deposit of its instrument of ratification.

The instruments of ratification shall be deposited with the Secretary General of the Council of Europe, who will notify all members of the names of those who have ratified.

Done at Paris, this 20th day of March 1952, in English and French, both texts being equally authentic, in a single copy which shall remain deposited in the archives of the Council of Europe. The Secretary General shall transmit certified copies to each of the signatory governments.

Protocol No. 4

to the Convention for the Protection of Human Rights and Fundamental Freedoms, securing certain rights and freedoms other than those already included in the Convention and in the first Protocol thereto

Strasbourg, 16 September 1963

Entry into force: 2 May 1968,
in accordance with Article 7

The governments signatory hereto, being members of the Council of Europe,

Being resolved to take steps to ensure the collective enforcement of certain rights and freedoms other than those already included in Section I of the Convention for the Protection of Human Rights and Fundamental Freedoms signed at Rome on 4 November 1950 (hereinafter referred to as "the Convention") and in Articles 1 to 3 of the First Protocol to the Convention, signed at Paris on 20 March 1952,

Have agreed as follows:

Article 1

No one shall be deprived of his liberty merely on the ground of inability to fulfil a contractual obligation.

Article 2

1. Everyone lawfully within the territory of a State shall, within that territory, have the right to liberty of movement and freedom to choose his residence.

2. Everyone shall be free to leave any country, including his own.

3. No restrictions shall be placed on the exercise of these rights other than such as are in accordance with law and are necessary in a democratic society in the interests of national security or public safety, for the maintenance of *ordre public,* for the prevention of crime, for the protection of health or morals, or for the protection of the rights and freedoms of others.

4. The rights set forth in paragraph 1 may also be subject, in particular areas, to restrictions imposed in accordance with law and justified by the public interest in a democratic society.

Article 3

1. No one shall be expelled, by means either of an individual or of a collective measure, from the territory of the State of which he is a national.

2. No one shall be deprived of the right to enter the territory of the State of which he is a national.

Article 4

Collective expulsion of aliens is prohibited.

Article 5

1. Any High Contracting Party may, at the time of signature or ratification of this Protocol, or at any time thereafter, communicate to the Secretary General of the Council of Europe a declaration stating the extent to which it undertakes that the provisions of this Protocol shall apply to such of the territories for the international relations of which it is responsible as are named therein.

2. Any High Contracting Party which has communicated a declaration in virtue of the preceding paragraph may, from time to time, communicate a further declaration modifying the terms of any former declaration or terminating the application of the provisions of this Protocol in respect of any territory.

3. A declaration made in accordance with this article shall be deemed to have been made in accordance with paragraph 1 of Article 63 of the Convention.

4. The territory of any State to which this Protocol applies by virtue of ratification or acceptance by that State, and each territory to which this Protocol is applied by virtue of a declaration by that State under this article, shall be treated as separate territories for the purpose of the references in Articles 2 and 3 to the territory of a State.

Article 6

1. As between the High Contracting Parties the provisions of Articles 1 to 5 of this Protocol shall be regarded as additional articles to the Convention, and all the provisions of the Convention shall apply accordingly.

2. Nevertheless, the right of individual recourse recognised by a declaration made under Article 25 of the Convention, or the acceptance of the compulsory jurisdiction of the Court by a declaration made under Article 46 of the Convention, shall not be effective in relation to this Protocol unless the High Contracting Party concerned has made a statement recognising such right, or accepting such jurisdiction, in respect of all or any of Articles 1 to 4 of the Protocol.

Article 7

1. This Protocol shall be open for signature by the members of the Council of Europe who are the signatories of the Convention; it shall be ratified at the same time as or after the ratification of the Convention. It shall enter into force after the deposit of five instruments of ratification. As regards any signatory ratifying subsequently, the Protocol shall enter into force at the date of the deposit of its instrument of ratification.

2. The instruments of ratification shall be deposited with the Secretary General of the Council of Europe, who will notify all members of the names of those who have ratified.

In witness whereof, the undersigned, being duly authorised thereto, have signed this Protocol.

Done at Strasbourg, this 16th day of September 1963, in English and in French, both texts being equally authoritative, in a single copy which shall remain deposited in the archives of the Council of Europe. The Secretary General shall transmit certified copies to each of the signatory States.

Protocol No. 6

to the Convention for the Protection of Human Rights and Fundamental Freedoms concerning the abolition of the death penalty

Strasbourg, 28 April 1983

Entry into force: 1 March 1985,
in accordance with Article 8

The member States of the Council of Europe, signatory to this Protocol to the Convention for the Protection of Human Rights and Fundamental Freedoms, signed at Rome on 4 November 1950 (hereinafter referred to as "the Convention"),

Considering that the evolution that has occurred in several member States of the Council of Europe expresses a general tendency in favour of abolition of the death penalty,

Have agreed as follows:

Article 1

The death penalty shall be abolished. No one shall be condemned to such penalty or executed.

Article 2

A State may make provision in its law for the death penalty in respect of acts committed in time of war or of imminent threat of war; such penalty shall be applied only in the instances laid down in the law and in accordance with its provisions. The State shall communicate to the Secretary General of the Council of Europe the relevant provisions of that law.

Article 3

No derogation from the provisions of this Protocol shall be made under Article 15 of the Convention.

Article 4

No reservation may be made under Article 64 of the Convention in respect of the provisions of this Protocol.

Article 5

1. Any State may at the time of signature or when depositing its instrument of ratification, acceptance or approval, specify the territory or territories to which this Protocol shall apply.

2. Any State may at any later date, by a declaration addressed to the Secretary General of the Council of Europe, extend the application of this Protocol to any other territory specified in the declaration. In respect of such territory the Protocol shall enter into force on the first day of the month following the date of receipt of such a declaration by the Secretary General.

3. Any declaration made under the two preceding paragraphs may, in respect of any territory specified in such declaration, be withdrawn by a notification addressed to the Secretary General. The withdrawal shall become effective on the first day of the month following the date of receipt of such notification by the Secretary General.

Article 6

As between the States Parties the provisions of articles 1 to 5 of this Protocol shall be regarded as additional articles to the Convention and all the provisions of the Convention shall apply accordingly.

Article 7

This Protocol shall be open for signature by the member States of the Council of Europe, signatories to the Convention. It shall be subject to ratification, acceptance or approval. A member State of the Council of Europe may not ratify, accept or approve this Protocol unless it has, simultaneously or previously, ratified the Convention. Instruments of ratification, acceptance or approval shall be deposited with the Secretary General of the Council of Europe.

Article 8

1. This Protocol shall enter into force on the first day of the month following the date on which five member States of the Council of Europe have expressed their consent to be bound by the Protocol in accordance with the provisions of Article 7.

2. In respect of any member State which subsequently expresses its consent to be bound by it, the Protocol shall enter into force on the first day of the month following the date of the deposit of the instrument of ratification, acceptance or approval.

Article 9

The Secretary General of the Council of Europe shall notify the member States of the Council of:

a. any signature;

b. the deposit of any instrument of ratification, acceptance or approval;

c. any date of entry into force of this Protocol in accordance with Articles 5 and 8;

d. any other act, notification or communication relating to this Protocol.

In witness whereof the undersigned, being duly authorised thereto, have signed this Protocol.

Done at Strasbourg, this 28th day of April 1983, in English and French, both texts being equally authentic, in a single copy which shall be deposited in the archives of the Council of Europe. The Secretary General of the Council of Europe shall transmit certified copies to each member State of the Council of Europe.

Protocol No. 7

to the Convention for the Protection of Human Rights and Fundamental Freedoms

Strasbourg, 22 November 1984

Entry into force: 1 November 1988,
in accordance with Article 9

The member States of the Council of Europe signatory hereto,

Being resolved to take further steps to ensure the collective enforcement of certain rights and freedoms by means of the Convention for the Protection of Human Rights and Fundamental Freedoms signed at Rome on 4 November 1950 (hereinafter referred to as "the Convention"),

Have agreed as follows:

Article 1

1. An alien lawfully resident in the territory of a State shall not be expelled therefrom except in pursuance of a decision reached in accordance with law and shall be allowed:

a. to submit reasons against his expulsion;
b. to have his case reviewed; and
c. to be represented for these purposes before the competent authority or a person or persons designated by that authority.

2. An alien may be expelled before the exercise of his rights under paragraph 1.*a*, *b* and *c* of this article, when such expulsion is necessary in the interests of public order or is grounded on reasons of national security.

Article 2

1. Everyone convicted of a criminal offence by a tribunal shall have the right to have his conviction or sentence reviewed by a higher tribunal. The exercise of this right, including the grounds on which it may be exercised, shall be governed by law.

2. This right may be subject to exceptions in regard to offences of a minor character, as prescribed by law, or in cases in which the person concerned was tried in the first instance by the highest tribunal or was convicted following an appeal against acquittal.

Article 3

When a person has by a final decision been convicted of a criminal offence and when subsequently his conviction has been reversed, or he has been pardoned, on the ground that a new or newly discovered fact shows conclusively that there has been a miscarriage of justice, the person who has suffered punishment as a result of such conviction shall be compensated according to the law or the practice of the State concerned, unless it is proved that the non-disclosure of the unknown fact in time is wholly or partly attributable to him.

Article 4

1. No one shall be liable to be tried or punished again in criminal proceedings under the jurisdiction of the same State for an offence for which he has already been finally acquitted or convicted in accordance with the law and penal procedure of that State.

2. The provisions of the preceding paragraph shall not prevent the reopening of the case in accordance with the law and penal procedure of the State concerned, if there is evidence of new or newly discovered facts, or if there has been a fundamental defect in the previous proceedings, which could affect the outcome of the case.

3. No derogation from this article shall be made under Article 15 of the Convention.

Article 5

Spouses shall enjoy equality of rights and responsibilities of a private law character between them, and in their relations with their children, as to marriage, during marriage and in the event of its dissolution. This article shall not prevent States from taking such measures as are necessary in the interests of the children.

Article 6

1. Any State may at the time of signature or when depositing its instrument of ratification, acceptance or approval, specify the territory or territories to which this Protocol shall apply and state the extent to which it undertakes that the provisions of this Protocol shall apply to such territory or territories.

2. Any State may at any later day, by a declaration addressed to the Secretary General of the Council of Europe, extend the application of this Protocol to any other territory specified in the declaration. In respect of such territory the Protocol shall enter into force on the first day of the month following the expiration of a period of two months after the date of receipt by the Secretary General of such declaration.

3. Any declaration made under the two preceding paragraphs may, in respect of any territory specified in such declaration, be withdrawn or modified by a notification addressed to the Secretary General. The withdrawal or modification shall become effective on the first day of the month following the expiration of a period of two months after the date of receipt of such notification by the Secretary General.

4. A declaration made in accordance with this article shall be deemed to have been made in accordance with paragraph 1 of Article 63 of the Convention.

5. The territory of any State to which this Protocol applies by virtue of ratification, acceptance or approval by that State, and each territory to which this Protocol is applied by virtue of a declaration by that State

under this article, may be treated as separate territories for the purpose of the reference in Article 1 to the territory of a State.

Article 7

1. As between the States Parties, the provisions of Articles 1 to 6 of this Protocol shall be regarded as additional articles to the Convention, and all the provisions of the Convention shall apply accordingly.

2. Nevertheless, the right of individual recourse recognised by a declaration made under Article 25 of the Convention, or the acceptance of the compulsory jurisdiction of the Court by a declaration made under Article 46 of the Convention, shall not be effective in relation to this Protocol unless the State concerned has made a statement recognising such right, or accepting such jurisdiction in respect of Articles 1 to 5 of this Protocol.

Article 8

This Protocol shall be open for signature by member States of the Council of Europe which have signed the Convention. It is subject to ratification, acceptance or approval. A member State of the Council of Europe may not ratify, accept or approve this Protocol without previously or simultaneously ratifying the Convention. Instruments of ratification, acceptance or approval shall be deposited with the Secretary General of the Council of Europe.

Article 9

1. This Protocol shall enter into force on the first day of the month following the expiration of a period of two months after the date on which seven member States of the Council of Europe have expressed their consent to be bound by the Protocol in accordance with the provisions of Article 8.

2. In respect of any member State which subsequently expresses its consent to be bound by it, the Protocol shall enter into force on the first day of the month following the expiration of a period of two months after the date of the deposit of the instrument of ratification, acceptance or approval.

Article 10

The Secretary General of the Council of Europe shall notify all the member States of the Council of Europe of:

a. any signature;
b. the deposit of any instrument of ratification, acceptance or approval;
c. any date of entry into force of this Protocol in accordance with Articles 6 and 9;
d. any other act, notification or declaration relating to this Protocol.

In witness whereof the undersigned, being duly authorised thereto, have signed this Protocol.

Done at Strasbourg, this 22nd day of November 1984, in English and French, both texts being equally authentic, in a single copy which shall be deposited in the archives of the Council of Europe. The Secretary General of the Council of Europe shall transmit certified copies to each member State of the Council of Europe.

Protocol No. 9

to the Convention for the Protection of Human Rights and Fundamental Freedoms

Rome, 6 November 1990

The member States of the Council of Europe, signatories to this Protocol to the Convention for the Protection of Human Rights and Fundamental Freedoms, signed at Rome on 4 November 1950 (hereinafter referred to as "the Convention"),

Being resolved to make further improvements to the procedure under the Convention,

Have agreed as follows:

Article 1

For Parties to the Convention which are bound by this Protocol, the Convention shall be amended as provided in Articles 2 to 5.

Article 2

Article 31, paragraph 2, of the Convention, shall read as follows:

"2. The report shall be transmitted to the Committee of Ministers. The report shall also be transmitted to the States concerned and, if it deals with a petition submitted under Article 25, the applicant. The States concerned and the applicant shall not be at liberty to publish it."

Article 3

Article 44 of the Convention shall read as follows:

"Only the High Contracting Parties, the Commission, and persons, non-governmental organisations or groups of individuals having submitted a petition under Article 25 shall have the right to bring a case before the Court."

Article 4

Article 45 of the Convention shall read as follows:

"The jurisdiction of the Court shall extend to all cases concerning the interpretation and application of the present Convention which are referred to it in accordance with Article 48."

Article 5

Article 48 of the Convention shall read as follows:

"1. The following may refer a case to the Court, provided that the High Contracting Party concerned, if there is only one, or the High Contracting Parties concerned, if there is more than one, are subject to the compulsory jurisdiction of the Court or, failing that, with the consent of the High Contracting Party concerned, if there is only one, or of the High Contracting Parties concerned if there is more than one:

a. the Commission;
b. a High Contracting Party whose national is alleged to be a victim;
c. a High Contracting Party which referred the case to the Commission;
d. a High Contracting Party against which the complaint has been lodged;
e. the person, non-governmental organisation or group of individuals having lodged the complaint with the Commission.

2. If a case is referred to the Court only in accordance with paragraph 1.*e*, it shall first be submitted to a panel composed of three members of the Court. There shall sit as an *ex officio* member of the panel the judge elected in respect of the High Contracting Party against which the complaint has been lodged, or, if there is none, a person of its choice who shall sit in the capacity of judge. If the complaint has been lodged against more than one High Contracting Party, the size of the panel shall be increased accordingly.

If the case does not raise a serious question affecting the interpretation or application of the Convention and does not for any other reason warrant consideration by the Court, the panel may, by a unanimous vote, decide that it shall not be considered by the Court. In that event, the Committee of Ministers shall decide, in accordance with the provisions of Article 32, whether there has been a violation of the Convention."

Article 6

1. This Protocol shall be open for signature by member States of the Council of Europe signatories to the Convention, which may express their consent to be bound by:

a. signature without reservation as to ratification, acceptance or approval; or

b. signature subject to ratification, acceptance or approval, followed by ratification, acceptance or approval.

2. The instruments of ratification, acceptance or approval shall be deposited with the Secretary General of the Council of Europe.

Article 7

1. This Protocol shall enter into force on the first day of the month following the expiration of a period of three months after the date on which ten member States of the Council of Europe have expressed their consent to be bound by the Protocol in accordance with the provisions of Article 6.

2. In respect of any member State which subsequently expresses its consent to be bound by it, the Protocol shall enter into force on the first day of the month following the expiration of a period of three months after the date of signature or of the deposit of the instrument of ratification, acceptance or approval.

Article 8

The Secretary General of the Council of Europe shall notify all the member States of the Council of Europe of:

a. any signature;

b. the deposit of any instrument of ratification, acceptance or approval;

c. any date of entry into force of this Protocol in accordance with Article 7;

d. any other act, notification or declaration relating to this Protocol.

In witness whereof, the undersigned, being duly authorised thereto, have signed this Protocol.

Done at Rome, this 6th day of November 1990, in English and French, both texts being equally authentic, in a single copy which shall be deposited in the archives of the Council of Europe. The Secretary General of the Council of Europe shall transmit certified copies to each member State of the Council of Europe.

4. European Agreement relating to persons participating in proceedings of the European Commission and Court of Human Rights

London, 6 May 1969

Entry into force: 17 April 1971,
in accordance with Article 8

The member States of the Council of Europe, signatory hereto,

Having regard to the Convention for the Protection of Human Rights and Fundamental Freedoms, signed at Rome on 4 November 1950 (hereinafter referred to as "the Convention");

Considering that it is expedient for the better fulfilment of the purposes of the Convention that persons taking part in proceedings before the European Commission of Human Rights (hereinafter referred to as "the Commission") or the European Court of Human Rights (hereinafter referred to as "the Court") shall be accorded certain immunities and facilities;

Desiring to conclude an agreement for this purpose,

Have agreed as follows:

Article 1

1. The persons to whom this Agreement applies are:

a. agents of the Contracting Parties and advisers and advocates assisting them;

b. persons taking part in proceedings instituted before the Commission under Article 25 of the Convention, whether in their own name or as representatives of one of the applicants enumerated in the said Article- 25;

c. barristers, solicitors or professors of law, taking part in proceedings in order to assist one of the persons enumerated in sub-paragraph *b* above;

d. persons chosen by the delegates of the Commission to assist them in proceedings before the Court;

e. witnesses, experts and other persons called upon by the Commission or the Court to take part in proceedings before the Commission or the Court.

2. For the purposes of this Agreement, the terms "Commission" and "Court" shall include a Sub-Commission or Chamber, or members of either body carrying out their duties under the terms of the Convention or of the rules of the Commission or of the Court, as the case may be; and the term "taking part in proceedings" shall include making communications with a view to a complaint against a State which has recognised the right of individual petition under Article 25 of the Convention.

3. In the course of the exercise by the Committee of Ministers of its functions under Article 32 of the Convention, any person mentioned in paragraph 1 of this article is called upon to appear before, or to submit written statements to the Committee of Ministers, the provisions of this Agreement shall apply in relation to him.

Article 2

1. The persons referred to in paragraph 1 of Article 1 of this Agreement shall have immunity from legal process in respect of oral or written statements made, or documents or other evidence submitted by them before or to the Commission or the Court.

2. This immunity does not apply to the communication, outside the Commission or the Court, by or on behalf of any person entitled to immunity under the preceding paragraph, of any such statements, documents or evidence or any part thereof submitted by that person to the Commission or the Court.

Article 3

1. The Contracting Parties shall respect the right of the persons referred to in paragraph 1 of Article 1 of this Agreement to correspond freely with the Commission and the Court.

2. As regards persons under detention, the exercise of this right shall in particular imply that:

a. if their correspondence is examined by the competent authorities, its despatch and delivery shall nevertheless take place without undue delay and without alteration;

b. such persons shall not be subject to disciplinary measures in any form on account of any communication sent through the proper channels to the Commission or the Court;

c. such persons shall have the right to correspond, and consult out of hearing of other persons, with a lawyer qualified to appear before the courts of the country where they are detained in regard to an application to the Commission, or any proceedings resulting therefrom.

3. In application of the preceding paragraphs, there shall be no interference by a public authority except such as is in accordance with the law and is necessary in a democratic society in the interests of national security, for the detection or prosecution of a criminal offence or for the protection of health.

Article 4

1.a. The Contracting Parties undertake not to hinder the free movement and travel, for the purpose of attending and returning from proceedings before the Commission or the Court, of persons referred to in paragraph 1 of Article 1 of this Agreement whose presence has in advance been authorised by the Commission or the Court.

b. No restrictions shall be placed on their movement and travel other than such as are in accordance with the law and necessary in a democratic society in the interests of national security or public safety, for the maintenance of *ordre public*, for the prevention of crime, for the protection of health or morals, or for the protection of the rights and freedoms of others.

2.a. Such persons shall not, in countries of transit and in the country where the proceedings take place, be prosecuted or detained or be subjected to any other restriction of their personal liberty in respect of acts or convictions prior to the commencement of the journey.

b. Any Contracting Party may at the time of signature or ratification of this Agreement declare that the provisions of this paragraph will not apply to its own nationals. Such a declaration may be withdrawn at any time by means of a notification addressed to the Secretary General of the Council of Europe.

3. The Contracting Parties undertake to re-admit on his return to their territory any such person who commenced his journey in the said territory.

4. The provisions of paragraphs 1 and 2 of this article shall cease to apply when the person concerned has had for a period of 15 consecutive days from the date when his presence is no longer required by the Commission or the Court the opportunity of returning to the country from which his journey commenced.

5. Where there is any conflict between the obligations of a Contracting Party resulting from paragraph 2 of this article and those resulting from a Council of Europe convention or from an extradition treaty or other treaty concerning mutual assistance in criminal matters with other Contracting Parties, the provisions of paragraph 2 of this article shall prevail.

Article 5

1. Immunities and facilities are accorded to the persons referred to in paragraph 1 of Article 1 of this Agreement solely in order to ensure for them the freedom of speech and the independence necessary for the discharge of their functions, tasks or duties, or the exercise of their rights in relation to the Commission and the Court.

2.a. The Commission or the Court, as the case may be, shall alone be competent to waive, in whole or in part, the immunity provided for in paragraph 1 of Article 2 of this Agreement; they have not only the right but the duty to waive immunity in any case where, in their opinion, such immunity would impede the course of justice and waiver in whole or in part would not prejudice the purpose defined in paragraph 1 of this article.

b. The immunity may be waived by the Commission or by the Court, either *ex officio* or at the request, addressed to the Secretary General of the Council of Europe, of any Contracting Party or of any person concerned.

c. Decisions waiving immunity or refusing the waiver shall be accompanied by a statement of reasons.

3. If a Contracting Party certifies that waiver of the immunity provided for in paragraph 1 of Article 2 of this Agreement is necessary for the purpose of proceedings in respect of an offence against national security, the Commission or the Court shall waive immunity to the extent specified in the certificate.

4. In the event of the discovery of a fact which might, by its nature, have a decisive influence and which at the time of the decision refusing waiver of immunity was unknown to the author of the request, the latter may make a new request to the Commission or the Court.

Article 6

Nothing in this Agreement shall be construed as limiting or derogating from any of the obligations assumed by the Contracting Parties under the Convention.

Article 7

1. This Agreement shall be open to signature by the member States of the Council of Europe, who may become Parties to it either by:

a. signature without reservation in respect of ratification or acceptance; or

b. signature with reservation in respect of ratification or acceptance, followed by ratification or acceptance.

2. Instruments of ratification or acceptance shall be deposited with the Secretary General of the Council of Europe.

Article 8

1. This Agreement shall enter into force one month after the date on which five member States of the Council shall have become Parties to the Agreement, in accordance with the provisions of Article 7.

2. As regards any member States who shall subsequently sign the Agreement without reservation in respect of ratification or acceptance or who shall ratify or accept it, the Agreement shall enter into force one month after the date of such signature or after the date of deposit of the instrument of ratification or acceptance.

Article 9

1. Any Contracting Party may, at the time of signature or when depositing its instrument of ratification or acceptance, specify the territory or territories to which this Agreement shall apply.

2. Any Contracting Party may, when depositing its instrument of ratification or acceptance or at any later date, by declaration addressed to the Secretary General of the Council of Europe, extend this Agreement to any other territory or territories specified in the declaration and for whose international relations it is responsible or on whose behalf it is authorised to give undertakings.

3. Any declaration made in pursuance of the preceding paragraph may, in respect of any territory mentioned in such declaration, be withdrawn according to the procedure laid down in Article 10 of this Agreement.

Article 10

1. This Agreement shall remain in force indefinitely.

2. Any Contracting Party may, insofar as it is concerned, denounce this Agreement by means of a notification addressed to the Secretary General of the Council of Europe.

3. Such denunciation shall take effect six months after the date of receipt by the Secretary General of such notification. Such a denunciation shall

not have the effect of releasing the Contracting Parties concerned from any obligation which may have arisen under this Agreement in relation to any person referred to in paragraph 1 of Article 1.

Article 11

The Secretary General of the Council of Europe shall notify the member States of the Council of:

a. any signature without reservation in respect of ratification or acceptance;

b. any signature with reservation in respect of ratification or acceptance;

c. the deposit of any instrument of ratification or acceptance;

d. any date of entry into force of this Agreement in accordance with Article 8 thereof;

e. any declaration received in pursuance of the provisions of paragraph 2 of Article 4 and of paragraphs 2 and 3 of Article 9;

f. any notification of withdrawal of a declaration in pursuance of the provisions of paragraph 2 of Article 4 and any notification received in pursuance of the provisions of Article 10 and the date on which any denunciation takes effect.

In witness whereof the undersigned, being duly authorised thereto, have signed this Agreement.

Done at London, this 6th day of May 1969, in the English and French languages, both texts being equally authoritative, in a single copy which shall remain deposited in the archives of the Council of Europe. The Secretary General of the Council of Europe shall transmit certified copies to each of the signatory States.

5. **European Social Charter**

Turin, 18 October 1961

Entry into force: 26 February 1965,
in accordance with Article 35

The governments signatory hereto, being members of the Council of Europe,

Considering that the aim of the Council of Europe is the achievement of greater unity between its members for the purpose of safeguarding and realising the ideals and principles which are their common heritage and of facilitating their economic and social progress, in particular by the maintenance and further realisation of human rights and fundamental freedoms;

Considering that in the European Convention for the Protection of Human Rights and Fundamental Freedoms signed at Rome on 4 November 1950, and the Protocol thereto signed at Paris on 20 March 1952, the member States of the Council of Europe agreed to secure to their populations the civil and political rights and freedoms therein specified;

Considering that the enjoyment of social rights should be secured without discrimination on grounds of race, colour, sex, religion, political opinion, national extraction or social origin;

Being resolved to make every effort in common to improve the standard of living and to promote the social well-being of both their urban and rural populations by means of appropriate institutions and action,

Have agreed as follows:

Part I

The Contracting Parties accept as the aim of their policy, to be pursued by all appropriate means, both national and international in character, the attainment of conditions in which the following rights and principles may be effectively realised:

1. Everyone shall have the opportunity to earn his living in an occupation freely entered upon.

2. All workers have the right to just conditions of work.

3. All workers have the right to safe and healthy working conditions.

4. All workers have the right to a fair remuneration sufficient for a decent standard of living for themselves and their families.

5. All workers and employers have the right to freedom of association in national or international organisations for the protection of their economic and social interests.

6. All workers and employers have the right to bargain collectively.

7. Children and young persons have the right to a special protection against the physical and moral hazards to which they are exposed.

8. Employed women, in case of maternity, and other employed women as appropriate, have the right to a special protection in their work.

9. Everyone has the right to appropriate facilities for vocational guidance with a view to helping him choose an occupation suited to his personal aptitude and interests.

10. Everyone has the right to appropriate facilities for vocational training.

11. Everyone has the right to benefit from any measures enabling him to enjoy the highest possible standard of health attainable.

12. All workers and their dependants have the right to social security.

13. Anyone without adequate resources has the right to social and medical assistance.

14. Everyone has the right to benefit from social welfare services.

15. Disabled persons have the right to vocational training, rehabilitation and resettlement, whatever the origin and nature of their disability.

16. The family as a fundamental unit of society has the right to appropriate social, legal and economic protection to ensure its full development.

17. Mothers and children, irrespective of marital status and family relations, have the right to appropriate social and economic protection.

18. The nationals of any one of the Contracting Parties have the right to engage in any gainful occupation in the territory of any one of the others on a footing of equality with the nationals of the latter, subject to restrictions based on cogent economic or social reasons.

19. Migrant workers who are nationals of a Contracting Party and their families have the right to protection and assistance in the territory of any other Contracting Party.

Part II

The Contracting Parties undertake, as provided for in Part III, to consider themselves bound by the obligations laid down in the following articles and paragraphs.

Article 1 – The right to work

With a view to ensuring the effective exercise of the right to work, the Contracting Parties undertake:

1. to accept as one of their primary aims and responsibilities the achievement and maintenance of as high and stable a level of employment as possible, with view to the attainment of full employment;

2. to protect effectively the right of the worker to earn his living in an occupation freely entered upon;

3. to establish or maintain free employment services for all workers;

4. to provide or promote appropriate vocational guidance, training and rehabilitation.

Article 2 – The right to just conditions of work

With a view to ensuring the effective exercise of the right to just conditions of work, the Contracting Parties undertake:

1. to provide for reasonable daily and weekly working hours, the working week to be progressively reduced to the extent that the increase of productivity and other relevant factors permit;

2. to provide for public holidays with pay;

3. to provide for a minimum of two weeks' annual holiday with pay;

4. to provide for additional paid holidays or reduced working hours for workers engaged in dangerous or unhealthy occupations as prescribed;

5. to ensure a weekly rest period which shall, as far as possible, coincide with the day recognised by tradition or custom in the country or region concerned as a day of rest.

Article 3 – The right to safe and healthy working conditions

With a view to ensuring the effective exercise of the right to safe and healthy working conditions, the Contracting Parties undertake:

1. to issue safety and health regulations;

2. to provide for the enforcement of such regulations by measures of supervision;

3. to consult, as appropriate, employers' and workers' organisations on measures intended to improve industrial safety and health.

Article 4 – The right to a fair remuneration

With a view to ensuring the effective exercise of the right to a fair remuneration, the Contracting Parties undertake:

1. to recognise the right of workers to a remuneration such as will give them and their families a decent standard of living;

2. to recognise the right of workers to an increased rate of remuneration for overtime work, subject to exceptions in particular cases;

3. to recognise the right of men and women workers to equal pay for work of equal value;

4. to recognise the right of all workers to a reasonable period of notice for termination of employment;

5. to permit deductions from wages only under conditions and to the extent prescribed by national laws or regulations or fixed by collective agreements or arbitration awards.
The exercise of these rights shall be achieved by freely concluded collective agreements, by statutory wage-fixing machinery, or by other means appropriate to national conditions.

Article 5 – The right to organise

With a view to ensuring or promoting the freedom of workers and employers to form local, national or international organisations for the protection of their economic and social interests and to join those organisations, the Contracting Parties undertake that national law shall not be such as to impair, nor shall it be so applied as to impair, this freedom. The extent to which the guarantees provided for in this article shall apply to the police shall be determined by national laws or regulations. The principle governing the application to the members of the armed forces of these guarantees and the extent to which they shall apply to persons in this category shall equally be determined by national laws or regulations.

Article 6 – The right to bargain collectively

With a view to ensuring the effective exercise of the right to bargain collectively, the Contracting Parties undertake:

1. to promote joint consultation between workers and employers;

2. to promote, where necessary and appropriate, machinery for voluntary negotiations between employers or employers' organisations and workers' organisations, with a view to the regulation of terms and conditions of employment by means of collective agreements;

3. to promote the establishment and use of appropriate machinery for conciliation and voluntary arbitration for the settlement of labour disputes;

and recognise:

4. the right of workers and employers to collective action in cases of conflicts of interest, including the right to strike, subject to obligations that might arise out of collective agreements previously entered into.

Article 7 – The right of children and young persons to protection

With a view to ensuring the effective exercise of the right of children and young persons to protection, the Contracting Parties undertake:

1. to provide that the minimum age of admission to employment shall be 15 years, subject to exceptions for children employed in

prescribed light work without harm to their health, morals or education;

2. to provide that a higher minimum age of admission to employment shall be fixed with respect to prescribed occupations regarded as dangerous or unhealthy;

3. to provide that persons who are still subject to compulsory education shall not be employed in such work as would deprive them of the full benefit of their education;

4. to provide that the working hours of persons under 16 years of age shall be limited in accordance with the needs of their development, and particularly with their need for vocational training;

5. to recognise the right of young workers and apprentices to a fair wage or other appropriate allowances;

6. to provide that the time spent by young persons in vocational training during the normal working hours with the consent of the employer shall be treated as forming part of the working day;

7. to provide that employed persons of under 18 years of age shall be entitled to not less than three weeks' annual holiday with pay;

8. to provide that persons under 18 years of age shall not be employed in night work with the exception of certain occupations provided for by national laws or regulations;

9. to provide that persons under 18 years of age employed in occupations prescribed by national laws or regulations shall be subject to regular medical control;

10. to ensure special protection against physical and moral dangers to which children and young persons are exposed, and particularly against those resulting directly or indirectly from their work.

Article 8 – The right of employed women to protection

With a view to ensuring the effective exercise of the right of employed women to protection, the Contracting Parties undertake:

1. to provide either by paid leave, by adequate social security benefits or by benefits from public funds for women to take leave before and after childbirth up to a total of at least 12 weeks;

2. to consider it as unlawful for an employer to give a woman notice of dismissal during her absence on maternity leave or to give her notice of dismissal at such a time that the notice would expire during such absence;

3. to provide that mothers who are nursing their infants shall be entitled to sufficient time off for this purpose;

4. a. to regulate the employment of women workers on night work in industrial employment;
b. to prohibit the employment of women workers in underground mining, and, as appropriate, on all other work which is unsuitable for them by reason of its dangerous, unhealthy, or arduous nature.

Article 9 – The right to vocational guidance

With a view to ensuring the effective exercise of the right to vocational guidance, the Contracting Parties undertake to provide or promote, as necessary, a service which will assist all persons, including the handicapped, to solve problems related to occupational choice and progress, with due regard to the individual's characteristics and their relation to occupational opportunity; this assistance should be available free of charge, both to young persons, including school children, and to adults.

Article 10 – The right to vocational training

With a view to ensuring the effective exercise of the right to vocational training, the Contracting Parties undertake:

1. to provide or promote, as necessary, the technical and vocational training of all persons, including the handicapped, in consultation with

employers' and workers' organisations, and to grant facilities for access to higher technical and university education, based solely on individual aptitude;

2. to provide or promote a system of apprenticeship and other systematic arrangements for training young boys and girls in their various employments;

3. to provide or promote, as necessary:

a. adequate and readily available training facilities for adult workers;
b. special facilities for the re-training of adult workers needed as a result of technological development or new trends in employment;

4. to encourage the full utilisation of the facilities provided by appropriate measures such as:

a. reducing or abolishing any fees or charges;
b. granting financial assistance in appropriate cases;
c. including in the normal working hours time spent on supplementary training taken by the worker, at the request of his employer, during employment;
d. ensuring, through adequate supervision, in consultation with the employers' and workers' organisations, the efficiency of apprenticeship and other training arrangements for young workers, and the adequate protection of young workers generally.

Article 11 – The right to protection of health

With a view to ensuring the effective exercise of the right to protection of health, the Contracting Parties undertake, either directly or in co-operation with public or private organisations, to take appropriate measures designed *inter alia:*

1. to remove as far as possible the causes of ill-health;

2. to provide advisory and educational facilities for the promotion of health and the encouragement of individual responsibility in matters of health;

3. to prevent as far as possible epidemic, endemic and other diseases.

Article 12 – The right to social security

With a view to ensuring the effective exercise of the right to social security, the Contracting Parties undertake:

1. to establish or maintain a system of social security;

2. to maintain the social security system at a satisfactory level at least equal to that required for ratification of International Labour Convention (No. 102) Concerning Minimum Standards of Social Security;

3. to endeavour to raise progressively the system of social security to a higher level;

4. to take steps, by the conclusion of appropriate bilateral and multilateral agreements, or by other means, and subject to the conditions laid down in such agreements, in order to ensure:

a. equal treatment with their own nationals of the nationals of other Contracting Parties in respect of social security rights, including the retention of benefits arising out of social security legislation, whatever movements the persons protected may undertake between the territories of the Contracting Parties;

b. the granting, maintenance and resumption of social security rights by such means as the accumulation of insurance or employment periods completed under the legislation of each of the Contracting Parties.

Article 13 – The right to social and medical assistance

With a view to ensuring the effective exercise of the right to social and medical assistance, the Contracting Parties undertake:

1. to ensure that any person who is without adequate resources and who is unable to secure such resources either by his own efforts or from other sources, in particular by benefits under a social security scheme, be

granted adequate assistance, and, in case of sickness, the care necessitated by this condition;

2. to ensure that persons receiving such assistance shall not, for that reason, suffer from a diminution of their political or social rights;

3. to provide that everyone may receive by appropriate public or private services such advice and personal help as may be required to prevent, to remove, or to alleviate personal or family want;

4. to apply the provisions referred to in paragraphs 1, 2 and 3 of this article on an equal footing with their nationals to nationals of other Contracting Parties lawfully within their territories, in accordance with their obligations under the European Convention on Social and Medical Assistance, signed at Paris on 11 December 1953.

Article 14 – The right to benefit from social welfare services

With a view to ensuring the effective exercise of the right to benefit from social welfare services, the Contracting Parties undertake:

1. to promote or provide services which, by using methods of social work, would contribute to the welfare and development of both individuals and groups in the community, and to their adjustment to the social environment;

2. to encourage the participation of individuals and voluntary or other organisations in the establishment and maintenance of such services.

Article 15 – The right of physically or mentally disabled persons to vocational training, rehabilitation and social resettlement

With a view to ensuring the effective exercise of the right of the physically or mentally disabled to vocational training, rehabilitation and resettlement, the Contracting Parties undertake:

1. to take adequate measures for the provision of training facilities, including, where necessary, specialised institutions, public or private;

2. to take adequate measures for the placing of disabled persons in employment, such as specialised placing services, facilities for sheltered employment and measures to encourage employers to admit disabled persons to employment.

Article 16 – The right of the family to social, legal and economic protection

With a view to ensuring the necessary conditions for the full development of the family, which is a fundamental unit of society, the Contracting Parties undertake to promote the economic, legal and social protection of family life by such means as social and family benefits, fiscal arrangements, provision of family housing, benefits for the newly married, and other appropriate means.

Article 17 – The right of mothers and children to social and economic protection

With a view to ensuring the effective exercise of the right of mothers and children to social and economic protection, the Contracting Parties will take all appropriate and necessary measures to that end, including the establishment or maintenance of appropriate institutions or services.

Article 18 – The right to engage in a gainful occupation in the territory of other Contracting Parties

With a view to ensuring the effective exercise of the right to engage in a gainful occupation in the territory of any other Contracting Party, the Contracting Parties undertake:

1. to apply existing regulations in a spirit of liberality;

2. to simplify existing formalities and to reduce or abolish chancery dues and other charges payable by foreign workers or their employers;

3. to liberalise, individually or collectively, regulations governing the employment of foreign workers;

and recognise:

4. the right of their nationals to leave the country to engage in a gainful occupation in the territories of the other Contracting Parties.

Article 19 – The right of migrant workers and their families to protection and assistance

With a view to ensuring the effective exercise of the right of migrant workers and their families to protection and assistance in the territory of any other Contracting Party, the Contracting Parties undertake:

1. to maintain or to satisfy themselves that there are maintained adequate and free services to assist such workers, particularly in obtaining accurate information, and to take all appropriate steps, so far as national laws and regulations permit, against misleading propaganda relating to emigration and immigration;

2. to adopt appropriate measures within their own jurisdiction to facilitate the departure, journey and reception of such workers and their families, and to provide, within their own jurisdiction, appropriate services for health, medical attention and good hygienic conditions during the journey;

3. to promote co-operation, as appropriate, between social services, public and private, in emigration and immigration countries;

4. to secure for such workers lawfully within their territories, in so far as such matters are regulated by law or regulations or are subject to the control of administrative authorities, treatment not less favourable than that of their own nationals in respect of the following matters:

a. remuneration and other employment and working conditions;
b. membership of trade unions and enjoyment of the benefits of collective bargaining;
c. accommodation;

5. to secure for such workers lawfully within their territories, treatment not less favourable than that of their own nationals with regard to employment taxes, dues or contributions payable in respect of employed persons;

6. to facilitate as far as possible the reunion of the family of a foreign worker permitted to establish himself in the territory;

7. to secure for such workers lawfully within their territories treatment not less favourable than that of their own nationals in respect of legal proceedings relating to matters referred to in this article;

8. to secure that such workers lawfully residing within their territories are not expelled unless they endanger national security or offend against public interest or morality;

9. to permit, within legal limits, the transfer of such parts of the earnings and savings of such workers as they may desire;

10. to extend the protection and assistance provided for in this article to self-employed migrants in so far as such measures apply.

Part III

Article 20 – Undertakings

1. Each of the Contracting Parties undertakes:

a. to consider Part I of this Charter as a declaration of the aims which it will pursue by all appropriate means, as stated in the introductory paragraph of that part;

b. to consider itself bound by at least five of the following articles of Part II of this Charter: Articles, 1, 5, 6, 12, 13, 16 and 19;

c. in addition to the articles selected by it in accordance with the preceding sub-paragraph, to consider itself bound by such a number of articles or numbered paragraphs of Part II of the Charter as it may select, provided that the total number of articles or numbered paragraphs by which it is bound is not less than 10 articles or 45 numbered paragraphs.

2. The articles or paragraphs selected in accordance with sub-paragraphs *b* and *c* of paragraph 1 of this article shall be notified to the Secretary General of the Council of Europe at the time when the instrument of ratification or approval of the Contracting Party concerned is deposited.

3. Any Contracting Party may, at a later date, declare by notification to the Secretary General that it considers itself bound by any articles or any numbered paragraphs of Part II of the Charter which it has not already accepted under the terms of paragraph 1 of this article. Such undertakings subsequently given shall be deemed to be an integral part of the ratification or approval, and shall have the same effect as from the thirtieth day after the date of the notification.

4. The Secretary General shall communicate to all the signatory governments and to the Director General of the International Labour Office any notification which he shall have received pursuant to this part of the Charter.

5. Each Contracting Party shall maintain a system of labour inspection appropriate to national conditions.

Part IV

Article 21 – Reports concerning accepted provisions

The Contracting Parties shall send to the Secretary General of the Council of Europe a report at two-yearly intervals, in a form to be determined by the Committee of Ministers, concerning the application of such provisions of Part II of the Charter as they have accepted.

Article 22 – Reports concerning provisions which are not accepted

The Contracting Parties shall send to the Secretary General, at appropriate intervals as requested by the Committee of Ministers, reports relating to the provisions of Part II of the Charter which they did not accept at the time of their ratification or approval or in a subsequent notification. The Committee of Ministers shall determine from time to time in respect of which provisions such reports shall be requested and the form of the reports to be provided.

Article 23 – Communication of copies

1. Each Contracting Party shall communicate copies of its reports referred to in Articles 21 and 22 to such of its national organisations as are members of the international organisations of employers and trade unions to be invited under Article 27, paragraph 2, to be represented at meetings of the Sub-committee of the Governmental Social Committee.

2. The Contracting Parties shall forward to the Secretary General any comments on the said reports received from these national organisations, if so requested by them.

Article 24 – Examination of the reports

The reports sent to the Secretary General in accordance with Articles 21 and 22 shall be examined by a committee of experts, who shall have also before them any comments forwarded to the Secretary General in accordance with paragraph 2 of Article 23.

Article 25 – Committee of Experts

1. The Committee of Experts shall consist of not more than seven members appointed by the Committee of Ministers from a list of independent experts of the highest integrity and of recognised competence in international social questions, nominated by the Contracting Parties.

2. The members of the committee shall be appointed for a period of six years. They may be reappointed. However, of the members first appointed, the terms of office of two members shall expire at the end of four years.

3. The members whose terms of office are to expire at the end of the initial period of four years shall be chosen by lot by the Committee of Ministers immediately after the first appointment has been made.

4. A member of the Committee of Experts appointed to replace a member whose term of office has not expired shall hold office for the remainder of his predecessor's term.

Article 26 – Participation of the International Labour Organisation

The International Labour Organisation shall be invited to nominate a representative to participate in a consultative capacity in the deliberations of the Committee of Experts.

Article 27 – Sub-committee of the Governmental Social Committee

1. The reports of the Contracting Parties and the conclusions of the Committee of Experts shall be submitted for examination to a sub-committee of the Governmental Social Committee of the Council of Europe.

2. The sub-committee shall be composed of one representative of each of the Contracting Parties. It shall invite no more than two international organisations of employers and no more than two international trade union organisations as it may designate to be represented as observers in a consultative capacity at its meetings. Moreover, it may consult no more than two representatives of international non-governmental organisations having consultative status with the Council of Europe, in respect of questions with which the organisations are particularly qualified to deal, such as social welfare, and the economic and social protection of the family.

3. The sub-committee shall present to the Committee of Ministers a report containing its conclusions and append the report of the Committee of Experts.

Article 28 – Consultative Assembly

The Secretary General of the Council of Europe shall transmit to the Consultative Assembly the conclusions of the Committee of Experts.

The Consultative Assembly shall communicate its views on these conclusions to the Committee of Ministers.

Article 29 – Committee of Ministers

By a majority of two-thirds of the members entitled to sit on the Committee, the Committee of Ministers may, on the basis of the report of the sub-committee, and after consultation with the Consultative Assembly, make to each Contracting Party any necessary recommendations.

Part V

Article 30 – Derogations in time of war or public emergency

1. In time of war or other public emergency threatening the life of the nation any Contracting Party may take measures derogating from its obligations under this Charter to the extent strictly required by the exigencies of the situation, provided that such measures are not inconsistent with its other obligations under international law.

2. Any Contracting Party which has availed itself of this right of derogation shall, within a reasonable lapse of time, keep the Secretary General of the Council of Europe fully informed of the measures taken and of the reasons therefor. It shall likewise inform the Secretary General when such measures have ceased to operate and the provisions of the Charter which it has accepted are again being fully executed.

3. The Secretary General shall in turn inform other Contracting Parties and the Director General of the International Labour Office of all communications received in accordance with paragraph 2 of this article.

Article 31 – Restrictions

1. The rights and principles set forth in Part I when effectively realised, and their effective exercise as provided for in Part II, shall not be subject to any restrictions or limitations not specified in those parts, except such as are prescribed by law and are necessary in a democratic society for the

protection of the rights and freedoms of others or for the protection of public interest, national security, public health, or morals.

2. The restrictions permitted under this Charter to the rights and obligations set forth herein shall not be applied for any purpose other than that for which they have been prescribed.

Article 32 – Relations between the Charter and domestic law or international agreements

The provisions of this Charter shall not prejudice the provisions of domestic law or of any bilateral or multilateral treaties, conventions or agreements which are already in force, or may come into force, under which more favourable treatment would be accorded to the persons protected.

Article 33 – Implementation by collective agreements

1. In member States where the provisions of paragraphs 1, 2, 3, 4 and 5 of Article 2, paragraphs 4, 6 and 7 of Article 7 and paragraphs 1, 2, 3 and 4 of Article 10 of Part II of this Charter are matters normally left to agreements between employers or employers' organisations and workers' organisations, or are normally carried out otherwise than by law, the undertakings of those paragraphs may be given and compliance with them shall be treated as effective if their provisions are applied through such agreements or other means to the great majority of the workers concerned.

2. In member States where these provisions are normally the subject of legislation, the undertakings concerned may likewise be given, and compliance with them shall be regarded as effective if the provisions are applied by law to the great majority of the workers concerned.

Article 34 – Territorial application

1. This Charter shall apply to the metropolitan territory of each Contracting Party. Each signatory government may, at the time of signature or of the deposit of its instrument of ratification or approval, specify, by

declaration addressed to the Secretary General of the Council of Europe, the territory which shall be considered to be its metropolitan territory for this purpose.

2. Any Contracting Party may, at the time of ratification or approval of this Charter or at any time thereafter, declare by notification addressed to the Secretary General of the Council of Europe, that the Charter shall extend in whole or in part to a non-metropolitan territory or territories specified in the said declaration for whose international relations it is responsible or for which it assumes international responsibility. It shall specify in the declaration the articles or paragraphs of Part II of the Charter which it accepts as binding in respect of the territories named in the declaration.

3. The Charter shall extend to the territory or territories named in the aforesaid declarations as from the thirtieth day after the date on which the Secretary General shall have received notification of such declaration.

4. Any Contracting Party may declare at a later date by notification addressed to the Secretary General of the Council of Europe, that, in respect of one or more of the territories to which the Charter has been extended in accordance with paragraph 2 of this article, it accepts as binding any articles or any numbered paragraphs which it has not already accepted in respect of that territory or territories. Such undertakings subsequently given shall be deemed to be an integral part of the original declaration in respect of the territory concerned, and shall have the same effect as from the thirtieth day after the date of the notification.

5. The Secretary General shall communicate to the other signatory governments and to the Director General of the International Labour Office any notification transmitted to him in accordance with this article.

Article 35 – Signature, ratification and entry into force

1. This Charter shall be open for signature by the members of the Council of Europe. It shall be ratified or approved. Instruments of ratification or

approval shall be deposited with the Secretary General of the Council of Europe.

2. This Charter shall come into force as from the thirtieth day after the date of deposit of the fifth instrument of ratification or approval.

3. In respect of any signatory government ratifying subsequently, the Charter shall come into force as from the thirtieth day after the date of deposit of its instrument of ratification or approval.

4. The Secretary General shall notify all the members of the Council of Europe and the Director General of the International Labour Office of the entry into force of the Charter, the names of the Contracting Parties which have ratified or approved it and the subsequent deposit of any instruments of ratification or approval.

Article 36 – Amendments

Any member of the Council of Europe may propose amendments to this Charter in a communication addressed to the Secretary General of the Council of Europe. The Secretary General shall transmit to the other members of the Council of Europe any amendments so proposed, which shall then be considered by the Committee of Ministers and submitted to the Consultative Assembly for opinion. Any amendments approved by the Committee of Ministers shall enter into force as from the thirtieth day after all the Contracting Parties have informed the Secretary General of their acceptance. The Secretary General shall notify all the members of the Council of Europe and the Director General of the International Labour Office of the entry into force of such amendments.

Article 37 – Denunciation

1. Any Contracting Party may denounce this Charter only at the end of a period of five years from the date on which the Charter entered into force for it, or at the end of any successive period of two years, and, in each case, after giving six months' notice to the Secretary General of the Council of Europe, who shall inform the other Parties and the Director General of the International Labour Office accordingly. Such denunci-

ation shall not affect the validity of the Charter in respect of the other Contracting Parties provided that at all times there are not less than five such Contracting Parties.

2. Any Contracting Party may, in accordance with the provisions set out in the preceding paragraph, denounce any article or paragraph of Part II of the Charter accepted by it provided that the number of articles or paragraphs by which this Contracting Party is bound shall never be less than 10 in the former case and 45 in the latter and that this number of articles or paragraphs shall continue to include the articles selected by the Contracting Party among those to which special reference is made in Article 20, paragraph 1, sub-paragraph *b*.

3. Any Contracting Party may denounce the present Charter or any of the articles or paragraphs of Part II of the Charter, under the conditions specified in paragraph 1 of this article in respect of any territory to which the said Charter is applicable by virtue of a declaration made in accordance with paragraph 2 of Article 34.

Article 38 – Appendix

The appendix to this Charter shall form an integral part of it.

In witness whereof, the undersigned, being duly authorised thereto, have signed this Charter.

Done at Turin, this 18th day of October 1961, in English and French, both texts being equally authoritative, in a single copy which shall be deposited within the archives of the Council of Europe. The Secretary General shall transmit certified copies to each of the signatories.

Appendix to the Social Charter

Scope of the Social Charter in terms of persons protected:

1. Without prejudice to Article 12, paragraph 4, and Article 13, paragraph 4, the persons covered by Articles 1 to 17 include foreigners only in so far as they are nationals of other Contracting Parties lawfully resident or working regularly within the territory of the Contracting Party concerned, subject to the understanding that these articles are to be interpreted in the light of the provisions of Articles 18 and 19.

This interpretation would not prejudice the extension of similar facilities to other persons by any of the Contracting Parties.

2. Each Contracting Party will grant to refugees as defined in the Convention relating to the Status of Refugees, signed at Geneva on 28 July 1951, and lawfully staying in its territory, treatment as favourable as possible, and in any case not less favourable than under the obligations accepted by the Contracting Party under the said Convention and under any other existing international instruments applicable to those refugees.

Part I, paragraph 18 and Part II, Article 18, paragraph 1

It is understood that these provisions are not concerned with the question of entry into the territories of the Contracting Parties and do not prejudice the provisions of the European Convention on Establishment, signed at Paris on 13 December 1955.

Part II

Article 1, paragraph 2

This provision shall not be interpreted as prohibiting or authorising any union security clause or practice.

Article 4, paragraph 4

This provision shall be so understood as not to prohibit immediate dismissal for any serious offence.

Article 4, paragraph 5

It is understood that a Contracting Party may give the undertaking required in this paragraph if the great majority of workers are not permitted to suffer deductions from wages either by law or through collective agreements or arbitration awards, the exception being those persons not so covered.

Article 6, paragraph 4

It is understood that each Contracting Party may, in so far as it is concerned, regulate the exercise of the right to strike by law, provided that any further restriction that this might place on the right can be justified under the terms of Article 31.

Article 7, paragraph 8

It is understood that a Contracting Party may give the undertaking required in this paragraph if it fulfils the spirit of the undertaking by providing by law that the great majority of persons under 18 years of age shall not be employed in night work.

Article 12, paragraph 4

The words "and subject to the conditions laid down in such agreements" in the introduction to this paragraph are taken to imply *inter alia* that with regard to benefits which are available independently of any insurance contribution a Contracting Party may require the completion of a prescribed period of residence before granting such benefits to nationals of other Contracting Parties.

Article 13, paragraph 4

Governments not Parties to the European Convention on Social and Medical Assistance may ratify the Social Charter in respect of this paragraph provided that they grant to nationals of other Contracting Parties a treatment which is in conformity with the provisions of the said convention.

Article 19, paragraph 6

For the purpose of this provision, the term "family of a foreign worker" is understood to mean at least his wife and dependent children under the age of 21 years.

Part III

It is understood that the Charter contains legal obligations of an international character, the application of which is submitted solely to the supervision provided for in Part IV thereof.

Article 20, paragraph 1

It is understood that the "numbered paragraphs" may include articles consisting of only one paragraph.

Part V

Article 30

The term "in time of war or other public emergency" shall be so understood as to cover also the *threat* of war.

6. **Additional Protocol to the European Social Charter**

Strasbourg, 5 May 1988

Preamble

The member States of the Council of Europe signatory hereto,

Resolved to take new measures to extend the protection of the social and economic rights guaranteed by the European Social Charter, opened for signature in Turin on 18 October 1961 (hereinafter referred to as "the Charter"),

Have agreed as follows:

Part I

The Parties accept as the aim of their policy to be pursued by all appropriate means, both national and international in character, the attainment of conditions in which the following rights and principles may be effectively realised:

1. All workers have the right to equal opportunities and equal treatment in matters of employment and occupation without discrimination on the grounds of sex.

2. Workers have the right to be informed and to be consulted within the undertaking.

3. Workers have the right to take part in the determination and improvement of the working conditions and working environment in the undertaking.

4. Every elderly person has the right to social protection.

Part II

The Parties undertake, as provided for in Part III, to consider themselves bound by the obligations laid down in the following articles:

Article 1 – Right to equal opportunities and equal treatment in matters of employment and occupation without discrimination on the grounds of sex

1. With a view to ensuring the effective exercise of the right to equal opportunities and equal treatment in matters of employment and occupation without discrimination on the grounds of sex, the Parties undertake to recognise that right and to take appropriate measures to ensure or promote its application in the following fields:
– access to employment, protection against dismissal and occupational resettlement;
– vocational guidance, training, retraining and rehabilitation;
– terms of employment and working conditions including remuneration;
– career development including promotion.

2. Provisions concerning the protection of women, particularly as regards pregnancy, confinement and the post-natal period, shall not be deemed to be discrimination as referred to in paragraph 1 of this article.

3. Paragraph 1 of this article shall not prevent the adoption of specific measures aimed at removing *de facto* inequalities.

4. Occupational activities which, by reason of their nature or the context in which they are carried out, can be entrusted only to persons of a particular sex may be excluded from the scope of this article or some of its provisions.

Article 2 – Right to information and consultation

1. With a view to ensuring the effective exercise of the right of workers to be informed and consulted within the undertaking, the Parties undertake to adopt or encourage measures enabling workers or their representatives, in accordance with national legislation and practice:

a. to be informed regularly or at the appropriate time and in a comprehensible way about the economic and financial situation of the undertaking employing them, on the understanding that the disclosure of certain information which could be prejudicial to the undertaking may be refused or subject to confidentiality; and

b. to be consulted in good time on proposed decisions which could substantially affect the interests of workers, particularly on those decisions which could have an important impact on the employment situation in the undertaking.

2. The Parties may exclude from the field of application of paragraph 1 of this article those undertakings employing less than a certain number of workers to be determined by national legislation or practice.

Article 3 – Right to take part in the determination and improvement of the working conditions and working environment

1. With a view to ensuring the effective exercise of the right of workers to take part in the determination and improvement of the working conditions and working environment in the undertaking, the Parties undertake to adopt or encourage measures enabling workers or their representatives, in accordance with national legislation and practice, to contribute:

a. to the determination and the improvement of the working conditions, work organisation and working environment;

b. to the protection of health and safety within the undertaking;

c. to the organisation of social and socio-cultural services and facilities within the undertaking;

d. to the supervision of the observance of regulations on these matters.

2. The Parties may exclude from the field of application of paragraph 1 of this article, those undertakings employing less than a certain number of workers to be determined by national legislation or practice.

Article 4 – Right of elderly persons to social protection

With a view to ensuring the effective exercise of the right of elderly persons to social protection, the Parties undertake to adopt or encourage, either directly or in co-operation with public or private organisations, appropriate measures designed in particular:

1. to enable elderly persons to remain full members of society for as long as possible, by means of:

a. adequate resources enabling them to lead a decent life and play an active part in public, social and cultural life;
b. provision of information about services and facilities available for elderly persons and their opportunities to make use of them;

2. to enable elderly persons to choose their life-style freely and to lead independent lives in their familiar surroundings for as long as they wish and are able, by means of:

a. provision of housing suited to their needs and their state of health or of adequate support for adapting their housing;
b. the health care and the services necessitated by their state;

3. to guarantee elderly persons living in institutions appropriate support, while respecting their privacy, and participation in decisions concerning living conditions in the institution.

Part III

Article 5 – Undertakings

1. Each of the Parties undertakes:

a. to consider Part I of this Protocol as a declaration of the aims which it will pursue by all appropriate means, as stated in the introductory paragraph of that part;

b. to consider itself bound by one or more articles of Part II of this Protocol.

2. The article or articles selected in accordance with sub-paragraph *b* of paragraph 1 of this article shall be notified to the Secretary General of the Council of Europe at the time when the instrument of ratification, acceptance or approval of the Contracting State concerned is deposited.

3. Any Party may, at a later date, declare by notification to the Secretary General that it considers itself bound by any articles of Part II of this Protocol which it has not already accepted under the terms of paragraph 1 of this article. Such undertakings subsequently given shall be deemed to be an integral part of the ratification, acceptance or approval, and shall have the same effect as from the thirtieth day after the date of the notification.

Part IV

Article 6 – Supervision of compliance with the undertakings given

The Parties shall submit reports on the application of those provisions of Part II of this Protocol which they have accepted in the reports submitted by virtue of Article 21 of the Charter.

Part V

Article 7 – Implementation of the undertakings given

1. The relevant provisions of Articles 1 to 4 of Part II of this Protocol may be implemented by:

a. laws and regulations;
b. agreements between employers or employers' organisations and workers' organisations;

c. a combination of those two methods; or
d. other appropriate means.

2. Compliance with the undertakings deriving from Articles 2 and 3 of Part II of this Protocol shall be regarded as effective if the provisions are applied, in accordance with paragraph 1 of this article, to the great majority of the workers concerned.

Article 8 – Relations between the Charter and this Protocol

1. The provisions of this Protocol shall not prejudice the provisions of the Charter.

2. Articles 22 to 32 and Article 36 of the Charter shall apply, *mutatis mutandis*, to this Protocol.

Article 9 – Territorial application

1. This Protocol shall apply to the metropolitan territory of each Party. Any State may, at the time of signature or when depositing its instrument of ratification, acceptance or approval, specify, by declaration addressed to the Secretary General of the Council of Europe, the territory which shall be considered to be its metropolitan territory for this purpose.

2. Any Contracting State may, at the time of ratification, acceptance or approval of this Protocol or at any time thereafter, declare by notification addressed to the Secretary General of the Council of Europe that the Protocol shall extend in whole or in part to a non-metropolitan territory or territories specified in the said declaration for whose international relations it is responsible or for which it assumes international responsibility. It shall specify in the declaration the article or articles of Part II of the Protocol which it accepts as binding in respect of the territories named in the declaration.

3. The Protocol shall extend to the territory or territories named in the aforesaid declaration as from the thirtieth day after the date on which the Secretary General shall have notification of such declaration.

4. Any Party may declare at a later date, by notification addressed to the Secretary General of the Council of Europe, that, in respect of one or more of the territories to which this Protocol has been extended in accordance with paragraph 2 of this article, it accepts as binding any articles which it has not already accepted in respect of that territory or territories. Such undertakings subsequently given shall be deemed to be an integral part of the original declaration in respect of the territory concerned, and shall have the same effect as from the thirtieth day after the date on which the Secretary General shall have notification of such declaration.

Article 10 – Signature, ratification, acceptance, approval and entry into force

1. This Protocol shall be open for signature by member States of the Council of Europe who are signatories to the Charter. It is subject to ratification, acceptance or approval. No member State of the Council of Europe shall ratify, accept or approve this Protocol except at the same time as or after ratification of the Charter. Instruments of ratification, acceptance or approval shall be deposited with the Secretary General of the Council of Europe.

2. The Protocol shall enter into force on the thirtieth day after the date of deposit of the third instrument of ratification, acceptance or approval.

3. In respect of any signatory State ratifying subsequently, the Protocol shall come into force as from the thirtieth day after the date of deposit of its instrument of ratification, acceptance or approval.

Article 11 – Denunciation

1. Any Party may denounce this Protocol only at the end of a period of five years from the date on which the Protocol entered into force for it, or at the end of any successive period of two years and, in each case, after giving six months' notice to the Secretary General of the Council of Europe. Such denunciation shall not affect the validity of the Protocol in respect of the other Parties provided that at all times there are not less than three such Parties.

2. Any Party may, in accordance with the provisions set out in the preceding paragraph, denounce any article of Part II of this Protocol accepted by it, provided that the number of articles by which this Party is bound shall never be less than one.

3. Any Party may denounce this Protocol or any of the articles of Part II of the Protocol, under the conditions specified in paragraph 1 of this article, in respect of any territory to which the Protocol is applicable by virtue of a declaration made in accordance with paragraphs 2 and 4 of Article 9.

4. Any Party bound by the Charter and this Protocol, which denounces the Charter in accordance with the provisions of paragraph 1 of Article 37 thereof, will be considered to have denounced the Protocol likewise.

Article 12 – Notifications

The Secretary General of the Council of Europe shall notify the member States of the Council and the Director General of the International Labour Office of:

a. any signature;
b. the deposit of any instrument of ratification, acceptance or approval;
c. any date of entry into force of this Protocol in accordance with Articles 9 and 10;
d. any other act, notification or communication relating to this Protocol.

Article 13 – Appendix

The appendix to this Protocol shall form an integral part of it.

In witness whereof the undersigned, being duly authorised thereto, have signed this Protocol.

Done at Strasbourg, this 5th day of May 1988, in English and French, both texts being equally authentic, in a single copy which shall be deposited in the archives of the Council of Europe. The Secretary General of the Council of Europe shall transmit certified copies to each member State of the Council of Europe.

Appendix to the Protocol

Scope of the Protocol in terms of persons protected

1. The persons covered by Articles 1 to 4 include foreigners only in so far as they are nationals of other Parties lawfully resident or working regularly within the territory of the Party concerned subject to the understanding that these articles are to be interpreted in the light of the provisions of Articles 18 and 19 of the Charter.
This interpretation would not prejudice the extension of similar facilities to other persons by any of the Parties.

2. Each Party will grant to refugees as defined in the Convention relating to the Status of Refugees, signed at Geneva on 28 July 1951 and in the Protocol of 31 January 1967, and lawfully staying in its territory, treatment as favourable as possible and in any case not less favourable than under the obligations accepted by the Party under the said instruments and under any other existing international instruments applicable to those refugees.

3. Each Party will grant to stateless persons as defined in the Convention on the Status of Stateless Persons done at New York on 28 September 1954, and lawfully staying in its territory, treatment as favourable as possible and in any case not less favourable than under the obligations accepted by the Party under the said instrument and under any other existing international instruments applicable to those stateless persons.

Article 1

It is understood that social security matters, as well as other provisions relating to unemployment benefit, old age benefit and survivor's benefit, may be excluded from the scope of this article.

Article 1, paragraph 4

This provision is not to be interpreted as requiring the Parties to embody in laws or regulations a list of occupations which, by reason of their nature or the context in which they are carried out, may be reserved to persons of a particular sex.

Articles 2 and 3

1. For the purpose of the application of these articles, the term "workers' representatives" means persons who are recognised as such under national legislation or practice.

2. The term "national legislation and practice" embraces as the case may be, in addition to laws and regulations, collective agreements, other agreements between employers and workers' representatives, customs, as well as relevant case-law.

3. For the purposes of the application of these articles, the term "undertaking" is understood as referring to a set of tangible and intangible components, with or without legal personality, formed to produce goods or provide services for financial gain and with power to determine its own market policy.

4. It is understood that religious communities and their institutions may be excluded from the application of these articles, even if these institutions are "undertakings" within the meaning of paragraph 3. Establishments pursuing activities which are inspired by certain ideals or guided by certain moral concepts, ideals and concepts which are protected by national legislation, may be excluded from the application of these articles to such an extent as is necessary to protect the orientation of the undertaking.

5. It is understood that, where in a State the rights set under Articles 2 and 3 are exercised in the various establishments of the undertaking, the Party concerned is to be considered as fulfilling the obligations deriving from these provisions.

Article 3

This provision affects neither the powers and obligations of States as regards the adoption of health and safety regulations for work-places, nor the powers and responsibilities of the bodies in charge of monitoring their application.

The terms "social and socio-cultural services and facilities" are understood as referring to the social and/or cultural facilities for workers provided by some undertakings such as welfare assistance, sports fields, rooms for nursing mothers, libraries, children's holiday camps, etc.

Article 4, paragraph 1

For the purpose of the application of this paragraph, the term "for as long as possible" refers to the elderly person's physical, psychological and intellectual capacities.

Article 7

It is understood that workers excluded in accordance with paragraph 2 of Article 2 and paragraph 2 of Article 3 are not taken into account in establishing the number of workers concerned.

7. **Protocol amending the European Social Charter**

Turin, 21 October 1991

The member States of the Council of Europe, signatory to this Protocol to the European Social Charter, opened for signature in Turin on 18 October 1961 (hereinafter referred to as "the Charter"),

Being resolved to take some measures to improve the effectiveness of the Charter, and particularly the functioning of its supervisory machinery;

Considering therefore that it is desirable to amend certain provisions of the Charter,

Have agreed as follows:

Article 1

Article 23 of the Charter shall read as follows:

"Article 23 – Communication of copies of reports and comments

1. When sending to the Secretary General a report pursuant to Articles 21 and 22, each Contracting Party shall forward a copy of that report to such of its national organisations as are members of the international organisations of employers and trade unions invited, under Article 27, paragraph 2, to be represented at meetings of the Governmental Committee. Those organisations shall send to the Secretary General any comments on the reports of the Contracting Parties. The Secretary General shall send a copy of those comments to the Contracting Parties concerned, who might wish to respond.

2. The Secretary General shall forward a copy of the reports of the Contracting Parties to the international non-governmental organisations which have consultative status with the Council of Europe and have particular competence in the matters governed by the present Charter.

3. The reports and comments referred to in Articles 21 and 22 and in the present article shall be made available to the public on request."

Article 2

Article 24 of the Charter shall read as follows:

"Article 24 – Examination of the reports

1. The reports sent to the Secretary General in accordance with Articles 21 and 22 shall be examined by a Committee of Independent Experts constituted pursuant to Article 25. The committee shall also have before it any comments forwarded to the Secretary General in accordance with paragraph 1 of Article 23. On completion of its examination, the Committee of Independent Experts shall draw up a report containing its conclusions.

2. With regard to the reports referred to in Article 21, the Committee of Independent Experts shall assess from a legal standpoint the compliance of national law and practice with the obligations arising from the Charter for the Contracting Parties concerned.

3. The Committee of Independent Experts may address requests for additional information and clarification directly to Contracting Parties. In this connection the Committee of Independent Experts may also hold, if necessary, a meeting with the representatives of a Contracting Party, either on its own initiative or at the request of the Contracting Party concerned. The organisations referred to in paragraph 1 of Article 23 shall be kept informed.

4. The conclusions of the Committee of Independent Experts shall be made public and communicated by the Secretary General to the Governmental Committee, to the Parliamentary Assembly and to the organisations which are mentioned in paragraph 1 of Article 23 and paragraph 2 of Article 27."

Article 3

Article 25 of the Charter shall read as follows:

"Article 25 – Committee of Independent Experts

1. The Committee of Independent Experts shall consist of at least nine members elected by the Parliamentary Assembly by a majority of votes cast from a list of experts of the highest integrity and of recognised competence in national and international social questions, nominated by the Contracting Parties. The exact number of members shall be determined by the Committee of Ministers.

2. The members of the committee shall be elected for a period of six years. They may stand for re-election once.

3. A member of the Committee of Independent Experts elected to replace a member whose term of office has not expired shall hold office for the remainder of his predecessor's term.

4. The members of the committee shall sit in their individual capacity. Throughout their term of office, they may not perform any function incompatible with the requirements of independence, impartiality and availability inherent in their office."

Article 4

Article 27 of the Charter shall read as follows:

"Article 27 – Governmental Committee

1. The reports of the Contracting Parties, the comments and information communicated in accordance with paragraphs 1 of Article 23 and 3 of Article 24, and the reports of the Committee of Independent Experts shall be submitted to a Governmental Committee.

2. The committee shall be composed of one representative of each of the Contracting Parties. It shall invite no more than two international organisations of employers and no more than two international trade union organisations to send observers in a consultative capacity to its

meetings. Moreover, it may consult representatives of international non-governmental organisations which have consultative status with the Council of Europe and have particular competence in the matters governed by the present Charter.

3. The Governmental Committee shall prepare the decisions of the Committee of Ministers. In particular, in the light of the reports of the Committee of Independent Experts and of the Contracting Parties, it shall select, giving reasons for its choice, on the basis of social, economic and other policy considerations the situations which should, in its view, be the subject of recommendations to each Contracting Party concerned, in accordance with Article 28 of the Charter. It shall present to the Committee of Ministers a report which shall be made public.

4. On the basis of its findings on the implementation of the Social Charter in general, the Governmental Committee may submit proposals to the Committee of Ministers aiming at studies to be carried out on social issues and on articles of the Charter which might possibly be updated."

Article 5

Article 28 of the Charter shall read as follows:

"Article 28 – Committee of Ministers

1. The Committee of Ministers shall adopt, by a majority of two-thirds of those voting, with entitlement to voting limited to the Contracting Parties, on the basis of the report of the Governmental Committee, a resolution covering the entire supervision cycle and containing individual recommendations to the Contracting Parties concerned.

2. Having regard to the proposals made by the Governmental Committee pursuant to paragraph 4 of Article 27, the Committee of Ministers shall take such decisions as it deems appropriate."

Article 6

Article 29 of the Charter shall read as follows:

"Article 29 – Parliamentary Assembly

The Secretary General of the Council of Europe shall transmit to the Parliamentary Assembly, with a view to the holding of periodical plenary debates, the reports of the Committee of Independent Experts and of the Governmental Committee, as well as the resolutions of the Committee of Ministers."

Article 7

1. This Protocol shall be open for signature by member States of the Council of Europe signatories to the Charter, which may express their consent to be bound by:

a. signature without reservation as to ratification, acceptance or approval; or
b. signature subject to ratification, acceptance or approval, followed by ratification, acceptance or approval.

2. Instruments of ratification, acceptance or approval shall be deposited with the Secretary General of the Council of Europe.

Article 8

This Protocol shall enter into force on the thirtieth day after the date on which all Contracting Parties to the Charter have expressed their consent to be bound by the Protocol in accordance with the provisions of Article 7.

Article 9

The Secretary General of the Council of Europe shall notify the member States of the Council of:

a. any signature;
b. the deposit of any instrument of ratification, acceptance or approval;
c. the date of entry into force of this Protocol in accordance with Article 8;

d. any other act, notification or communication relating to this Protocol.

In witness whereof the undersigned, being duly authorised thereto, have signed this Protocol.

Done at Turin, this 21st day of October 1991, in English and French, both texts being equally authentic, in a single copy which shall be deposited in the archives of the Council of Europe. The Secretary General of the Council of Europe shall transmit certified copies to each member State of the Council of Europe.

8. **European Convention for the Prevention of Torture and Inhuman or Degrading Treatment or Punishment**

Strasbourg, 26 November 1987

Entry into force: 1 February 1989,
in accordance with Article 19

The member States of the Council of Europe, signatory hereto,

Having regard to the provisions of the Convention for the Protection of Human Rights and Fundamental Freedoms,

Recalling that, under Article 3 of the same Convention, "no one shall be subjected to torture or to inhuman or degrading treatment or punishment";

Noting that the machinery provided for in that Convention operates in relation to persons who allege that they are victims of violations of Article 3;

Convinced that the protection of persons deprived of their liberty against torture and inhuman or degrading treatment or punishment could be strengthened by non-judicial means of a preventive character based on visits,

Have agreed as follows:

Chapter I

Article 1

There shall be established a European Committee for the Prevention of Torture and Inhuman or Degrading Treatment or Punishment (hereinafter referred to as "the Committee"). The Committee shall, by means of visits, examine the treatment of persons deprived of their liberty with a view to strengthening, if necessary, the protection of such persons from torture and from inhuman or degrading treatment or punishment.

Article 2

Each Party shall permit visits, in accordance with this Convention, to any place within its jurisdiction where persons are deprived of their liberty by a public authority.

Article 3

In the application of this Convention, the Committee and the competent national authorities of the Party concerned shall co-operate with each other.

Chapter II

Article 4

1. The Committee shall consist of a number of members equal to that of the Parties.

2. The members of the Committee shall be chosen from among persons of high moral character, known for their competence in the field of human rights or having professional experience in the areas covered by this Convention.

3. No two members of the Committee may be nationals of the same State.

4. The members shall serve in their individual capacity, shall be independent and impartial, and shall be available to serve the Committee effectively.

Article 5

1. The members of the Committee shall be elected by the Committee of Ministers of the Council of Europe by an absolute majority of votes, from a list of names drawn up by the Bureau of the Consultative Assembly of the Council of Europe; each national delegation of the Parties in the Consultative Assembly shall put forward three candidates, of whom two at least shall be its nationals.

2. The same procedure shall be followed in filling casual vacancies.

3. The members of the Committee shall be elected for a period of four years. They may only be re-elected once. However, among the members elected at the first election, the terms of three members shall expire at the end of two years. The members whose terms are to expire at the end of the initial period of two years shall be chosen by lot by the Secretary General of the Council of Europe immediately after the first election has been completed.

Article 6

1. The Committee shall meet in camera. A quorum shall be equal to the majority of its members. The decisions of the Committee shall be taken by a majority of the members present, subject to the provisions of Article 10, paragraph 2.

2. The Committee shall draw up its own rules of procedure.

3. The Secretariat of the Committee shall be provided by the Secretary General of the Council of Europe.

Chapter III

Article 7

1. The Committee shall organise visits to places referred to in Article 2. Apart from periodic visits, the Committee may organise such other visits as appear to it to be required in the circumstances.

2. As a general rule, the visits shall be carried out by at least two members of the Committee. The Committee may, if it considers it necessary, be assisted by experts and interpreters.

Article 8

1. The Committee shall notify the Government of the Party concerned of its intention to carry out a visit. After such notification, it may at any time visit any place referred to in Article 2.

2. A Party shall provide the Committee with the following facilities to carry out its task:

a. access to its territory and the right to travel without restriction;
b. full information on the places where persons deprived of their liberty are being held;
c. unlimited access to any place where persons are deprived of their liberty, including the right to move inside such places without restriction;
d. other information available to the Party which is necessary for the Committee to carry out its task. In seeking such information, the Committee shall have regard to applicable rules of national law and professional ethics.

3. The Committee may interview in private persons deprived of their liberty.

4. The Committee may communicate freely with any person whom it believes can supply relevant information.

5. If necessary, the Committee may immediately communicate observations to the competent authorities of the Party concerned.

Article 9

1. In exceptional circumstances, the competent authorities of the Party concerned may make representations to the Committee against a visit at the time or to the particular place proposed by the Committee. Such representations may only be made on grounds of national defence, public

safety, serious disorder in places where persons are deprived of their liberty, the medical condition of a person or that an urgent interrogation relating to a serious crime is in progress.

2. Following such representations, the Committee and the Party shall immediately enter into consultations in order to clarify the situation and seek agreement on arrangements to enable the Committee to exercise its functions expeditiously. Such arrangements may include the transfer to another place of any person whom the Committee proposed to visit. Until the visit takes place, the Party shall provide information to the Committee about any person concerned.

Article 10

1. After each visit, the Committee shall draw up a report on the facts found during the visit, taking account of any observations which may have been submitted by the Party concerned. It shall transmit to the latter its report containing any recommendations it considers necessary. The Committee may consult with the Party with a view to suggesting, if necessary, improvements in the protection of persons deprived of their liberty.

2. If the Party fails to co-operate or refuses to improve the situation in the light of the Committee's recommendations, the Committee may decide, after the Party has had an opportunity to make known its views, by a majority of two-thirds of its members to make a public statement on the matter.

Article 11

1. The information gathered by the Committee in relation to a visit, its report and its consultations with the Party concerned shall be confidential.

2. The Committee shall publish its report, together with any comments of the Party concerned, whenever requested to do so by that Party.

3. However, no personal data shall be published without the express consent of the person concerned.

Article 12

Subject to the rules of confidentiality in Article 11, the Committee shall every year submit to the Committee of Ministers a general report on its activities which shall be transmitted to the Consultative Assembly and made public.

Article 13

The members of the Committee, experts and other persons assisting the Committee are required, during and after their terms of office, to maintain the confidentiality of the facts or information of which they have become aware during the discharge of their functions.

Article 14

1. The names of persons assisting the Committee shall be specified in the notification under Article 8, paragraph 1.

2. Experts shall act on the instructions and under the authority of the Committee. They shall have particular knowledge and experience in the areas covered by this Convention and shall be bound by the same duties of independence, impartiality and availability as the members of the Committee.

3. A Party may exceptionally declare that an expert or other person assisting the Committee may not be allowed to take part in a visit to a place within its jurisdiction.

Chapter IV

Article 15

Each Party shall inform the Committee of the name and address of the authority competent to receive notifications to its Government, and of any liaison officer it may appoint.

Article 16

The Committee, its members and experts referred to in Article 7, paragraph 2, shall enjoy the privileges and immunities set out in the annex to this Convention.

Article 17

1. This Convention shall not prejudice the provisions of domestic law or any international agreement which provide greater protection for persons deprived of their liberty.

2. Nothing in this Convention shall be construed as limiting or derogating from the competence of the organs of the European Convention on Human Rights or from the obligations assumed by the Parties under that Convention.

3. The Committee shall not visit places which representatives or delegates of protecting powers or the International Committee of the Red Cross effectively visit on a regular basis by virtue of the Geneva Conventions of 12 August 1949 and the Additional Protocols of 8 June 1977 thereto.

Chapter V

Article 18

This Convention shall be open for signature by the member States of the Council of Europe. It is subject to ratification, acceptance or approval. Instruments of ratification, acceptance or approval shall be deposited with the Secretary General of the Council of Europe.

Article 19

1. This Convention shall enter into force on the first day of the month following the expiration of a period of three months after the date on which seven member States of the Council of Europe have expressed their consent to be bound by the Convention in accordance with the provisions of Article 18.

2. In respect of any member State which subsequently expresses its consent to be bound by it, the Convention shall enter into force on the first day of the month following the expiration of a period of three months after the date of the deposit of the instrument of ratification, acceptance or approval.

Article 20

1. Any State may, at the time of signature or when depositing its instrument of ratification, acceptance or approval, specify the territory or territories to which this Convention shall apply.

2. Any State may at any later date, by a declaration addressed to the Secretary General of the Council of Europe, extend the application of this Convention to any other territory specified in the declaration. In respect of such territory the Convention shall enter into force on the first day of the month following the expiration of a period of three months after the date of receipt of such declaration by the Secretary General.

3. Any declaration made under the two preceding paragraphs may, in respect of any territory specified in such declaration, be withdrawn by a notification addressed to the Secretary General. The withdrawal shall become effective on the first day of the month following the expiration of a period of three months after the date of receipt of such notification by the Secretary General.

Article 21

No reservation may be made in respect of the provisions of this Convention.

Article 22

1. Any Party may, at any time, denounce this Convention by means of a notification addressed to the Secretary General of the Council of Europe.

2. Such denunciation shall become effective on the first day of the month following the expiration of a period of twelve months after the date of receipt of the notification by the Secretary General.

Article 23

The Secretary General of the Council of Europe shall notify the member States of the Council of Europe of:

a. any signature;

b. the deposit of any instrument of ratification, acceptance or approval;

c. any date of entry into force of this Convention in accordance with Articles 19 and 20;

d. any other act, notification or communication relating to this Convention, except for action taken in pursuance of Articles 8 and 10.

In witness thereof, the undersigned, being duly authorised thereto, have signed this Convention.

Done at Strasbourg, this 26th day of November 1987, in English and French, both texts being equally authentic, in a single copy which shall be deposited in the archives of the Council of Europe. The Secretary General of the Council of Europe shall transmit certified copies to each member State of the Council of Europe.

Annex

Privileges and immunities (Article 16)

1. For the purpose of this annex, references to members of the Committee shall be deemed to include references to experts mentioned in Article 7, paragraph 2.

2. The members of the Committee shall, while exercising their functions and during journeys made in the exercise of their functions, enjoy the following privileges and immunities:

a. immunity from personal arrest or detention and from seizure of their personal baggage and, in respect of words spoken or written and all acts done by them in their official capacity, immunity from legal process of every kind;

b. exemption from any restrictions on their freedom of movement on exit from and return to their country of residence, and entry into and exit from the country in which they exercise their functions, and from alien registration in the country which they are visiting or through which they are passing in the exercise of their functions.

3. In the course of journeys undertaken in the exercise of their functions, the members of the Committee shall, in the matter of customs and exchange control, be accorded:

a. by their own government, the same facilities as those accorded to senior officials travelling abroad on temporary official duty;

b. by the governments of other Parties, the same facilities as those accorded to representatives of foreign governments on temporary official duty.

4. Documents and papers of the Committee, in so far as they relate to the business of the Committee, shall be inviolable.
The official correspondence and other official communications of the Committee may not be held up or subjected to censorship.

5. In order to secure for the members of the Committee complete freedom of speech and complete independence in the discharge of their duties, the immunity from legal process in respect of words spoken or written and all acts done by them in discharging their duties shall continue to be accorded, notwithstanding that the persons concerned are no longer engaged in the discharge of such duties.

6. Privileges and immunities are accorded to the members of the Committee, not for the personal benefit of the individuals themselves but in order to safeguard the independent exercise of their functions. The Committee alone shall be competent to waive the immunity of

its members; it has not only the right, but is under a duty, to waive the immunity of one of its members in any case where, in its opinion, the immunity would impede the course of justice, and where it can be waived without prejudice to the purpose for which the immunity is accorded.

Other texts

1. Declaration on human rights

Adopted by the Committee of Ministers on 27 April 1978 at its 62nd Session

The member states of the Council of Europe,

1. Mindful of their adherence to the principles of parliamentary democracy and of their commitment, under the Statute of the Council of Europe, to the respect of human rights and fundamental freedoms;

2. Considering that the European Convention for the Protection of Human Rights and Fundamental Freedoms, which has now been in force for twenty-five years, has given concrete expression to this commitment by providing for a collective guarantee of a number of rights affirmed in the Universal Declaration of Human Rights proclaimed by the United Nations General Assembly thirty years ago, particularly through the Convention's control mechanism which is based on objective criteria and entrusted to independent institutions;

3. Considering that, by virtue of that European Convention, effective international protection is accorded to any person who comes under the jurisdiction of the Contracting States, which implies protection irrespective of nationality or place of residence;

4. In the conviction that the protection of human rights and fundamental freedoms, both at national and international level, is a continuing task and that the individual rights arising out of man's human dignity conserve their prime value and importance throughout the changes and evolution of society;

5. Believing that it is of paramount importance that the institutions established by the European Convention on Human Rights remain an ef-

fective instrument for ensuring the observance of the engagements which result from it;

6. Recalling, moreover, that within the Council of Europe proposals are under consideration to extend the lists of rights of the individual to be protected by the European Convention on Human Rights and other relevant European conventions, including rights in the social, economic and cultural fields;

7. Noting in this respect the initial contribution that the European Social Charter has made in the field of social and economic rights and being prepared to consider the possibility of further enlarging in the framework of the Council of Europe the protection of those rights;

8. Aware of the close interrelationship between the protection and advancement of human rights and fundamental freedoms within states, and the strengthening of justice and peace in the world,

I. Reaffirm the importance of the role of the European Convention on Human Rights in the international protection of human rights and fundamental freedoms, and their effective exercise, in Europe;

II. Decide to give priority to the work undertaken in the Council of Europe of exploring the possibility of extending the lists of rights of the individual, notably rights in the social, economic and cultural fields, which should be protected by European conventions or any other appropriate means;

III. Resolve to play an active part in the protection and further realisation of human rights and fundamental freedoms including, in a wider concept, those in the social, economic and cultural fields, thus contributing to the strengthening of world peace and security and international co-operation as well as to the economic and social development of all peoples.

2. **Declaration regarding intolerance – A threat to democracy**

Adopted by the Committee of Ministers on 14 May 1981 at its 68th Session

The Committee of Ministers of the Council of Europe,

1. Convinced that tolerance and respect for the dignity and intrinsic equality of all human beings are the very basis of a democratic and pluralistic society;

2. Profoundly disturbed by the resurgence of various forms of intolerance;

3. Reaffirming its determination to safeguard the effective political democracy referred to in the preamble to the Convention for the Protection of Human Rights and Fundamental Freedoms;

4. Recalling that human rights and fundamental freedoms are the very foundation of justice and peace throughout the world;

5. Bearing in mind that the Convention for the Protection of Human Rights and Fundamental Freedoms has successfully afforded effective international protection, without discrimination, to everyone within the jurisdiction of the Contracting States;

6. Recalling that, in accordance with the United Nations International Convention on the Elimination of All Forms of Racial Discrimination and following the Committee of Ministers Resolution (68) 30 of 31 October 1968 on measures to be taken against incitement to racial, national and religious hatred, several member states have either adopted new legislation or reinforced existing legislation against acts inspired by racism;

7. Welcoming the adoption by the Consultative Assembly of Resolution 743 (1980) on the need to combat resurgent fascist propaganda and its racist aspects;

8. Considering that the best way of countering all forms of intolerance is to preserve and consolidate democratic institutions, to foster citizens' confidence in those institutions and to encourage them to take an active part in their operation;

9. Convinced of the vital part played by education and information in any action against intolerance, whose origin frequently lies in ignorance, source of incomprehension, hatred and even violence,

I. Vigorously condemns all forms of intolerance, regardless of their origin, inspiration or aims, and the acts of violence to which they give rise, especially when human lives are at stake;

II. Rejects all ideologies entailing contempt for the individual or a denial of the intrinsic equality of all human beings;

III. Solemnly recalls its unswerving attachment to the principles of pluralistic democracy and respect for human rights, the cornerstone of membership of the Council of Europe, as well as to the Convention for the Protection of Human Rights and Fundamental Freedoms, the essential instrument in the effective exercise of these rights;

IV. Decides:

i. to reinforce efforts, at national and international levels, and particularly in the framework of the Council of Europe, to prevent the spread of totalitarian and racist ideologies and to act effectively against all forms of intolerance;

ii. to take, with this objective in mind, all appropriate measures and to implement a programme of activities including, in particular, the study of legal instruments applicable in the matter with a view to their reinforcement where appropriate;

iii. to promote an awareness of the requirements of human rights and the ensuing responsibilities in a democratic society, and to this end, in addition to human rights education, to encourage the creation in schools, from the primary level upwards, of a climate of active understanding of and respect for the qualities and culture of others;

V. Agrees that member states will make every effort so that the principles enounced above prevail within other international organisations;

VI. Appeals to all institutions, movements and associations and to all political and social forces to contribute towards a sustained effort against the threat to democracy represented by intolerance.

3. **Declaration on the freedom of expression and information**

Adopted by the Committee of Ministers on 29 April 1982 at its 70th Session

The member states of the Council of Europe,

1. Considering that the principles of genuine democracy, the rule of law and respect for human rights form the basis of their co-operation, and that the freedom of expression and information is a fundamental element of those principles;

2. Considering that this freedom has been proclaimed in national constitutions and international instruments, and in particular in Article 19 of the Universal Declaration of Human Rights and Article 10 of the European Convention on Human Rights;

3. Recalling that through that Convention they have taken steps for the collective enforcement of the freedom of expression and information by entrusting the supervision of its application to the organs provided for by the Convention;

4. Considering that the freedom of expression and information is necessary for the social, economic, cultural and political development of every human being, and constitutes a condition for the harmonious progress of social and cultural groups, nations and the international community;

5. Convinced that the continued development of information and communication technology should serve to further the right, regardless of frontiers, to express, to seek, to receive and to impart information and ideas, whatever their source;

6. Convinced that states have the duty to guard against infringements of the freedom of expression and information and should adopt policies designed to foster as much as possible a variety of media and a

plurality of information sources, thereby allowing a plurality of ideas and opinions;

7. Noting that, in addition to the statutory measures referred to in paragraph 2 of Article 10 of the European Convention on Human Rights, codes of ethics have been voluntarily established and are applied by professional organisations in the field of the mass media;

8. Aware that a free flow and wide circulation of information of all kinds across frontiers is an important factor for international understanding, for bringing peoples together and for the mutual enrichment of cultures,

I. Reiterate their firm attachment to the principles of freedom of expression and information as a basic element of democratic and pluralist society;

II. Declare that in the field of information and mass media they seek to achieve the following objectives:

a. protection of the right of everyone, regardless of frontiers, to express himself, to seek and receive information and ideas, whatever their source, as well as to impart them under the conditions set out in Article 10 of the European Convention on Human Rights;

b. absence of censorship or any arbitrary controls or constraints on participants in the information process, on media content or on the transmission and dissemination of information;

c. the pursuit of an open information policy in the public sector, including access to information, in order to enhance the individual's understanding of, and his ability to discuss freely, political, social, economic and cultural matters;

d. the existence of a wide variety of independent and autonomous media, permitting the reflection of diversity of ideas and opinions;

e. the availability and access on reasonable terms to adequate facilities for the domestic and international transmission and dissemination of information and ideas;

f. the promotion of international co-operation and assistance, through public and private channels, with a view to fostering the free flow of information and improving communication infrastructures and expertise;

III. Resolve to intensify their co-operation in order:

a. to defend the right of everyone to the exercise of the freedom of expression and information;

b. to promote, through teaching and education, the effective exercise of the freedom of expression and information;

c. to promote the free flow of information, thus contributing to international understanding, a better knowledge of convictions and traditions, respect for the diversity of opinions and the mutual enrichment of cultures;

d. to share their experience and knowledge in the media field;

e. to ensure that new information and communication techniques and services, where available, are effectively used to broaden the scope of freedom of expression and information.

4. Recommendation No. R (87) 8 of the Committee of Ministers to member states regarding conscientious objection to compulsory military service[1]

Adopted by the Committee of Ministers on 9 April 1987 at the 406th meeting of the Ministers' Deputies

The Committee of Ministers, under the terms of Article 15.*b* of the Statute of the Council of Europe,

Considering that the aim of the Council of Europe is to achieve a greater unity between its members;

Recalling that respect for human rights and fundamental freedoms is the common heritage of member states of the Council of Europe, as is borne out, in particular, by the European Convention on Human Rights;

Considering that it is desirable to take common action for the further realisation of human rights and fundamental freedoms;

Noting that in the majority of member states of the Council of Europe military service is a basic obligation of citizens;

---

1. When this recommendation was adopted:

– in application of Article 10.2.*c* of the Rules of Procedure for the meetings of the Ministers' Deputies, the Representative of Greece reserved the right of his Government to comply with it or not, and the Representative of Cyprus reserved the right of his Government to comply or not with paragraph 9 of the text;

– in application of Article 10.2.*d* of the Rules of Procedure for the meetings of the Ministers' Deputies, the Representative of Italy recorded his abstention and in an explanatory statement said that his Government was of the opinion that the text as adopted fell short of the suggestions made by the Assembly, and therefore appeared to be deficient;

– in application of Article 10.2.*d* of the Rules of Procedure for the meetings of the Ministers' Deputies, the Representatives of Switzerland and Turkey recorded their abstentions and in explanatory statements said that their Governments would be unable to comply with the text.

Considering the problems raised by conscientious objection to compulsory military service;

Wishing that conscientious objection to compulsory military service be recognised in all the member states of the Council of Europe and governed by common principles;

Noting that, in some member states where conscientious objection to compulsory military service is not yet recognised, specific measures have been taken with a view to improving the situation of the individuals concerned,

Recommends that the governments of member states, in so far as they have not already done so, bring their national law and practice into line with the following principles and rules:

A. *Basic principle*

1. Anyone liable to conscription for military service, who, for compelling reasons of conscience, refuses to be involved in the use of arms, shall have the right to be released from the obligation to perform such service, on the conditions set out hereafter. Such persons may be liable to perform alternative service;

B. *Procedure*

2. States may lay down a suitable procedure for the examination of applications for conscientious objector status or accept a declaration giving reasons by the person concerned;

3. With a view to the effective application of the principles and rules of this recommendation, persons liable to conscription shall be informed in advance of their rights. For this purpose, the state shall provide them with all relevant information directly or allow private organisations concerned to furnish that information;

4. Applications for conscientious objector status shall be made in ways and within time-limits to be determined having due regard to the requirement that the procedure for the examination of an application should, as a rule, be completed before the individual concerned is actually enlisted in the forces;

5. The examination of applications shall include all the necessary guarantees for a fair procedure;

6. An applicant shall have the right to appeal against the decision at first instance;

7. The appeal authority shall be separate from the military administration and composed so as to ensure its independence;

8. The law may also provide for the possibility of applying for and obtaining conscientious objector status in cases where the requisite conditions for conscientious objection appear during military service or periods of military training after initial service;

C. *Alternative service*

9. Alternative service, if any, shall be in principle civilian and in the public interest. Nevertheless, in addition to civilian service, the state may also provide for unarmed military service, assigning to it only those conscientious objectors whose objections are restricted to the personal use of arms;

10. Alternative service shall not be of a punitive nature. Its duration shall, in comparison to that of military service, remain within reasonable limits;

11. Conscientious objectors performing alternative service shall not have less social and financial rights than persons performing military service. Legislative provisions or regulations which relate to the taking into account of military service for employment, career or pension purposes shall apply to alternative service.

5. **Declaration on equality of women and men**

Adopted by the Committee of Ministers on 16 November 1988 at its 83rd Session

The Council of Europe member states,

1. Recalling that equality of women and men is a principle of human rights, upheld as a fundamental right in many international instruments to which they have subscribed and secured by national constitutions and laws;

2. Mindful of their undertaking, by virtue of the Statute of the Council of Europe, to observe such fundamental rights;

3. Convinced that the betterment and progress of humanity absolutely depend on due consideration of the aspirations, interests and talents of both sexes;

4. Observing that in present-day society inequalities between women and men persist *de jure* and *de facto;*

5. Aware that sex-related discrimination in the political, economic, social, educational, cultural and any other fields constitutes impediments to the recognition, enjoyment and exercise of human rights and fundamental freedoms;

6. Convinced that resolute overall policies should be pursued for the effective achievement of equality between women and men, such policies to involve the authorities, groups and individuals,

I. Reaffirm their commitment to the principle of equality of women and men, as a *sine que non* of democracy and an imperative of social justice;

II. Condemn all forms of sexism, as they have the effect of perpetuating the idea of superiority or inferiority of one of the sexes, and justifying the preponderance or dominance of one over the other;

III. Deplore the under-utilisation of human resources by the community resulting from the persistence of sexist attitudes and behaviour patterns;

IV. Welcome past and present activities aimed at the achievement of equal rights and opportunities for women and men at worldwide, regional and national levels;

V. Assert their resolve and undertaking:

a. to pursue and develop policies aimed at achieving real equality between women and men in all walks of life;

b. to continue work in the Council of Europe to further the effective achievement of equality between women and men;

c. to promote awareness of the imperatives of democracy and human rights in respect of equality of women and men;

VI. Declare that the strategies to be applied for this purpose must enable women and men to receive equal treatment under the law and equal opportunities to exercise their rights and develop their individual gifts and talents. These strategies should provide for suitable measures including temporary special measures aimed at accelerating *de facto* equality between women and men relating to the following in particular:

a. protection of individual rights;

b. participation in political, economic, social and cultural life;

c. access to all levels of the civil service;

d. access to education and freedom of choice in education and initial and further vocational training;

e. rights of couples;

f. eradication of violence in the family and in society;

g. rights and duties with regard to children;

h. access to all professions, occupational advancement, and remuneration;

i. promotion of economic independence;

j. access to information;

VII. Stress the importance for the achievement of the above-mentioned strategies of informing and educating people in a suitable way, and making them realise the injustices and adverse effects of inequalities of rights, treatment and opportunities, together with the need for unrelenting vigilance in order to prevent or remedy any act or form of discrimination founded on sex;

VIII. Invite the member states not yet having done so to become parties:

a. to Protocol No. 7 to the Convention for the Protection of Human Rights and Fundamental Freedoms and to the European Social Charter and its additional Protocol;

b. to the United Nations Convention on the Elimination of All Forms of Discrimination against Women;

and to apply the Nairobi Forward-looking Strategies for the Advancement of Women adopted by the World Conference to Review and Appraise the Achievements of the United Nations Decade for Women: Equality, Development and Peace (Nairobi, Kenya, 15-26 July 1985).

6. Resolution 690 (1979) of the Parliamentary Assembly on the Declaration on the Police

Adopted by the Parliamentary Assembly on 8 May 1979

The Assembly,

1. Considering that the full exercise of human rights and fundamental freedoms, guaranteed by the European Convention on Human Rights and other national and international instruments, has as a necessary basis the existence of a peaceful society which enjoys the advantages of order and public safety;

2. Considering that, in this respect, police play a vital role in all the member states, that they are frequently called upon to intervene in conditions which are dangerous for their members, and that their duties are made yet more difficult if the rules of conduct of their members are not sufficiently precisely defined;

3. Being of the opinion that it is inappropriate for those who have committed violations of human rights whilst members of police forces, or those who have belonged to any police force that has been disbanded on account of inhumane practices, to be employed as policemen;

4. Being of the opinion that the European system for the protection of human rights would be improved if there were generally accepted rules concerning the professional ethics of the police which take account of the principles of human rights and fundamental freedoms;

5. Considering that it is desirable that police officers have the active moral and physical support of the community they are serving;

6. Considering that police officers should enjoy status and rights comparable to those of members of the civil service;

7. Believing that it may be desirable to lay down guidelines for the behaviour of police officers in case of war and other emergency situations, and in the event of occupation by a foreign power,

8. Adopts the following Declaration on the Police, which forms an integral part of this resolution;

9. Instructs its Committee on Parliamentary and Public Relations and its Legal Affairs Committee as well as the Secretary General of the Council of Europe to give maximum publicity to the declaration.

Appendix

Declaration on the Police

A. *Ethics*[1]

1. A police officer shall fulfil the duties the law imposes upon him by protecting his fellow citizens and the community against violent, predatory and other harmful acts, as defined by law.

2. A police officer shall act with integrity, impartiality and dignity. In particular he shall refrain from and vigorously oppose all acts of corruption.

3. Summary executions, torture and other forms of inhuman or degrading treatment or punishment remain prohibited in all circumstances. A police officer is under an obligation to disobey or disregard any order or instruction involving such measures.

4. A police officer shall carry out orders properly issued by his hierarchical superior, but he shall refrain from carrying out any order he knows, or ought to know, is unlawful.

---

1. Parts A and B of the declaration cover all individuals and organisations, including such bodies as secret services, military police forces, armed forces or militias performing police duties, that are responsible for enforcing the law, investigating offences, and maintaining public order and state security.

5. A police officer must oppose violations of the law. If immediate or irreparable and serious harm should result from permitting the violation to take place he shall take immediate action, to the best of his ability.

6. If no immediate or irreparable and serious harm is threatened, he must endeavour to avert the consequences of this violation, or its repetition, by reporting the matter to his superiors. If no results are obtained in that way he may report to higher authority.

7. No criminal or disciplinary action shall be taken against a police officer who has refused to carry out an unlawful order.

8. A police officer shall not co-operate in the tracing, arresting, guarding or conveying of persons who, while not being suspected of having committed an illegal act, are searched for, detained or prosecuted because of their race, religion or political belief.

9. A police officer shall be personally liable for his own acts and for acts of commission or omission he has ordered and which are unlawful.

10. There shall be a clear chain of command. It should always be possible to determine which superior may be ultimately responsible for acts or omissions of a police officer.

11. Legislation must provide for a system of legal guarantees and remedies against any damage resulting from police activities.

12. In performing his duties, a police officer shall use all necessary determination to achieve an aim which is legally required or allowed, but he may never use more force than is reasonable.

13. Police officers shall receive clear and precise instructions as to the manner and circumstances in which they should make use of arms.

14. A police officer having the custody of a person needing medical attention shall secure such attention by medical personnel and, if necessary,

take measures for the preservation of the life and health of this person. He shall follow the instructions of doctors and other competent medical workers when they place a detainee under medical care.

15. A police officer shall keep secret all matters of a confidential nature coming to his attention, unless the performance of duty or legal provisions require otherwise.

16. A police officer who complies with the provisions of this declaration is entitled to the active moral and physical support of the community he is serving.

B. *Status*

1. Police forces are public services created by law, which shall have the responsibility of maintaining and enforcing the law.

2. Any citizen may join the police forces if he satisfies the relevant conditions.

3. A police officer shall receive thorough general training, professional training and in-service training, as well as appropriate instruction in social problems, democratic freedoms, human rights and in particular the European Convention on Human Rights.

4. The professional, psychological and material conditions under which a police officer must perform his duties shall be such as to protect his integrity, impartiality and dignity.

5. A police officer is entitled to a fair remuneration, and special factors are to be taken into account, such as greater risks and responsibilities and more irregular working schedules.

6. Police officers shall have the choice of whether to set up professional organisations, join them and play an active part therein. They may also play an active part in other organisations.

7. A police professional organisation, provided it is representative, shall have the right:

– to take part in negotiations concerning the professional status of police officers;
– to be consulted on the administration of police units
– to initiate legal proceedings for the benefit of a group of police officers or on behalf of a particular police officer.

8. Membership of a police professional organisation and playing an active part therein shall not be detrimental to any police officer.

9. In case of disciplinary or penal proceedings taken against him, a police officer has the right to be heard and to be defended by a lawyer. The decision shall be taken within a reasonable time. He shall also be able to avail himself of the assistance of a professional organisation to which he belongs.

10. A police officer against whom a disciplinary measure has been taken or penal sanction imposed shall have the right of appeal to an independent and impartial body or court.

11. The rights of a police officer before courts or tribunals shall be the same as those of any other citizen.

C. *War and other emergency situations – Occupation by a foreign power*[1]

1. A police officer shall continue to perform his tasks of protecting persons and property during war and enemy occupation in the interests of the civilian population. For that reason he shall not have the status of "combatant", and the provisions of the Third Geneva Convention of 12 August 1949, relative to the treatment of prisoners of war, shall not apply.

---

1. This chapter does not apply to the military police.

2. The provisions of the Fourth Geneva Convention of 12 August 1949, relative to the protection of civilian persons in time of war, apply to the civilian police.

3. The occupying power shall not order police officers to perform tasks other than those mentioned in Article 1 of this chapter.

4. During occupation a police officer shall not:

– take part in measures against members of resistance movements;

– take part in applying measures designed to employ the population for military purposes and for guarding military installations.

5. If a police officer resigns during enemy occupation because he is forced to execute illegitimate orders of the occupying power which are contrary to the interests of the civilian population, such as those listed above, and because he sees no other way out, he shall be reintegrated into the police force as soon as the occupation is over without losing any of the rights or benefits he would have enjoyed if he had stayed in the police force.

6. Neither during nor after the occupation may any penal or disciplinary sanction be imposed on a police officer for having executed in good faith an order of an authority regarded as competent, where the execution of such an order was normally the duty of the police force.

7. The occupying power shall not take any disciplinary or judicial action against police officers by reason of the execution, prior to the occupation, of orders given by the competent authorities.

II. Texts prepared within the Organization of American States

1. American Declaration of the Rights and Duties of Man

Bogotá, 2 May 1948

Ninth International Conference of American States,

Whereas: The American peoples have acknowledged the dignity of the individual, and their national constitutions recognize that juridical and political institutions, which regulate life in human society, have as their principal aim the protection of the essential rights of man and the creation of circumstances that will permit him to achieve spiritual and material progress and attain happiness;

The American States have on repeated occasions recognized that the essential rights of man are not derived from the fact that he is a national of a certain state, but are based upon attributes of his human personality;

The international protection of the rights of man should be the principal guide of an evolving American law;

The affirmation of essential human rights by the American States together with the guarantees given by the internal regimes of the states establish the initial system of protection considered by the American States as being suited to the present social and juridical conditions, not without a recognition on their part that they should increasingly strengthen that system in the international field as conditions become more favourable,

Agrees to adopt the following American Declaration of the Rights and Duties of Man.

Preamble

All men are born free and equal, in dignity and in rights, and, being endowed by nature with reason and conscience, they should conduct themselves as brothers one to another.

The fulfilment of duty by each individual is a prerequisite to the rights of all. Rights and duties are interrelated in every social and political activity of man. While rights exalt individual liberty, duties express the dignity of that liberty.

Duties of a juridical nature presuppose others of a moral nature which support them in principle and constitute their basis.

Inasmuch as spiritual development is the supreme end of human existence and the highest expression thereof, it is the duty of man to serve that end with all his strength and resources.

Since culture is the highest social and historical expression of that spiritual development, it is the duty of man to preserve, practice and foster culture by every means within his power.

And, since moral conduct constitutes the noblest flowering of culture, it is the duty of every man always to hold it in high respect.

Chapter I – Rights

Article 1 – Right to life, liberty and personal security

Every human being has the right to life, liberty and the security of his person.

Article 2 – Right to equality before the law

All persons are equal before the law and have the rights and duties established in this declaration, without distinction as to race, sex, language, creed or any other factor.

Article 3 – Right to religious freedom and worship

Every person has the right freely to profess a religious faith, and to manifest and practise it both in public and in private.

Article 4 – Right to freedom of investigation, opinion, expression and dissemination

Every person has the right to freedom of investigation, of opinion, and of the expression and dissemination of ideas, by any medium whatsoever.

Article 5 – Right to protection of honour, personal reputation, and private and family life

Every person has the right to the protection of the law against abusive attacks upon his honour, his reputation, and his private and family life.

Article 6 – Right to a family and to the protection thereof

Every person has the right to establish a family, the basic element of society, and to receive protection therefor.

Article 7 – Right to protection for mothers and children

All women, during pregnancy and the nursing period, and all children have the right to special protection, care and aid.

Article 8 – Right to residence and movement

Every person has the right to fix his residence within the territory of the state of which he is a national, to move about freely within such territory, and not to leave it except by his own will.

Article 9 – Right to inviolability of the home

Every person has the right to the inviolability of his home.

Article 10 – Right to the inviolability and transmission of correspondence

Every person has the right to the inviolability and transmission of his correspondence.

Article 11 – Right to the preservation of health and to well-being

Every person has the right to the preservation of his health through sanitary and social measures relating to food, clothing, housing and medical care, to the extent permitted by public and community resources.

Article 12 – Right to education

Every person has the right to an education, which should be based on the principles of liberty, morality and human solidarity.

Likewise every person has the right to an education that will prepare him to attain a decent life, to raise his standard of living and to be a useful member of society.

The right to an education includes the right to equality of opportunity in every case, in accordance with natural talents, merit and the desire to utilize the resources that the state or the community is in a position to provide.

Every person has the right to receive, free, at least a primary education.

Article 13 – Right to the benefits of culture

Every person has the right to take part in the cultural life of the community, to enjoy the arts and to participate in the benefits that result from intellectual progress, especially scientific discoveries.

He likewise has the right to the protection of his moral and material interests as regards his inventions or any literary, scientific or artistic works of which he is the author.

Article 14 – Right to work and to fair remuneration

Every person has the right to work, under proper conditions, and to follow his vocation freely, in so far as existing conditions of employment permit.

Every person who works has the right to receive such remuneration as will, in proportion to his capacity and skill, assure him a standard of living suitable for himself and for his family.

Article 15 – Right to leisure time and to the use thereof

Every person has the right to leisure time, to wholesome recreation, and to the opportunity for advantageous use of his free time to his spiritual, cultural and physical benefit.

Article 16 – Right to social security

Every person has the right to social security which will protect him from the consequences of unemployment, old age, and any disabilities arising from causes beyond his control that make it physically or mentally impossible for him to earn a living.

Article 17 – Right to recognition of juridical personality and of civil rights

Every person has the right to be recognized everywhere as a person having rights and obligations, and to enjoy the basic civil rights.

Article 18 – Right to a fair trial

Every person may resort to the courts to ensure respect for his legal rights. There should likewise be available to him a simple, brief procedure whereby the courts will protect him from acts of authority that, to his prejudice, violate any fundamental constitutional rights.

Article 19 – Right to nationality

Every person has the right to the nationality to which he is entitled by law and to change it, if he so wishes, for the nationality of any other country that is willing to grant it to him.

Article 20 – Right to vote and to participate in government

Every person having legal capacity is entitled to participate in the government of his country, directly or through his representatives, and to take part in popular elections, which shall be by secret ballot, and shall be honest, periodic and free.

Article 21 – Right of assembly

Every person has the right to assemble peaceably with others in a formal public meeting or an informal gathering, in connection with matters of common interest of any nature.

Article 22 – Right of association

Every person has the right to associate with others to promote, exercise and protect his legitimate interests of a political, economic, religious, social, cultural, professional, labour union or other nature.

Article 23 – Right to property

Every person has a right to own such private property as meets the essential needs of decent living and helps to maintain the dignity of the individual and of the home.

Article 24 – Right to petition

Every person has the right to submit respectful petitions to any competent authority, for reasons of either general or private interest, and the right to obtain a prompt decision thereon.

Article 25 – Right of protection from arbitrary arrest

No person may be deprived of his liberty except in the cases and according to the procedures established by pre-existing law.

No person may be deprived of liberty for non-fulfilment of obligations of a purely civil character.

Every individual who has been deprived of his liberty has the right to have the legality of his detention ascertained without delay by a court, and the right to be tried without undue delay or, otherwise, to be released. He also has the right to humane treatment during the time he is in custody.

Article 26 – Right to due process of law

Every accused person is presumed to be innocent until proved guilty.

Every person accused of an offence has the right to be given an impartial and public hearing, and to be tried by courts previously established in accordance with pre-existing laws, and not to receive cruel, infamous or unusual punishment.

Article 27 – Right of asylum

Every person has the right, in case of pursuit not resulting from ordinary crimes, to seek and receive asylum in foreign territory, in accordance with the laws of each country and with international agreements.

Article 28 – Scope of the rights of man

The rights of man are limited by the rights of others, by the security of all, and by the just demands of the general welfare and the advancement of democracy.

Chapter II – Duties

Article 29 – Duties to society

It is the duty of the individual so to conduct himself in relation to others that each and every one may fully form and develop his personality.

Article 30 – Duties towards children and parents

It is the duty of every person to aid, support, educate and protect his minor children, and it is the duty of children to honour their parents always and to aid, support and protect them when they need it.

Article 31 – Duty to receive instruction

It is the duty of every person to acquire at least an elementary education.

Article 32 – Duty to vote

It is the duty of every person to vote in the popular elections of the country of which he is a national, when he is legally capable of doing so.

Article 33 – Duty to obey the law

It is the duty of every person to obey the law and other legitimate commands of the authorities of his country and those of the country in which he may be.

Article 34 – Duty to serve the community and the nation

It is the duty of every able-bodied person to render whatever civil and military service his country may require for its defence and preservation, and, in case of public disaster, to render such services as may be in his power.

It is likewise his duty to hold any public office to which he may be elected by popular vote in the state of which he is a national.

Article 35 – Duties with respect to social security and welfare

It is the duty of every person to cooperate with the State and the community with respect to social security and welfare, in accordance with his ability and with existing circumstances.

Article 36 – Duty to pay taxes

It is the duty of every person to pay the taxes established by law for the support of public services.

Article 37 – Duty to work

It is the duty of every person to work, as far as his capacity and possibilities permit, in order to obtain the means of livelihood or to benefit his community.

Article 38 – Duty to refrain from political activities in a foreign country

It is the duty of every person to refrain from taking part in political activities that, according to law, are reserved exclusively to the citizens of the state in which he is an alien.

2. **American Convention on Human Rights**

"Pact of San José, Costa Rica"

San José, Costa Rica, 22 November 1969

Preamble

The American States signatory to the present Convention,

Reaffirming their intention to consolidate in this hemisphere, within the framework of democratic institutions, a system of personal liberty and social justice based on respect for the essential rights of man;

Recognizing that the essential rights of man are not derived from one's being a national of a certain State, but are based upon attributes of the human personality, and that they therefore justify international protection in the form of a convention reinforcing or complementing the protection provided by the domestic law of the American States;

Considering that these principles have been set forth in the Charter of the Organization of American States, in the American Declaration of the Rights and Duties of Man, and in the Universal Declaration of Human Rights, and that they have been reaffirmed and refined in other international instruments, worldwide as well as regional in scope;

Reiterating that, in accordance with the Universal Declaration of Human Rights, the ideal of free men enjoying freedom from fear and want can be achieved only if conditions are created whereby everyone may enjoy his economic, social and cultural rights, as well as his civil and political rights; and

Considering that the Third Special Inter-American Conference (Buenos Aires, 1967) approved the incorporation into the Charter of the Organization itself of broader standards with respect to economic, social and educational rights and resolved that an inter-American convention on human rights should determine the structure, competence and procedure of the organs responsible for these matters,

Have agreed upon the following:

Part I – State obligations and rights protected

Chapter I – General obligations

Article 1 – Obligation to respect rights

1. The States Parties to this Convention undertake to respect the rights and freedoms recognized herein and to ensure to all persons subject to their jurisdiction the free and full exercise of those rights and freedoms, without any discrimination for reasons of race, colour, sex, language, religion, political or other opinion, national or social origin, economic status, birth, or any other social condition.

2. For the purposes of this Convention, "person" means every human being.

Article 2 – Domestic legal effects

Where the exercise of any of the rights or freedoms referred to in Article 1 is not already ensured by legislative or other provisions, the States Parties undertake to adopt, in accordance with their constitutional processes and the provisions of this Convention, such legislative or other measures as may be necessary to give effect to those rights or freedoms.

Chapter II – Civil and political rights

Article 3 – Right to juridical personality

Every person has the right to recognition as a person before the law.

Article 4 – Right to life

1. Every person has the right to have his life respected. This right shall be protected by law, and, in general, from the moment of conception. No one shall be arbitrarily deprived of his life.

2. In countries that have not abolished the death penalty, this may be imposed only for the most serious crimes and pursuant to a final judgment rendered by a competent court and in accordance with a law establishing such punishment, enacted prior to the commission of the crime. Its application shall not be extended to crimes to which it does not presently apply.

3. The death penalty shall not be re-established in States that have abolished it.

4. In no case shall capital punishment be inflicted for political offences or related common crimes.

5. Capital punishment shall not be imposed upon persons who, at the time the crime was committed, were under 18 years of age or over 70 years of age; nor shall it be applied to pregnant women.

6. Every person condemned to death shall have the right to apply for amnesty, pardon, or commutation of sentence, which may be granted in all cases. Capital punishment shall not be imposed while such a petition is pending decision by the competent authority.

Article 5 – Right to humane treatment

1. Every person has the right to have his physical, mental and moral integrity respected.

2. No one shall be subjected to torture or to cruel, inhuman, or degrading punishment or treatment. All persons deprived of their liberty shall be treated with respect for the inherent dignity of the human person.

3. Punishment shall not be extended to any person other than the criminal.

4. Accused persons shall, save in exceptional circumstances, be segregated from convicted persons, and shall be subject to separate treatment appropriate to their status as unconvicted persons.

5. Minors while subject to criminal proceedings shall be separated from adults and brought before specialized tribunals, as speedily as possible, so that they may be treated in accordance with their status as minors.

6. Punishments consisting of deprivation of liberty shall have as an essential aim the reform and social readaptation of the prisoners.

Article 6 – Freedom from slavery

1. No one shall be subject to slavery or to involuntary servitude, which are prohibited in all their forms, as are the slave trade and traffic in women.

2. No one shall be required to perform forced or compulsory labour. This provision shall not be interpreted to mean that, in those countries in which the penalty established for certain crimes is deprivation of liberty at forced labour, the carrying out of such a sentence imposed by a competent court is prohibited. Forced labour shall not adversely affect the dignity or the physical or intellectual capacity of the prisoner.

3. For the purposes of this article, the following do not constitute forced or compulsory labour:

a. any work or service normally required of a person imprisoned in execution of a sentence or formal decision passed by the competent judicial authority. Such work or service shall be carried out under the supervision and control of public authorities, and any persons performing such work or service shall not be placed at the disposal of any private party, company, or juridical person;

b. any military service and, in countries in which conscientious objectors are recognized, national service that the law may provide for in lieu of that service;

c. any service exacted in time of danger or calamity that threatens the existence or the well-being of the community; or

d. any work or service that forms part of normal civic obligations.

Article 7 – Right to personal liberty

1. Every person has the right to personal liberty and security.

2. No one shall be deprived of his physical liberty except for the reasons and under the conditions established beforehand by the constitution of the State Party concerned or a law established pursuant thereto.

3. No one shall be subject to arbitrary arrest or imprisonment.

4. Anyone who is detained shall be informed of the reasons for his detention and shall be promptly notified of the charge or charges against him.

5. Any person detained shall be brought promptly before a judge or other officer authorized by law to exercise judicial power and shall be entitled to trial within a reasonable time or to be released without prejudice to the continuation of the proceedings. His release may be subject to guarantees to assure his appearance for trial.

6. Anyone who is deprived of his liberty shall be entitled to recourse to a competent court, in order that the court may decide without delay on the lawfulness of his arrest or detention and order his release if the arrest or detention is unlawful. In States Parties whose laws provide that anyone who believes himself to be threatened with deprivation of his liberty is entitled to recourse to a competent court in order that it may decide on the lawfulness of such threat, this remedy may not be restricted or abolished. The interested party or another person on his behalf is entitled to seek these remedies.

7. No one shall be detained for debt. This principle shall not limit the orders of a competent judicial authority issued for non fulfillment of duties of support.

Article 8 – Right to a fair trial

1. Every person has the right to a hearing, with due guarantees and within a reasonable time, by a competent, independent and impartial tribunal, previously established by law, in the substantiation of any accusation of a criminal nature made against him or for the determination of his rights and obligations of a civil, labour, fiscal or any other nature.

2. Every person accused of a serious crime has the right to be presumed innocent so long as his guilt has not been proven according to law. During the proceedings, every person is entitled, with full equality, to the following minimum guarantees:

a. the right of the accused to be assisted without charge by a translator or interpreter, if he does not understand or does not speak the language of the tribunal or court;
b. prior notification in detail to the accused of the charges against him;
c. adequate time and means for the preparation of his defence;
d. the right of the accused to defend himself personally or to be assisted by legal counsel of his own choosing, and to communicate freely and privately with his counsel;
e. the inalienable right to be assisted by counsel provided by the State, paid or not as the domestic law provides, if the accused does not defend himself personally or engage his own counsel within the time period established by law;
f. the right of the defence to examine witnesses present in the court and to obtain the appearance, as witnesses, of experts or other persons who may throw light on the facts;
g. the right not to be compelled to be a witness against himself or to plead guilty; and
h. the right to appeal the judgment to a higher court.

3. A confession of guilt by the accused shall be valid only if it is made without coercion of any kind.

4. An accused person, acquitted by a nonappealable judgment, shall not be subjected to a new trial for the same cause.

5. Criminal procedure shall be public, except in so far as may be necessary to protect the interests of justice.

Article 9 – Freedom from ex post facto *laws*

No one shall be convicted of any act or omission that did not constitute a criminal offence, under the applicable law, at the time it was committed. A heavier penalty shall not be imposed than the one that was applicable at the time the criminal offence was committed. If subsequently to the commission of the offence the law provides for the imposition of a lighter punishment, the guilty person shall benefit therefrom.

Article 10 – Right to compensation

Every person shall have the right to be compensated in accordance with the law in the event sentenced by a final judgment through a miscarriage of justice.

Article 11 – Right to privacy

1. Everyone has the right to have his honour respected and his dignity recognized.

2. No one may be the object of arbitrary or abusive interference with his private life, his family, his home, or his correspondence, or of unlawful attacks on his honour or reputation.

3. Everyone has the right to the protection of the law against such interference or attacks.

Article 12 – Freedom of conscience and religion

1. Everyone has the right to freedom of conscience and of religion. This right includes freedom to maintain or to change one's religion or beliefs,

and freedom to profess or disseminate one's religion or beliefs either individually or together with others, in public or in private.

2. No one shall be subject to restrictions that might impair his freedom to maintain or to change his religion or beliefs.

3. Freedom to manifest one's religion and beliefs may be subject only to the limitations prescribed by law that are necessary to protect public safety, order, health, or morals, or the rights or freedoms of others.

4. Parents or guardians, as the case may be, have the right to provide for religious and moral education of their children, or wards, that is in accord with their own convictions.

Article 13 – Freedom of thought and expression

1. Everyone has the right to freedom of thought and expression. This right includes freedom to seek, receive and impart information and ideas of all kinds, regardless of frontiers, either orally, in writing, in print, in the form of art, or through any other medium of one's choice.

2. The exercise of the right provided for in the foregoing paragraph shall not be subject to prior censorship but shall be subject to subsequent imposition of liability, which shall be expressly established by law to the extent necessary in order to ensure:

a. respect for the rights or reputations of others; or
b. the protection of national security, public order, or public health or morals.

3. The right of expression may not be restricted by indirect methods or means, such as the abuse of government or private controls over newsprint, radio broadcasting frequencies, or implements or equipment used in the dissemination of information, or by any other means tending to impede the communication and circulation of ideas and opinions.

4. Notwithstanding the provisions of paragraph 2 above, public entertainments may be subject by law to prior censorship, for the sole purpose

of regulating access to them for the moral protection of childhood and adolescence.

5. Any propaganda for war and any advocacy of national, racial, or religious hatred that constitute incitements to lawless violence or any other similar illegal action against any person or group of persons on any grounds including those of race, colour, religion, language or national origin shall be considered as offences punishable by law.

Article 14 – Right of reply

1. Anyone injured by inaccurate or offensive statements or ideas disseminated to the public in general by a legally regulated medium of communication has the right to reply or to make a correction using the same communication outlet, under such conditions as the law may establish.

2. The correction or reply shall not in any case remit other legal liabilities that may have been incurred.

3. For the effective protection of honour and reputation, every publication and every newspaper, motion picture, radio, and television company, shall have a person responsible who is not protected by immunities or special privileges.

Article 15 – Right of assembly

The right of peaceful assembly, without arms, is recognized. No restrictions may be placed on the exercise of this right other than those imposed in conformity with the law and necessary in a democratic society in the interest of national security or public safety or public order, or to protect public health or morals or the rights or freedoms of others.

Article 16 – Freedom of association

1. Everyone has the right to associate freely for ideological, religious, political, economic, labour, social, cultural, sports or other purposes.

2. The exercise of this right shall be subject only to such restrictions established by law as may be necessary in a democratic society, in the interest of national security, public safety or public order, or to protect public health or morals or the rights and freedoms of others.

3. The provisions of this article do not bar the imposition of legal restrictions, including even deprivation of the exercise of the right of association, on members of the armed forces and the police.

Article 17 – Rights of the family

1. The family is the natural and fundamental group unit of society and is entitled to protection by society and the State.

2. The right of men and women of marriageable age to marry and to raise a family shall be recognized, if they meet the conditions required by domestic laws, in so far as such conditions do not affect the principle of non-discrimination established in this Convention.

3. No marriage shall be entered into without the free and full consent of the intending spouses.

4. The States Parties shall take appropriate steps to ensure the equality of rights and the adequate balancing of responsibilities of the spouses as to marriage, during marriage, and in the event of its dissolution. In case of dissolution, provision shall be made for the necessary protection of any children solely on the basis of their own best interests.

5. The law shall recognize equal rights for children born out of wedlock and those born in wedlock.

Article 18 – Right to a name

Every person has the right to a given name and to the surnames of his parents or that of one of them. The law shall regulate the manner in which this right shall be ensured for all, by the use of assumed names if necessary.

Article 19 – Rights of the child

Every minor child has the right to the measures of protection required by his condition as a minor, on the part of his family, society and the State.

Article 20 – Right to nationality

1. Every person has the right to a nationality.

2. Every person has the right to the nationality of the State in whose territory he was born if he does not have the right to any other nationality.

3. No one shall be arbitrarily deprived of his nationality or of the right to change it.

Article 21 – Right to property

1. Everyone has the right to the use and enjoyment of his property. The law may subordinate such use and enjoyment to the interest of society.

2. No one shall be deprived of his property except upon payment of just compensation, for reasons of public utility or social interest, and in the cases and according to the forms established by law.

3. Usury and any other form of exploitation of man by man shall be prohibited by law.

Article 22 – Freedom of movement and residence

1. Every person lawfully in the territory of a State Party shall have the right to move about in it and to reside in it subject to the provisions of the law.

2. Every person has the right to leave the country freely, including his own.

3. The exercise of the foregoing rights may be restricted only pursuant to a law, to the extent indispensable in a democratic society in order to

prevent crime or to protect national security, public safety, public order, public morals, public health, or the rights or freedoms of others.

4. The exercise of the rights recognized in paragraph 1 may also be restricted by law in designated zones for reasons of public interest.

5. No one can be expelled from the territory of the State of which he is a national or be deprived of the right to enter it.

6. An alien lawfully in the territory of a State Party to this Convention may be expelled from it only pursuant to a decision reached in accordance with law.

7. Every person has the right to seek and be granted asylum in a foreign territory, in accordance with the legislation of the State and international conventions, in the event he is being pursued for political or related common crimes.

8. In no case may an alien be deported or returned to a country, regardless of whether or not it is his country of origin, if in that country his right to life or personal freedom is in danger of being violated because of his race, nationality, religion, social status, or political opinions.

9. The collective expulsion of aliens is prohibited.

Article 23 – Right to participate in government

1. Every citizen shall enjoy the following rights and opportunities:

a. to take part in the conduct of public affairs, directly or through freely chosen representatives;

b. to vote and to be elected in genuine periodic elections, which shall be by universal and equal suffrage and by secret ballot that guarantees the free expression of the will of the voters; and

c. to have access, under general conditions of equality, to the public service of his country.

2. The law may regulate the exercise of the rights and opportunities referred to in the preceding paragraph, exclusively on the basis of age, nationality, residence, language, education, civil and mental capacity and conviction by a competent judge in criminal proceedings.

Article 24 – Right to equal protection

All persons are equal before the law. Consequently, they are entitled, without discrimination, to equal protection of the law.

Article 25 – Right to judicial protection

1. Everyone has the right to simple and prompt recourse, or any other effective recourse, to a competent court or tribunal for protection against acts that violate his fundamental rights recognized by the Constitution or laws of the State or by this Convention, even though such violation may have been committed by persons acting in the course of their official duties.

2. The States Parties undertake:

a. to ensure that any person claiming such remedy shall have his right thereto determined by the competent authority provided for by the legal system of the State;
b. to develop the possibilities of judicial remedy; and
c. to ensure that the competent authorities shall enforce such remedies when granted.

Chapter III – Economic, social and cultural rights

Article 26 – Progressive development

The States Parties undertake to adopt measures, both internally and through international co-operation, especially those of an economic and technical nature, with a view to achieving progressively by legislation or other appropriate means, the full realization of the rights implicit in the economic, social, educational, scientific and cultural standards set forth in the Charter of the Organization of American States as amended by the Protocol of Buenos Aires.

Chapter IV – Suspension of guarantees – Interpretation and application

Article 27 – Suspension of guarantees

1. In time of war, public danger, or other emergency that threatens the independence or security of a State Party, it may take measures derogating from its obligations under the present Convention to the extent and for the period of time strictly required by the exigencies of the situation, provided that such measures are not inconsistent with its other obligations under international law and do not involve discrimination on the ground of race, colour, sex, language, religion or social origin.

2. The foregoing provision does not authorize any suspension of the following articles: Article 3 (Right to juridical personality), Article 4 (Right to life), Article 5 (Right to humane treatment), Article 6 (Freedom from slavery), Article 9 (Freedom from *ex post facto* laws), Article 12 (Freedom of conscience and religion), Article 17 (Rights of the family), Article 18 (Right to a name), Article 19 (Rights of the child), Article 20 (Right to nationality), and Article 23 (Right to participate in government), or of the judicial guarantees essential for the protection of such rights.

3. Any State Party availing itself of the right of suspension shall immediately inform the other States Parties, through the Secretary General of the Organization of American States, of the provisions the application of which it has suspended, the reasons that gave rise to the suspension and the date set for the termination of such suspension.

Article 28 – Federal clause

1. Where a State Party is constituted as a federal State, the national government of such State Party shall implement all the provisions of the

Convention over whose subject matter it exercises legislative and judicial jurisdiction.

2. With respect to the provisions over whose subject matter the constituent units of the federal State have jurisdiction, the national government shall immediately take suitable measures, in accordance with its constitution and its laws, to the end that the competent authorities of the constituent units may adopt appropriate provisions for the fulfilment of this Convention.

3. Whenever two or more States Parties agree to form a federation or other type of association, they shall take care that the resulting federal or other compact contains the provisions necessary for continuing and rendering effective the standards of this Convention in the new State that is organised.

Article 29 – Restrictions regarding interpretation

No provision of this Convention shall be interpreted as:

a. permitting any State Party, group, or person to suppress the enjoyment or exercise of the rights and freedoms recognized in this Convention, or to restrict them to a greater extent than is provided for herein;
b. restricting the enjoyment or exercise of any right or freedom recognized by virtue of the laws of any State Party or by virtue of another convention to which one of the said States is a party;
c. precluding other rights or guarantees that are inherent in the human personality or derived from representative democracy as a form of government; or
d. excluding or limiting the effect that the American Declaration of the Rights and Duties of Man and other international acts of the same nature may have.

Article 30 – Scope of restrictions

The restrictions that, pursuant to this Convention, may be placed on the enjoyment or exercise of the rights or freedoms recognized herein may not be applied except in accordance with laws enacted for reasons of general interest and for the purpose of which the restrictions have been established.

Article 31 – Recognition of other rights

Other rights and freedoms recognized by virtue of the procedures established in Articles 76 and 77 may be included in the system of protection of this Convention.

Chapter V – Personal responsibilities

Article 32 – Relations between duties and rights

1. Every person has responsibilities to his family, his community and mankind.

2. The rights of each person are limited by the rights of others, by the security of all, and by the just demands of the general welfare, in a democratic society.

Part II – Means of protection

Chapter VI – Competent organs

Article 33

The following organs shall be competent to hear matters relating to the fulfilment of the commitments made by the States Parties to this Convention:

a. the Inter-American Commission on Human Rights, referred to as "the Commission"; and
b. the Inter-American Court of Human Rights, referred to as "the Court".

Chapter VII – Inter-American Commission on Human Rights

Section 1 – Organization

Article 34

The Inter-American Commission on Human Rights shall be composed of seven members, who shall be persons of high moral character and recognized competence in the field of human rights.

Article 35

The Commission shall represent all the member countries of the Organization of American States.

Article 36

1. The members of the Commission shall be elected in a personal capacity by the General Assembly of the Organization from a list of candidates proposed by the governments of the member States.

2. Each of those governments may propose up to three candidates, who may be nationals of the States proposing them or of any other member State of the Organization of American States. When a slate of three is proposed, at least one of the candidates shall be a national of a State other than the one proposing the slate.

Article 37

1. The members of the Commission shall be elected for a term of four years and may be re-elected only once, but the terms of three of the members chosen in the first election shall expire at the end of two years. Immediately following that election the General Assembly shall determine the names of those three members by lot.

2. No two nationals of the same State may be members of the Commission.

Article 38

Vacancies that may occur on the Commission for reasons other than the normal expiration of a term shall be filled by the Permanent Council of the Organization in accordance with the provisions of the Statute of the Commission.

Article 39

The Commission shall prepare its Statute, which shall be submitted to the General Assembly for approval, and it shall also establish its own Regulations.

Article 40

Secretariat services for the Commission shall be furnished by the appropriate specialized unit of the General Secretariat of the Organization. This unit shall be provided with the resources required to accomplish the tasks assigned to it by the Commission.

Section 2 – Functions

Article 41

The main function of the Commission shall be to promote respect for and defence of human rights. In the exercise of its mandate, it shall have the following functions and powers:

a. to develop an awareness of human rights among the peoples of America;

b. to make recommendations to the governments of the member States, when it considers such action advisable, for the adoption of progressive measures in favour of human rights within the framework of their domestic law and constitution precepts as well as appropriate measures to further the observance of those rights;

c. to prepare such studies or reports as it considers advisable in the performance of its duties;

d. to request the governments of the member States to supply it with information on the measures adopted by them in matters of human rights;

e. to respond, through the General Secretariat of the Organization of American States, to inquiries made by the member States on matters related to human rights and, within the limits of its possibilities, to provide those States with the advisory services they request;

f. to take action on petitions and other communications pursuant to its authority, in accordance with the provisions of Articles 44 through 51 of this Convention; and

g. to submit an annual report to the General Assembly of the Organization of American States.

Article 42

The States Parties shall transmit to the Commission a copy of each of the reports and studies that they submit annually to the Executive Committees of the Inter-American Economic and Social Council and the Inter-American Council for Education, Science and Culture, in their respective fields, so that the Commission may watch over the promotion of the rights implicit in the economic, social, educational, scientific and cultural standards set forth in the Charter of the Organization of American States as amended by the Protocol of Buenos Aires.

Article 43

The States Parties undertake to provide the Commission with such information as it may request of them as to the manner in which their domestic law ensures the effective application of any provisions of this Convention.

Section 3 – Competence

Article 44

Any person or group of persons, or any non-governmental entity legally recognized in one or more member States of the Organization, may lodge petitions with the Commission containing denunciations or complaints of violation of this Convention by a State Party.

Article 45

1. Any State Party may, when it deposits its instrument of ratification of or adherence to this Convention, or at any later time, declare that it recognizes the competence of the Commission to receive and examine communications in which a State Party alleges that another State Party has committed a violation of a human right set forth in this Convention.

2. Communications presented by virtue of this article may be admitted and examined only if they are presented by a State Party that has made a declaration recognizing the aforementioned competence of the Commission. The Commission shall not admit any communication against a State Party that has not made such a declaration.

3. A declaration concerning recognition of competence may be made to be valid for an indefinite time, for a specified period or for a specific case.

4. Declarations shall be deposited with the General Secretariat of the Organization of American States, which shall transmit copies thereof to member States of that Organization.

Article 46

1. Admission by the Commission of a petition or communication lodged in accordance with Articles 44 or 45 shall be subject to the following requirements:

a. that the remedies under domestic law have been pursued and exhausted in accordance with generally recognized principles of international law;

b. that the petition is lodged within a period of six months from the date on which the party alleging violation of his rights was notified of the final decision;

c. that the subject of the petition or communication is not pending before another international procedure for settlement; and

d. that, in the case of Article 44, the petition contains the name, nationality, profession, domicile and signature of the person or persons or of the legal representative of the entity lodging the petition.

2. The provisions of paragraphs 1.*a* and 1.*b* of this article shall not be applicable when:

a. the domestic legislation of the State concerned does not afford due process of law for the protection of the right or rights that have allegedly been violated;

b. the party alleging violation of his right has been denied access to the remedies of domestic jurisdiction or has been prevented from exhausting them; or

c. there has been unwarranted delay in rendering a final judgment under the aforementioned remedies.

Article 47

The Commission shall consider inadmissible any petition or communication submitted under Articles 44 or 45 if:

a. any of the requirements indicated in Article 46 has not been met;

b. the petition or communication does not state facts that tend to establish a violation of the rights guaranteed by this Convention;

c. the statements of the petitioner or the State indicate that the petition or communication is manifestly groundless or obviously out of order; or

d. the petition or communication is substantially the same as one previously studied by the Commission or another international organization.

Section 4 – Procedure

Article 48

1. When the Commission receives a petition or communication alleging violation of any of the rights protected by this Convention, it shall proceed as follows:

a. if it considers the petition or communication admissible, it shall request information from the government of the State which has been indicated as being the authority responsible for the alleged violations and shall furnish that government a transcript of the pertinent portions of the petition or communication. This information shall be submitted within a reasonable period to be determined by the Commission in accordance with the circumstances of each case;

b. after the information has been received, or after the period established has elapsed and the information has not been received, the Commission shall ascertain whether the grounds for the petition or communication still exist. If they do not, the Commission shall order the record to be closed;

c. the Commission may also declare the petition or communication inadmissible or out of order on the basis of information or evidence subsequently received;

d. if the record has not been closed, the Commission shall, with the knowledge of the parties, examine the matter set forth in the petition or communication in order to verify the facts. If necessary and advisable, the Commission shall conduct an investigation, for the effective conduct of which it shall request, and the States concerned shall furnish to it, all necessary facilities;

e. the Commission may request the States concerned to furnish any pertinent information and, if so requested, shall hear oral statements or receive written statements from the parties concerned;

f. the Commission shall place itself at the disposal of the parties concerned with a view to reaching a friendly settlement of the matter on the basis of respect for the human rights recognized in this Convention.

2. However, in serious and urgent cases, only the presentation of a petition or communication that fulfils all the formal requirements of admissibility shall be necessary in order for the Commission to conduct an investigation with the prior consent of the State in whose territory a violation has allegedly been committed.

Article 49

If a friendly settlement has been reached in accordance with paragraph 1.*f* of Article 48, the Commission shall draw up a report, which shall be transmitted to the petitioner and to the States Parties to this Convention, and then communicated to the Secretary General of the Organization of American States for publication. This report shall contain a brief statement of the facts and of the solution reached. If any party in the case so requests, the fullest possible information shall be provided to it.

Article 50

1. If a settlement is not reached, the Commission shall, within the time-limit established by its Statute, draw up a report setting forth the facts and stating its conclusions. If the report, in whole or in part, does not represent the unanimous agreement of the members of the Commission, any member may attach to it a separate opinion. The written and oral statements made by the parties in accordance with paragraph 1.*e* of Article 48 shall also be attached to the report.

2. The report shall be transmitted to the States concerned, which shall not be at liberty to publish it.

3. In transmitting the report, the Commission may make such proposals and recommendations as it sees fit.

Article 51

1. If, within a period of three months from the date of the transmittal of the report of the Commission to the States concerned, the matter has not either been settled or submitted by the Commission or by the State concerned to the Court and its jurisdiction accepted, the Commission may,

by the vote of an absolute majority of its members, set forth its opinion and conclusions concerning the question submitted for its consideration.

2. Where appropriate, the Commission shall make pertinent recommendations and shall prescribe a period within which the State is to take the measures that are incumbent upon it to remedy the situation examined.

3. When the prescribed period has expired, the Commission shall decide by the vote of an absolute majority of its members whether the State has taken adequate measures and whether to publish its report.

Chapter VIII – Inter-American Court of Human Rights

Section 1 – Organization

Article 52

1. The Court shall consist of seven judges, nationals of the member States of the Organization, elected in an individual capacity from among jurists of the highest moral authority and of recognized competence in the field of human rights, who possess the qualifications required for the exercise of the highest judicial functions in conformity with the law of the State of which they are nationals or of the State that proposes them as candidates.

2. No two judges may be nationals of the same State.

Article 53

1. The judges of the Court shall be elected by secret ballot by an absolute majority vote of the States Parties to the Convention in the General Assembly of the Organization, from a panel of candidates proposed by those States.

2. Each of the States Parties may propose up to three candidates, nationals of the State that proposes them or of any other member State

of the Organization of American States. When a slate of three is proposed, at least one of the candidates shall be a national of a State other than the one proposing the slate.

Article 54

1. The judges of the Court shall be elected for a term of six years and may be re-elected only once. The term of three of the judges chosen in the first election shall expire at the end of three years. Immediately after the election, the names of the three judges shall be determined by lot in the General Assembly.

2. A judge elected to replace a judge whose term has not expired shall complete the term of the latter.

3. The judges shall continue in office until the expiration of their term. However, they shall continue to serve with regard to cases that they have begun to hear and that are still pending, for which purposes they shall not be replaced by the newly elected judges.

Article 55

1. If a judge is a national of any of the States Parties to a case submitted to the Court, he shall retain his right to hear that case.

2. If one of the judges called upon to hear a case should be a national of one of the States Parties to the case, any other State Party in the case may appoint a person of its choice to serve on the Court as an *ad hoc* judge.

3. If among the judges called upon to hear a case none is a national of any of the States Parties to the case, each of the latter may appoint an *ad hoc* judge.

4. An *ad hoc* judge shall possess the qualifications indicated in Article 52.

5. If several States Parties to the Convention should have the same interest in a case, they shall be considered as a single party for pur-

poses of the above provisions. In case of doubt, the Court shall decide.

Article 56

Five judges shall constitute a quorum for the transaction of business by the Court.

Article 57

The Commission shall appear at all cases before the Court.

Article 58

1. The Court shall have its seat at the place determined by the States Parties to the Convention in the General Assembly of the Organization; however, it may convene in the territory of any member State of the Organization of American States when a majority of the Court consider it desirable, and with the prior consent of the State concerned. The seat of the Court may be changed by the States Parties to the Convention in the General Assembly by a two-thirds vote.

2. The Court shall appoint its own Secretary.

3. The Secretary shall have his office at the place where the Court has its seat and shall attend the meetings that the Court may hold away from its seat.

Article 59

The Court shall establish its own Secretariat, which shall function under the direction of the Secretary of the Court, in accordance with the administrative standards of the General Secretariat of the Organization in all matters not incompatible with the independence of the Court. The staff of the Court's Secretariat shall be appointed by the Secretary General of the Organization, in consultation with the Secretary of the Court.

Article 60

The Court shall draw up its Statute which it shall submit to the General Assembly for approval. It shall adopt its own Rules of Procedure.

Section 2 – Jurisdiction and functions

Article 61

1. Only the States Parties and the Commission shall have the right to submit a case to the Court.

2. In order for the Court to hear a case, it is necessary that the procedures set forth in Articles 48 to 50 shall have been exhausted.

Article 62

1. A State Party may, upon depositing its instrument of ratification or accession to this Convention or at any subsequent time, declare that it recognizes as binding, *ipso facto* and not requiring special agreement, the jurisdiction of the Court on all matters relating to the interpretation or application of this Convention.

2. Such declaration may be made unconditionally or on the condition of reciprocity, for a specified period or for specific cases. It shall be presented to the Secretary General of the Organization, who shall transmit copies thereof to the other member States of the Organization and to the Secretary of the Court.

3. The jurisdiction of the Court shall comprise all cases concerning the interpretation and application of the provisions of this Convention that are submitted to it, provided that the States Parties to the case recognize or have recognized such jurisdiction, whether by special declaration pursuant to the preceding paragraphs or by a special agreement.

Article 63

1. If the Court finds that there has been a violation of a right or freedom protected by this Convention, the Court shall rule that the injured party

be ensured the enjoyment of his right or freedom that was violated. It shall also rule, if appropriate, that the consequences of the measure or situation that constituted the breach of such right or freedom be remedied and that fair compensation be paid to the injured party.

2. In cases of extreme gravity and urgency, and when necessary to avoid irreparable damage to persons, the Court shall adopt such provisional measures as it deems pertinent in the matters it has under consideration. With respect to a case not yet submitted to the Court, it may act at the request of the Commission.

Article 64

1. The member States of the Organization may consult the Court regarding the interpretation of this Convention or of other treaties concerning the protection of human rights in the American States. Within their spheres of competence, the organs listed in Chapter X of the Charter of the Organization of American States, as amended by the Protocol of Buenos Aires, may in like manner consult the Court.

2. The Court, at the request of a member State of the Organization, may provide that State with opinions regarding the compatibility of any of its domestic laws with the aforesaid international instruments.

Article 65

To each regular session of the General Assembly of the Organization of American States the Court shall submit, for the Assembly's consideration, a report on its work during the previous year. It shall specify, in particular, the cases in which a State has not complied with its judgments and make any pertinent recommendations.

Section 3 – Procedure

Article 66

1. Reasons shall be given for the judgment of the Court.

2. If the judgment does not represent in whole or in part the unanimous opinion of the judges, any judge shall be entitled to have his dissenting or separate opinion attached to the judgment.

Article 67

The judgment of the Court shall be final and not subject to appeal. In case of disagreement as to the meaning or scope of the judgment, the Court shall interpret it at the request of any of the parties, provided the request is made within ninety days from the date of notification of the judgment.

Article 68

1. The States Parties to the Convention undertake to comply with the judgment of the Court in any case to which they are parties.

2. That part of a judgment that stipulates compensatory damages may be executed in the country concerned in accordance with domestic procedure governing the execution of judgments against the State.

Article 69

The parties to the case shall be notified of the judgment of the Court and it shall be transmitted to the States Parties to the Convention.

Chapter IX – Common provisions

Article 70

1. The judges of the Court and the members of the Commission shall enjoy, from the moment of their election and throughout their term of office, the immunities extended to diplomatic agents in accordance with international law. During the exercise of their official function they shall, in addition, enjoy the diplomatic privileges necessary for the performance of their duties.

2. At no time shall the judges of the Court or the members of the Commission be held liable for any decisions or opinions issued in the exercise of their functions.

Article 71

The position of judge of the Court or member of the Commission is incompatible with any other activity that might affect the independence or impartiality of a judge or member, as determined in the respective statutes.

Article 72

The judges of the Court and the members of the Commission shall receive emoluments and travel allowances in the form and under the conditions set forth in their statutes, with due regard for the importance and independence of their office. Such emoluments and travel allowances shall be determined in the budget of the Organization of American States, which shall also include the expenses of the Court and its Secretariat. To this end, the Court shall draw up its own budget and submit it to the General Assembly through the General Secretariat. The latter may not introduce any changes in it.

Article 73

The General Assembly may, only at the request of the Commission or the Court, as the case may be, determine sanctions to be applied against members of the Commission or judges of the Court when there are justifiable grounds for such action as set forth in the respective statutes. A vote of a two-thirds majority of the member States of the Organization shall be required for a decision in the case of members of the Commission and, in the case of judges of the Court, a two-thirds majority vote of the States Parties to the Convention shall also be required.

Part III – General and transitory provisions

Chapter X – Signature, ratification, reservations, amendments, protocols, and denunciation

Article 74

1. This Convention shall be open for signature and ratification by or adherence of any member State of the Organization of American States.

2. Ratification of or adherence to this Convention shall be made by the deposit of an instrument of ratification or adherence with the General Secretariat of the Organization of American States. As soon as eleven States have deposited their instruments of ratification or adherence, the Convention shall enter into force. With respect to any State that ratifies or adheres thereafter, the Convention shall enter into force on the date of the deposit of its instrument of ratification or adherence.

3. The Secretary General shall inform all member States of the Organization of the entry into force of the Convention.

Article 75

This Convention shall be subject to reservations only in conformity with the provisions of the Vienna Convention on the Law of Treaties signed on 23 May 1969.

Article 76

1. Proposals to amend this Convention may be submitted to the General Assembly for the action it deems appropriate by any State Party directly, and by the Commission or the Court through the Secretary General.

2. Amendments shall enter into force for the States ratifying them on the date when two-thirds of the States Parties to this Convention have deposited their respective instruments of ratification. With respect to the other States Parties, the amendments shall enter into force

on the dates on which they deposit their respective instruments of ratification.

Article 77

1. In accordance with Article 31, any State Party and the Commission may submit proposed protocols to this Convention for consideration by the States Parties at the General Assembly with a view to gradually including other rights and freedoms within its system of protection.

2. Each protocol shall determine the manner of its entry into force and shall be applied only among the States Parties to it.

Article 78

1. The States Parties may denounce this Convention at the expiration of a five-year period starting from the date of its entry into force and by means of notice given one year in advance. Notice of the denunciation shall be addressed to the Secretary General of the Organization of American States, who shall inform the other States Parties.

2. Such a denunciation shall not have the effect of releasing the State Party concerned from the obligations contained in this Convention with respect to any act that may constitute a violation of those obligations and that has been taken by that State prior to the effective date of denunciation.

Chapter XI – Transitory provisions

Section 1 – Inter-American Commission on Human Rights

Article 79

Upon the entry into force of this Convention, the Secretary General shall, in writing, request each member State of the Organization to present, within ninety days, its candidates for membership on the Inter-American Commission on Human Rights. The Secretary General shall prepare a list in alphabetical order of the candidates presented, and transmit it to the member States of the Organization at least thirty days prior to the next session of the General Assembly.

Article 80

The members of the Commission shall be elected by secret ballot of the General Assembly from the list of candidates referred to in Article 79. The candidates who obtain the largest number of votes and an absolute majority of the votes of the representatives of the member States shall be declared elected. Should it become necessary to have several ballots in order to elect all the members of the Commission, the candidates who receive the smallest number of votes shall be eliminated successively, in the manner determined by the General Assembly.

Section 2 – Inter-American Court of Human Rights

Article 81

Upon the entry into force of this Convention, the Secretary General shall, in writing, request each State Party to present, within ninety days, its candidates for membership on the Inter-American Court of Human Rights. The Secretary General shall prepare a list in alphabetical order of the candidates presented and transmit it to the States Parties at least thirty days prior to the next session of the General Assembly.

Article 82

The judges of the Court shall be elected from the list of candidates referred to in Article 81, by secret ballot of the States Parties to the Convention in the General Assembly. The candidates who obtain the largest number of votes and an absolute majority of the votes of the representatives of the States Parties shall be declared elected. Should it become necessary to have several ballots in order to elect all the judges of the Court, the candidates who receive the smallest number of votes shall be eliminated successively, in the manner determined by the States Parties.

Statements and reservations

Statement of Chile

The Delegation of Chile signs this Convention, subject to its subsequent parliamentary approval and ratification, in accordance with the constitutional rules in force.

Statement of Ecuador

The Delegation of Ecuador has the honour of signing the American Convention on Human Rights. It does not believe that it is necessary to make any specific reservation at this time, without prejudice to the general power set forth in the Convention itself that leaves the governments free to ratify it or not.

Reservation of Uruguay

Article 80, paragraph 2, of the Uruguay Constitution provides that citizenship is suspended for a person indicted according to law in a criminal prosecution that may result in a sentence of imprisonment. This restriction of the exercise of the rights recognized in Article 23 of the Convention is not envisaged among the circumstances provided for in this respect by paragraph 2 of Article 23, for which reason the Delegation of Uruguay expresses a reservation on this matter.

3. Additional Protocol to the American Convention on Human Rights in the area of Economic, Social and Cultural Rights

"Protocol of San Salvador"

San Salvador, 17 November 1988

Preamble

The States Parties to the American Convention on Human Rights "Pact of San José, Costa Rica",

Reaffirming their intention to consolidate in this hemisphere, within the framework of democratic institutions, a system of personal liberty and social justice based on respect for the essential rights of man;

Recognizing that the essential rights of man are not derived from one's being a national of a certain State, but are based upon attributes of the human person, for which reason they merit international protection in the form of a convention reinforcing or complementing the protection provided by the domestic law of the American States;

Considering the close relationship that exists between economic, social and cultural rights, and civil and political rights, in that the different categories of rights constitute an indivisible whole based on the recognition of the dignity of the human person, for which reason both require permanent protection and promotion if they are to be fully realized, and the violation of some rights in favour of the realization of others can never be justified;

Recognizing the benefits that stem from the promotion and development of cooperation among states and international relations;

Recalling that, in accordance with the Universal Declaration of Human Rights and the American Convention on Human Rights, the ideal of free human beings enjoying freedom from fear and want can only be achieved if conditions are created whereby everyone may enjoy his economic, social and cultural rights as well as his civil and political rights;

Bearing in mind that, although fundamental economic, social and cultural rights have been recognized in earlier international instruments of both world and regional scope, it is essential that those rights be reaffirmed, developed, perfected and protected in order to consolidate in America, on the basis of full respect for the rights of the individual, the democratic representative form of government as well as the right of its peoples to development, self-determination, and the free disposal of their wealth and natural resources; and

Considering that the American Convention on Human Rights provides that draft additional protocols to that Convention may be submitted for consideration to the States Parties, meeting together on the occasion of the General Assembly of the Organization of American States, for the purpose of gradually incorporating other rights and freedoms into the protective system thereof,

Have agreed upon the following Additional Protocol to the American Convention on Human Rights "Protocol of San Salvador":

Article 1 – Obligation to adopt measures

The States Parties to this Additional Protocol to the American Convention on Human Rights undertake to adopt the necessary measures, both domestically and through cooperation among the States, especially economic and technical, to the extent allowed by their available resources and taking into account their degree of development, for the purpose of achieving progressively and pursuant to their internal legislations the full observance of the rights recognized in this Protocol.

Article 2 – Obligation to enact domestic legislation

If the exercise of the rights set forth in this Protocol is not already guaranteed by legislative or other provisions, the States Parties undertake to adopt, in accordance with their constitutional processes and the provisions of this Protocol, such legislative or other measures as may be necessary for making those rights a reality.

Article 3 – Obligation of non-discrimination

The States Parties to this Protocol undertake to guarantee the exercise of the rights set forth herein without discrimination of any kind for reasons related to race, color, sex, language, religion, political or other opinions, national or social origin, economic status, birth or any other social condition.

Article 4 – Inadmissibility of restrictions

A right which is recognized or in effect in a State by virtue of its internal legislation or international conventions may not be restricted or curtailed on the pretext that this Protocol does not recognize the right or recognizes it to a lesser degree.

Article 5 – Scope of restrictions and limitations

The States Parties may establish restrictions and limitations on the enjoyment and exercise of the rights established herein by means of laws promulgated for the purpose of preserving the general welfare in a democratic society only to the extent that they are not incompatible with the purpose and reason underlying those rights.

Article 6 – Right to work

1. Everyone has the right to work, which includes the opportunity to secure the means for living a dignified and decent existence by performing a freely elected or accepted lawful activity.

2. The States Parties undertake to adopt measures that will make the right to work fully effective, especially with regard to the achievement of full employment, vocational guidance and the development of technical and vocational training projects, in particular those directed to the disabled. The States Parties also undertake to implement and strengthen programs that help to ensure suitable family care, so that women may enjoy a real opportunity to exercise the right to work.

Article 7 – Just, equitable and satisfactory conditions of work

The States Parties to this Protocol recognize that the right to work to which the foregoing article refers presupposes that everyone shall enjoy that right under just, equitable and satisfactory conditions, which the States Parties undertake to guarantee in their internal legislation, particularly with respect to:

a. remuneration which guarantees, as a minimum, to all workers dignified and decent living conditions for them and their families and fair and equal wages for equal work, without distinction;

b. the right of every worker to follow his vocation and to devote himself to the activity that best fulfils his expectations and to change employment in accordance with the pertinent national regulations;

c. the right of every worker to promotion or upward mobility in his employment, for which purpose account shall be taken of his qualifications, competence, integrity and seniority;

d. stability of employment, subject to the nature of each industry and occupation and the causes for just separation. In cases of unjustified dismissal, the worker shall have the right to indemnity or to reinstatement on the job or any other benefits provided by domestic legislation;

e. safety and hygiene at work;

f. the prohibition of night work or unhealthy or dangerous working conditions and, in general, of all work which jeopardizes health, safety or morals, for persons under 18 years of age. As regards minors under the age of 16, the work day shall be subordinated to the provisions regarding compulsory education and in no case shall work constitute an impediment to school attendance or a limitation on benefiting from education received;

g. a reasonable limitation of working hours, both daily and weekly. The days shall be shorter in the case of dangerous or unhealthy work or of night work;

h. rest, leisure and paid vacations as well as remuneration for national holidays.

Article 8 – Trade union rights

1. The States Parties shall ensure:

a. the right of workers to organise trade unions and to join the union of their choice for the purpose of protecting and promoting their interests. As an extention of that right, the States Parties shall permit trade unions to establish national federations or confederations, or to affiliate with those that already exist, as well as to form international trade union organizations and to affiliate with that of their choice. The States Parties shall also permit trade unions, federations and confederations to function freely;

b. the right to strike.

2. The exercise of the rights set forth above may be subject only to restrictions established by law, provided that such restrictions are characteristic of a democratic society and necessary for safeguarding public order or for protecting public health or morals or the rights and freedoms of others. Members of the armed forces and the police and of other essential public services shall be subject to limitations and restrictions established by law.

3. No one may be compelled to belong to a trade union.

Article 9 – Right to social security

1. Everyone shall have the right to social security protecting him from the consequences of old age and of disability which prevents him, physically or mentally, from securing the means for a dignified and decent existence. In the event of the death of a beneficiary, social security benefits shall be applied to his dependants.

2. In the case of persons who are employed, the right to social security shall cover at least medical care and an allowance or retirement benefit in the case of work accidents or occupational disease and, in the case of women, paid maternity leave before and after childbirth.

Article 10 – Right to health

1. Everyone shall have the right to health, understood to mean the enjoyment of the highest level of physical, mental and social well-being.

2. In order to ensure the exercise of the right to health, the States Parties agree to recognize health as a public good and, particularly, to adopt the following measures to ensure that right:

a. primary health care, that is, essential health care made available to all individuals and families in the community;
b. extension of the benefits of health services to all individuals subject to the State's jurisdiction;
c. universal immunization against the principal infectious diseases;
d. prevention and treatment of endemic, occupational and other diseases;
e. education of the population on the prevention and treatment of health problems; and
f. satisfaction of the health needs of the highest risk groups and of those whose poverty makes them the most vulnerable.

Article 11 – Right to a healthy environment

1. Everyone shall have the right to live in a healthy environment and to have access to basic public services.

2. The States Parties shall promote the protection, preservation and improvement of the environment.

Article 12 – Right to food

1. Everyone has the right to adequate nutrition which guarantees the possibility of enjoying the highest level of physical, emotional and intellectual development.

2. In order to promote the exercise of this right and eradicate malnutrition, the States Parties undertake to improve methods of production, supply and distribution of food, and to this end, agree to

promote greater international cooperation in support of the relevant national policies.

Article 13 – Right to education

1. Everyone has the right to education.

2. The States Parties to this Protocol agree that education should be directed towards the full development of the human personality and human dignity and should strengthen respect for human rights, ideological pluralism, fundamental freedoms, justice and peace. They further agree that education ought to enable everyone to participate effectively in a democratic and pluralistic society and achieve a decent existence and should foster understanding, tolerance and friendship among all nations and all racial, ethnic or religious groups and promote activities for the maintenance of peace.

3. The States Parties to this Protocol recognize that in order to achieve the full exercise of the right to education:

a. primary education should be compulsory and accessible to all without cost;
b. secondary education in its different forms, including technical and vocational secondary education, should be made generally available and accessible to all by every appropriate means, and in particular, by the progressive introduction of free education;
c. higher education should be made equally accessible to all on the basis of individual capacity, by every appropriate means and, in particular, by the progressive introduction of free education;
d. basic education should be encouraged or intensified as far as possible for those persons who have not received or completed the whole cycle of primary instruction;
e. programs of special education should be established for the handicapped, so as to provide special instruction and training to persons with physical disabilities or mental deficiencies.

4. In conformity with the domestic legislation of the States Parties, parents should have the right to select the type of education to be given

to their children, provided that it conforms to the principles set forth above.

5. Nothing in this Protocol shall be interpreted as a restriction of the freedom of individuals and entities to establish and direct educational institutions in accordance with the domestic legislation of the States Parties.

Article 14 – Right to the benefits of culture

1. The States Parties to this Protocol recognize the right of everyone:

a. to take part in the cultural and artistic life of the community;
b. to enjoy the benefits of scientific and technological progress;
c. to benefit from the protection of moral and material interests deriving from any scientific, literary or artistic production of which he is the author.

2. The steps to be taken by the States Parties to this Protocol to ensure the full exercise of this right shall include those necessary for the conservation, development and dissemination of science, culture and art.

3. The States Parties to this Protocol undertake to respect the freedom indispensable for scientific research and creative activity.

4. The States Parties to this Protocol recognize the benefits to be derived from the encouragement and development of international cooperation and relations in the fields of science, arts and culture, and accordingly agree to foster greater international cooperation in these fields.

Article 15 – Right to the formation and the protection of families

1. The family is the natural and fundamental element of society and ought to be protected by the State, which should see to the improvement of its spiritual and material conditions.

2. Everyone has the right to form a family, which shall be exercised in accordance with the provisions of the pertinent domestic legislation.

3. The States Parties hereby undertake to accord adequate protection to the family unit and in particular:

a. to provide special care and assistance to mothers during a reasonable period before and after childbirth;
b. to guarantee adequate nutrition for children at the nursing stage and during school attendance years;
c. to adopt special measures for the protection of adolescents in order to ensure the full development of their physical, intellectual and moral capacities;
d. to undertake special programs of family training so as to help create a stable and positive environment in which children will receive and develop the values of understanding, solidarity, respect and responsibility.

Article 16 – Rights of children

Every child, whatever his parentage, has the right to the protection that his status as a minor requires from his family, society and the State. Every child has the right to grow under the protection and responsibility of his parents; save in exceptional, judicially recognized circumstances, a child of young age ought not to be separated from his mother. Every child has the right to free and compulsory education, at least in the elementary phase, and to continue his training at higher levels of the educational system.

Article 17 – Protection of the elderly

Everyone has the right to special protection in old age. With this in view the States Parties agree to take progressively the necessary steps to make this right a reality and, particularly, to:

a. provide suitable facilities, as well as food and specialized medical care, for elderly individuals who lack them and are unable to provide them for themselves;
b. undertake work programs specifically designed to give the elderly the opportunity to engage in a productive activity suited to their abilities and consistent with their vocations or desires;

c. foster the establishment of social organizations aimed at improving the quality of life for the elderly.

Article 18 – Protection of the handicapped

Everyone affected by a diminution of his physical or mental capacities is entitled to receive special attention designed to help him achieve the greatest possible development of his personality. The States Parties agree to adopt such measures as may be necessary for this purpose and, especially, to:

a. undertake programs specifically aimed at providing the handicapped with the resources and environment needed for attaining this goal, including work programs consistent with their possibilities and freely accepted by them or their legal representatives, as the case may be;
b. provide special training to the families of the handicapped in order to help them solve the problems of coexistence and convert them into active agents in the physical, mental and emotional development of the latter;
c. include the consideration of solutions to specific requirements arising from the needs of this group as a priority component of their urban development plans;
d. encourage the establishment of social groups in which the handicapped can be helped to enjoy a fuller life.

Article 19 – Means of protection

1. Pursuant to the provisions of this article and the corresponding rules to be formulated for this purpose by the General Assembly of the Organization of American States, the States Parties to this Protocol undertake to submit periodic reports on the progressive measures they have taken to ensure due respect for the rights set forth in this Protocol.

2. All reports shall be submitted to the Secretary General of the OAS, who shall transmit them to the Inter-American Economic and Social Council and the Inter-American Council for Education, Science and Culture so that may examine them in accordance with the provisions of this article.

The Secretary General shall send a copy of such reports to the Inter-American Commission of Human Rights.

3. The Secretary General of the Organization of American States shall also transmit to the specialized organizations of the inter-American system, of which the States Parties to the present Protocol are members, copies or pertinent portions of the reports submitted, in so far as they relate to matters within the purview of those organizations, as established by their constituent instruments.

4. The specialized organisations of the inter-American system may submit reports to the Inter-American Economic and Social Council and the Inter-American Council for Education, Science and Culture relative to compliance with the provisions of the present Protocol in their fields of activity.

5. The annual reports submitted to the General Assembly by the Inter-American Economic and Social Council and the Inter-American Council for Education, Science and Culture shall contain a summary of the information received from the States Parties to the present Protocol and the specialized organizations concerning the progressive measures adopted in order to ensure respect for the rights acknowledged in the Protocol itself and the general recommendations they consider to be appropriate in this respect.

6. Any instance in which the rights established in paragraph *a* of Article 8 and in Article 13 are violated by action directly attributable to a State Party to this Protocol may give rise, through participation of the Inter-American Commission on Human Rights and, when applicable, of the Inter-American Court of Human Rights, to application of the system of individual petitions governed by Articles 44 through 51 and 61 through 69 of the American Convention on Human Rights.

7. Without prejudice to the provisions of the preceding paragraph, the Inter-American Commission on Human Rights may formulate such observations and recommendations as it deems pertinent concerning the status of the economic, social and cultural rights established in the

present Protocol in all or some of the States Parties which it may include in its annual report to the General Assembly or in a special report, whichever it considers more appropriate.

8. The Councils and the Inter-American Commission on Human Rights, in discharging the functions conferred upon them in this article, shall take into account the progressive nature of the observance of the rights subject to protection by this Protocol.

Article 20 – Reservations

The States Parties may, at the time of approval, signature, ratification or accession, make reservations to one or more specific provisions of this Protocol, provided that such reservations are not incompatible with the object and purpose of the Protocol.

Article 21 – Signature, ratification or accession – Entry into effect

1. This Protocol shall remain open to signature and ratification or accession by any State Party to the American Convention on Human Rights.

2. Ratification of or accession to this Protocol shall be effected by depositing an instrument of ratification or accession with the General Secretariat of the Organization of American States.

3. The Protocol shall enter into effect when eleven States have deposited their respective instruments of ratification or accession.

4. The Secretary General shall notify all the member States of the Organization of American States of the entry of the Protocol into effect.

Article 22 – Inclusion of other rights and expansion of those recognized

1. Any State Party and the Inter-American Commission on Human Rights may submit for the consideration of the States Parties meeting on the occasion of the General Assembly proposed amendments to include the

recognition of other rights or freedoms or to extend or expand rights or freedoms recognized in this Protocol.

2. Such amendments shall enter into effect for the States that ratify them on the date of deposit of the instrument of ratification corresponding to the number representing two-thirds of the States Parties to this Protocol. For all other States Parties they shall enter into effect on the date on which they deposit their respective instrument of ratification.

4. Protocol to the American Convention on Human Rights to abolish the death penalty

Santiago, Chile, 8 June 1990

Preamble

The States Parties to this Protocol,

Considering:

That Article 4 of the American Convention on Human Rights recognizes the right to life and restricts the application of the death penalty;

That everyone has the inalienable right to respect for his life, a right that cannot be suspended for any reason;

That the tendency among the American States is to be in favor of abolition of the death penalty;

That application of the death penalty has irrevocable consequences, forecloses the correction of judicial error, and precludes any possibility of changing or rehabilitating those convicted;

That the abolition of the death penalty helps to ensure more effective protection of the rights to life;

That an international agreement must be arrived at that will entail a progressive development of the American Convention on Human Rights; and

That States Parties to the American Convention on Human Rights have expressed their intention to adopt an international agreement with a view to consolidating the practice of not applying the death penalty in the Americas,

Have agreed to sign the following Protocol to the American Convention on Human Rights to abolish the death penalty:

Article 1

The States Parties to this Protocol shall not apply the death penalty in their territory to any person subject to their jurisdiction.

Article 2

1. No reservations may be made to this Protocol. However, at the time of ratification or accession, the States Parties to this instrument may declare that they reserve the right to apply the death penalty in wartime in accordance with international law, for extremely serious crimes of a military nature.

2. The State Party making this reservation shall, upon ratification or accession, inform the Secretary General of the Organization of American States of the pertinent provisions of its national legislation applicable in wartime, as referred to in the preceding paragraph.

3. The said State Party shall notify the Secretary General of the Organization of American States of the beginning or end of any state of war in effect in its territory.

Article 3

This Protocol shall be open for signature and ratification or accession by any State Party to the American Convention on Human Rights.

Ratification of this Protocol or accession thereto shall be made through the deposit of an instrument of ratification or accession with the General Secretariat of the Organization of American States.

Article 4

This Protocol shall enter into force among the States that ratify or accede to it when they deposit their respective instruments of ratification or accession with the General Secretariat of the Organization of American States.

III. Text prepared within the Organization of African Unity

African Charter on Human and Peoples' Rights

Adopted at the 18th Conference of Heads of State and Government, Nairobi, Kenya, 27 June 1981

Entry into force: 21 October 1986,
in accordance with Article 63

Preamble

The African States members of the Organization of African Unity, parties to the present Convention entitled "African Charter on Human and Peoples' Rights",

Recalling Decision 115 (XVI) of the Assembly of Heads of State and Government at its Sixteenth Ordinary Session held in Monrovia, Liberia, from 17 to 20 July 1979 on the preparation of a "preliminary draft on an African Charter on Human and Peoples' Rights providing *inter alia* for the establishment of bodies to promote and protect human and peoples' rights";

Considering the Charter of the Organization of African Unity, which stipulates that "freedom, equality, justice and dignity are essential objectives for the achievement of the legitimate aspirations of the African peoples";

Reaffirming the pledge they solemnly made in Article 2 of the said Charter to eradicate all forms of colonialism from Africa, to co-ordinate and intensify their co-operation and efforts to achieve a better life for the peoples of Africa and to promote international co-operation having due regard to the Charter of the United Nations and the Universal Declaration of Human Rights;

Taking into consideration the virtues of their historical tradition and the values of African civilization which should inspire and characterize their reflection on the concept of human and peoples' rights;

Recognizing, on the one hand, that fundamental human rights stem from the attributes of human beings, which justifies their national and international protection and, on the other hand, that the reality and respect of peoples' rights should necessarily guarantee human rights;

Considering that the enjoyment of rights and freedoms also implies the performance of duties on the part of everyone;

Convinced that it is henceforth essential to pay a particular attention to the right to development and that civil and political rights cannot be dissociated from economic, social and cultural rights in their conception as well as universality and that the satisfaction of economic, social and cultural rights is a guarantee for the enjoyment of civil and political rights;

Conscious of their duty to achieve the total liberation of Africa, the peoples of which are still struggling for their dignity and genuine independence, and undertaking to eliminate colonialism, neo-colonialism, *apartheid*, Zionism and to dismantle aggressive foreign military bases and all forms of discrimination, particularly those based on race, ethnic group, colour, sex, language, religion or political opinions;

Reaffirming their adherence to the principles of human and peoples' rights and freedoms contained in the declarations, conventions and other instruments adopted by the Organization of African Unity, the Movement of Non-Aligned Countries and the United Nations;

Firmly convinced of their duty to promote and protect human and peoples' rights and freedoms taking into account the importance traditionally attached to these rights and freedoms in Africa,

Have agreed as follows:

Part I – Rights and duties

Chapter I – Human and peoples' rights

Article 1

The member States of the Organization of African Unity parties to the present Charter shall recognize the rights, duties and freedoms enshrined in this Charter and shall undertake to adopt legislative or other measures to give effect to them.

Article 2

Every individual shall be entitled to the enjoyment of the rights and freedoms recognized and guaranteed in the present Charter without distinction of any kind such as race, ethnic group, colour, sex, language, religion, political or any other opinion, national and social origin, fortune, birth or other status.

Article 3

1. Every individual shall be equal before the law.

2. Every individual shall be entitled to equal protection of the law.

Article 4

Human beings are inviolable. Every human being shall be entitled to respect for his life and the integrity of his person. No one may be arbitrarily deprived of this right.

Article 5

Every individual shall have the right to the respect of the dignity inherent in a human being and to the recognition of his legal status. All forms of exploitation and degradation of man particularly slavery, slave trade, torture, cruel, inhuman or degrading punishment and treatment shall be prohibited.

Article 6

Every individual shall have the right to liberty and to the security of his person. No one may be deprived of his freedom except for reasons and conditions previously laid down by law. In particular, no one may be arbitrarily arrested or detained.

Article 7

1. Every individual shall have the right to have his cause heard. This comprises:

a. the right to an appeal to competent national organs against acts of violating his fundamental rights as recognized and guaranteed by conventions, laws, regulations and customs in force;
b. the right to be presumed innocent until proved guilty by a competent court or tribunal;
c. the right to defence, including the right to be defended by counsel of his choice;
d. the right to be tried within a reasonable time by an impartial court or tribunal.

2. No one may be condemned for an act or omission which did not constitute a legally punishable offence at the time it was committed. No penalty may be inflicted for an offence for which no provision was made at the time it was committed. Punishment is personal and can be imposed only on the offender.

Article 8

Freedom of conscience, the profession and free practice of religion shall be guaranteed. No one may, subject to law and order, be submitted to measures restricting the exercise of these freedoms.

Article 9

1. Every individual shall have the right to receive information.

2. Every individual shall have the right to express and disseminate his opinions within the law.

Article 10

1. Every individual shall have the right to free association provided that he abides by the law.

2. Subject to the obligation of solidarity provided for in Article 29 no one may be compelled to join an association.

Article 11

Every individual shall have the right to assemble freely with others. The exercise of this right shall be subject only to necessary restrictions provided for by law, in particular those enacted in the interest of national security, the safety, health, ethics and rights and freedoms of others.

Article 12

1. Every individual shall have the right to freedom of movement and residence within the borders of a State provided he abides by the law.

2. Every individual shall have the right to leave any country including his own, and to return to his country. This right may only be subject to restrictions, provided for by law for the protection of national security, law and order, public health or morality.

3. Every individual shall have the right, when persecuted, to seek and obtain asylum in other countries in accordance with the laws of those countries and international conventions.

4. A non-national legally admitted in a territory of a State Party to the present Charter may only be expelled from it by virtue of a decision taken in accordance with the law.

5. The mass expulsion of non-nationals shall be prohibited. Mass expulsion shall be that which is aimed at national, racial, ethnic or religious groups.

Article 13

1. Every citizen shall have the right to participate freely in the government of his country, either directly or through freely chosen representatives in accordance with the provisions of the law.

2. Every citizen shall have the right of equal access to the public service of his country.

3. Every individual shall have the right of access to public property and services in strict equality of all persons before the law.

Article 14

The right to property shall be guaranteed. It may only be encroached upon in the interest of public need or in the general interest of the community and in accordance with the provisions of appropriate laws.

Article 15

Every individual shall have the right to work under equitable and satisfactory conditions, and shall receive equal pay for equal work.

Article 16

1. Every individual shall have the right to enjoy the best attainable state of physical and mental health.

2. States parties to the present Charter shall take the necessary measures to protect the health of their people and to ensure that they receive medical attention when they are sick.

Article 17

1. Every individual shall have the right to education.

2. Every individual may freely take part in the cultural life of his community.

3. The promotion and protection of morals and traditional values recognized by the community shall be the duty of the State.

Article 18

1. The family shall be the natural unit and basis of society. It shall be protected by the State which shall take care of its physical health and morals.

2. The State shall have the duty to assist the family, which is the custodian of morals and traditional values recognized by the community.

3. The State shall ensure the elimination of every discrimination against women and also ensure the protection of the rights of the woman and the child as stipulated in international declarations and conventions.

4. The aged and the disabled shall also have the right to special measures of protection in keeping with their physical or moral needs.

Article 19

All peoples shall be equal; they shall enjoy the same respect and shall have the same rights. Nothing shall justify the domination of a people by another.

Article 20

1. All peoples shall have the right to existence. They shall have the unquestionable and inalienable right to self-determination. They shall freely determine their political status and shall pursue their economic and social development according to the policy they have freely chosen.

2. Colonized or oppressed peoples shall have the right to free themselves from the bonds of domination by resorting to any means recognized by the international community.

3. All peoples shall have the right to the assistance of the States Parties to the present Charter in their liberation struggle against foreign domination, be it political, economic or cultural.

Article 21

1. All peoples shall freely dispose of their wealth and natural resources. This right shall be exercised in the exclusive interest of the people. In no case shall a people be deprived of it.

2. In case of spoliation the dispossessed people shall have the right to the lawful recovery of its property as well as to an adequate compensation.

3. The free disposal of wealth and natural resources shall be exercised without prejudice to the obligation of promoting international economic co-operation based on mutual respect, equitable exchange and the principles of international law.

4. States Parties to the present Charter shall individually and collectively exercise the right to free disposal of their wealth and natural resources with a view to strengthening African unity and solidarity.

5. States Parties to the present Charter shall undertake to eliminate all forms of foreign economic exploitation particularly that practised by international monopolies so as to enable their peoples to fully benefit from the advantages derived from their national resources.

Article 22

1. All peoples shall have the right to their economic, social and cultural development with due regard to their freedom and identity and in the equal enjoyment of the common heritage of mankind.

2. States shall have the duty, individually or collectively, to ensure the exercise of the right to development.

Article 23

1. All peoples shall have the right to national and international peace and security. The principles of solidarity and friendly relations implicitly affirmed by the Charter of the United Nations and reaffirmed by that of the Organization of African Unity shall govern relations between States.

2. For the purpose of strengthening peace, solidarity and friendly relations, States Parties to the present Charter shall ensure that:

a. any individual enjoying the right of asylum under Article 12 of the present Charter shall not engage in subversive activities against his country of origin or any other State Party to the present Charter;

b. their territories shall not be used as bases for subversive or terrorist activities against the people of any other State Party to the present Charter.

Article 24

All peoples shall have the right to a general satisfactory environment favourable to their development.

Article 25

States Parties to the present Charter shall have the duty to promote and ensure, through teaching, education and publication, the respect of the rights and freedoms contained in the present Charter and to see to it that these freedoms and rights as well as corresponding obligations and duties are understood.

Article 26

States Parties to the present Charter shall have the duty to guarantee the independence of the Courts and shall allow the establishment and improvement of appropriate national institutions entrusted with the promotion and protection of the rights and freedoms guaranteed by the present Charter.

Chapter II – Duties

Article 27

1. Every individual shall have duties towards his family and society, the State and other legally recognized communities and the international community.

2. The rights and freedoms of each individual shall be exercised with due regard to the rights of others, collective security, morality and common interest.

Article 28

Every individual shall have the duty to respect and consider his fellow beings without discrimination, and to maintain relations aimed at promoting, safeguarding and reinforcing mutual respect and tolerance.

Article 29

The individual shall also have the duty:

1. To preserve the harmonious development of the family and to work for the cohesion and respect of the family; to respect his parents at all times, to maintain them in case of need;

2. To serve his national community by placing his physical and intellectual abilities at its service;

3. Not to compromise the security of the State whose national or resident he is;

4. To preserve and strengthen social and national solidarity, particularly when the latter is threatened;

5. To preserve and strengthen the national independence and the territorial integrity of his country and to contribute to its defence in accordance with the law;

6. To work to the best of his abilities and competence, and to pay taxes imposed by law in the interest of the society;

7. To preserve and strengthen positive African cultural values in his relations with other members of the society, in the spirit of tolerance, dialogue and consultation and, in general, to contribute to the promotion of the moral well-being of society;

8. To contribute to the best of his abilities, at all times and at all levels, to the promotion and achievement of African unity.

Part II – Measures of safeguard

Chapter I – Establishment and organization of the African Commission on Human and Peoples' Rights

Article 30

An African Commission on Human and Peoples' Rights, hereinafter called "the Commission", shall be established within the Organization of African Unity to promote human and peoples' rights and ensure their protection in Africa.

Article 31

1. The Commission shall consist of eleven members chosen from amongst African personalities of the highest reputation, known for their high morality, integrity, impartiality and competence in matters of human and peoples' rights; particular consideration being given to persons having legal experience.

2. The members of the Commission shall serve in their personal capacity.

Article 32

The Commission shall not include more than one national of the same State.

Article 33

The members of the Commission shall be elected by secret ballot by the Assembly of Heads of State and Government, from a list of persons nominated by the States Parties to the present Charter.

Article 34

Each State Party to the present Charter may not nominate more than two candidates. The candidates must have the nationality of one of the States Parties to the present Charter. When two candidates are nominated by a State, one of them may not be a national of that State.

Article 35

1. The Secretary General of the Organization of African Unity shall invite States Parties to the present Charter at least four months before the elections to nominate candidates.

2. The Secretary General of the Organization of African Unity shall make an alphabetical list of the persons thus nominated and communicate it to the Heads of State and Government at least one month before the elections.

Article 36

The members of the Commission shall be elected for a six-year period and shall be eligible for re-election. However, the term of office of four of the members elected at the first election shall terminate after two years and the term of office of the three others at the end of four years.

Article 37

Immediately after the first election, the Chairman of the Assembly of Heads of State and Government of the Organization of African Unity shall draw lots to decide the names of those members referred to in Article 36.

Article 38

After their election, the members of the Commission shall make a solemn declaration to discharge their duties impartially and faithfully.

Article 39

1. In case of death or resignation of a member of the Commission, the Chairman of the Commission shall immediately inform the Secretary General of the Organization of African Unity, who shall declare the seat vacant from the date of death or from the date on which the resignation takes effect.

2. If, in the unanimous opinion of other members of the Commission, a member has stopped discharging his duties for any reason other than a temporary absence, the Chairman of the Commission shall inform the Secretary General of the Organization of African Unity, who shall then declare the seat vacant.

3. In each of the cases anticipated above, the Assembly of Heads of State and Government shall replace the member whose seat became vacant for the remaining period of his term unless the period is less than six months.

Article 40

Every member of the Commission shall be in office until the date his successor assumes office.

Article 41

The Secretary General of the Organization of African Unity shall appoint the Secretary of the Commission. He shall also provide the staff and services necessary for the effective discharge of the duties of the Commission. The Organization of African Unity shall bear the costs of the staff and services.

Article 42

1. The Commission shall elect its Chairman and Vice-Chairman for a two-year period. They shall be eligible for re-election.

2. The Commission shall lay down its rules of procedure.

3. Seven members shall form a quorum.

4. In case of an equality of votes, the Chairman shall have a casting vote.

5. The Secretary General may attend the meetings of the Commission. He shall neither participate in deliberations nor shall he be entitled to vote. The Chairman of the Commission may, however, invite him to speak.

Article 43

In discharging their duties, members of the Commission shall enjoy diplomatic privileges and immunities provided for in the General Convention on the Privileges and Immunities of the Organization of African Unity.

Article 44

Provision shall be made for the emoluments and allowances of the members of the Commission in the Regular Budget of the Organization of African Unity.

Chapter II – Mandate of the Commission

Article 45

The functions of the Commission shall be:

1. To promote human and peoples' rights and in particular:

a. to collect documents, undertake studies and researches on African problems in the field of human and peoples' rights, organize seminars, symposia and conferences, disseminate information, encourage national and local institutions concerned with human and peoples' rights, and, should the case arise, give its views or make recommendations to governments;

b. to formulate and lay down principles and rules aimed at solving legal problems relating to human and peoples' rights and fundamental freedoms upon which African Governments may base their legislations;

c. co-operate with other African and international institutions concerned with the promotion and protection of human and peoples' rights.

2. Ensure the protection of human and peoples' rights under conditions laid down by the present Charter.

3. Interpret all the provisions of the present Charter at the request of a State Party, an institution of the OAU or an African organization recognised by the OAU.

4. Perform any other tasks which may be entrusted to it by the Assembly of Heads of State and Government.

Chapter III – Procedure of the Commission

Article 46

The Commission may resort to any appropriate method of investigation; it may hear from the Secretary General of the Organization of African Unity or any other person capable of enlightening it.

Communication from States

Article 47

If a State Party to the present Charter has good reasons to believe that another State Party to this Charter has violated the provisions of the Charter, it may draw, by written communication, the attention of that State to the matter. This communication shall also be addressed to the Secretary General of the OAU and to the Chairman of the Commission. Within three months of the receipt of the communication, the State to which the communication is addressed shall give the enquiring State, written explanation or statement elucidating the matter. This should include as much as possible relevant information relating to the laws and rules of procedure applied and applicable, and the redress already given or course of action available.

Article 48

If, within three months from the date on which the original communication is received by the State to which it is addressed, the issue is not settled to the satisfaction of the two States involved through bilateral negotiation or by any other peaceful procedure, either State shall have the right to submit the matter to the Commission through the Chairman and shall notify the other States involved.

Article 49

Notwithstanding the provisions of Article 47, if a State Party to the present Charter considers that another State Party has violated the provisions of the Charter, it may refer the matter directly to the Commission by addressing a communication to the Chairman, to the Secretary General of the Organization of African Unity and the State concerned.

Article 50

The Commission can only deal with a matter submitted to it after making sure that all local remedies, if they exist, have been exhausted, unless it is obvious to the Commission that the procedure of achieving these remedies would be unduly prolonged.

Article 51

1. The Commission may ask the States concerned to provide it with all relevant information.

2. When the Commission is considering the matter, States concerned may be represented before it and submit written or oral representation.

Article 52

After having obtained from the States concerned and from other sources all the information it deems necessary and after having tried all appropriate means to reach an amicable solution based on the respect of human and peoples' rights, the Commission shall prepare, within a reasonable period of time from the notification referred to in Article 48, a report stating the facts and its findings. This report shall be sent to the States concerned and communicated to the Assembly of Heads of State and Government.

Article 53

While transmitting its report, the Commission may make to the Assembly of Heads of State and Government such recommendations as it deems useful.

Article 54

The Commission shall submit to each ordinary session of the Assembly of Heads of State and Government a report on its activities.

Other communications

Article 55

1. Before each session, the Secretary of the Commission shall make a list of the communications other than those of States Parties to the present Charter and transmit them to the members of the Commission, who shall indicate which communications should be considered by the Commission.

2. A communication shall be considered by the Commission if a simple majority of its members so decide.

Article 56

Communications relating to human and peoples' rights referred to in Article 55, received by the Commission, shall be considered if they:

1. Indicate their authors even if the latter request anonymity;

2. Are compatible with the Charter of the Organization of African Unity or with the present Charter;

3. Are not written in disparaging or insulting language directed against the State concerned and its institutions or to the Organization of African Unity;

4. Are not based exclusively on news disseminated through the mass media;

5. Are sent after exhausting local remedies, if any, unless it is obvious that this procedure is unduly prolonged;

6. Are submitted within a reasonable period from the time local remedies are exhausted or from the date the Commission is seized of the matter; and

7. Do not deal with cases which have been settled by the States involved in accordance with the principles of the Charter of the United Nations, or the Charter of the Organization of African Unity or the provisions of the present Charter.

Article 57

Prior to any substantive consideration, all communications shall be brought to the knowledge of the State concerned by the Chairman of the Commission.

Article 58

1. When it appears after deliberations of the Commission that one or more communications apparently relate to special cases which reveal the existence of a series of serious or massive violations of human and peoples' rights, the Commission shall draw the attention of the Assembly of Heads of State and Government to these special cases.

2. The Assembly of Heads of State and Government may then request the Commission to undertake an in-depth study of these cases and

make a factual report, accompanied by its findings and recommendations.

3. A case of emergency duly noticed by the Commission shall be submitted by the latter to the Chairman of the Assembly of Heads of State and Government who may request an in-depth study.

Article 59

1. All measures taken within the provisions of the present chapter shall remain confidential until such a time as the Assembly of Heads of State and Government shall otherwise decide.

2. However, the report shall be published by the Chairman of the Commission upon the decision of the Assembly of Heads of State and Government.

3. The report on the activities of the Commission shall be published by its Chairman after it has been considered by the Assembly of Heads of State and Government.

Chapter IV – Applicable principles

Article 60

The Commission shall draw inspiration from international law on human and peoples' rights, particularly from the provisions of various African instruments on human and peoples' rights, the Charter of the United Nations, the Charter of the Organization of African Unity, the Universal Declaration of Human Rights, other instruments adopted by the United Nations and by African countries in the field of human and peoples' rights, as well as from the provisions of various instruments adopted within the specialized agencies of the United Nations of which the parties to the present Charter are members.

Article 61

The Commission shall also take into consideration, as subsidiary measures to determine the principles of law, other general or special international conventions, laying down rules expressly recognized by member States of the Organization of African Unity, African practices consistent with international norms on human and peoples' rights, customs generally accepted as law, general principles of law recognized by African States as well as legal precedents and doctrine.

Article 62

Each State Party shall undertake to submit every two years, from the date the present Charter comes into force, a report on the legislative or other measures taken with a view to giving effect to the rights and freedoms recognized and guaranteed by the present Charter.

Article 63

1. The present Charter shall be open to signature, ratification or adherence of the member States of the Organization of African Unity.

2. The instruments of ratification or adherence to the present Charter shall be deposited with the Secretary General of the Organization of African Unity.

3. The present Charter shall come into force three months after the reception by the Secretary General of the instruments of ratification or adherence of a simple majority of the member States of the Organization of African Unity.

Part III – General provisions

Article 64

1. After the coming into force of the present Charter, members of the Commission shall be elected in accordance with the relevant articles of the present Charter.

2. The Secretary General of the Organization of African Unity shall convene the first meeting of the Commission at the headquarters of the Organization within three months of the constitution of the Commission. Thereafter, the Commission shall be convened by its Chairman whenever necessary but at least once a year.

Article 65

For each of the States that will ratify or adhere to the present Charter after its coming into force, the Charter shall take effect three months after the date of the deposit by that State of its instrument of ratification or adherence.

Article 66

Special protocols or agreements may, if necessary, supplement the provisions of the present Charter.

Article 67

The Secretary General of the Organization of African Unity shall inform member States of the Organization of the deposit of each instrument of ratification or adherence.

Article 68

The present Charter may be amended if a State Party makes a written request to that effect to the Secretary General of the Organization of African Unity. The Assembly of Heads of State and Government may only consider the draft amendment after all the States Parties have been duly informed of it and the Commission has given its opinion on it at the request of the sponsoring State. The amendment shall be approved by a simple majority of the States Parties. It shall come into force for each State which has accepted it in accordance with its constitutional procedure three months after the Secretary General has received notice of the acceptance.

IV. Conference on Security and Co-operation in Europe (CSCE)

1. Final Act, Helsinki

Helsinki, 1 August 1975

(Extracts)

Questions relating to security in Europe

The States participating in the Conference on Security and Co-operation in Europe,

Reaffirming their objective of promoting better relations among themselves and ensuring conditions in which their people can live in true and lasting peace free from any threat to or attempt against their security;

Convinced of the need to exert efforts to make *détente* both a continuing and an increasingly viable and comprehensive process, universal in scope, and that the implementation of the results of the Conference on Security and Co-operation in Europe will be a major contribution to this process;

Considering that solidarity among peoples, as well as the common purpose of the participating States in achieving the aims as set forth by the Conference on Security and Co-operation in Europe, should lead to the development of better and closer relations among them in all fields and thus to overcoming the confrontation stemming from the character of their past relations, and to better mutual understanding;

Mindful of their common history and recognizing that the existence of elements common to their traditions and values can assist them in developing their relations, and desiring to search, fully taking into account the individuality and diversity of their positions and views, for possibilities of joining their efforts with a view to overcoming distrust and increasing confidence, solving the problems that separate them and co-operating in the interest of mankind;

Recognizing the indivisibility of security in Europe as well as their common interest in the development of co-operation throughout Europe and among themselves and expressing their intention to pursue efforts accordingly;

Recognising the close link between peace and security in Europe and in the world as a whole and conscious of the need for each of them to make its contribution to the strengthening of world peace and security and to the promotion of fundamental rights, economic and social progress and well-being for all peoples,

Have adopted the following:

1.

a. *Declaration on principles guiding relations between participating States*

The participating States,

Reaffirming their commitment to peace, security and justice and the continuing development of friendly relations and co-operation;

Recognizing that this commitment, which reflects the interest and aspirations of peoples, constitutes for each participating State a present and future responsibility, heightened by experience of the past;

Reaffirming, in conformity with their membership in the United Nations and in accordance with the purposes and principles of the United Nations, their full and active support for the United Nations and for the enhancement of its role and effectiveness in strengthening international peace, security and justice, and in promoting the solution of international problems, as well as the development of friendly relations and co-operation among States;

Expressing their common adherence to the principles which are set forth below and are in conformity with the Charter of the United Nations, as well as their common will to act, in the application of these principles, in conformity with the purposes and principles of the Charter of the United Nations,

Declare their determination to respect and put into practice, each of them in its relations with all other participating States, irrespective of their political, economic or social systems as well as of their size, geographical location or level of economic development, the following principles, which all are of primary significance, guiding their mutual relations.

I. *Sovereign equality, respect for the rights inherent in sovereignty*

The participating States will respect each other's sovereign equality and individuality as well as all the rights inherent in and encompassed by its sovereignty, including in particular the right of every State to juridical equality, to territorial integrity and to freedom and political independence. They will also respect each other's right freely to choose and develop its political, social, economic and cultural systems as well as its right to determine its laws and regulations.

Within the framework of international law, all the participating States have equal rights and duties. They will respect each other's right to define and conduct as it wishes its relations with other States in accordance with international law and in the spirit of the present Declaration. They consider that their frontiers can be changed, in accordance with international law, by peaceful means and by agreement. They also have the right to belong or not to belong to international organizations, to be or not to be a party to bilateral or multilateral treaties including the right to be or not to be a party to treaties of alliance; they also have the right to neutrality.

II. *Refraining from the threat or use of force*

The participating States will refrain in their mutual relations, as well as in their international relations in general, from the threat or use of force against the territorial integrity or political independence of any State, or in any other manner inconsistent with the purposes of the United Nations and with the present Declaration. No consideration may be invoked to serve to warrant resort to the threat or use of force in contravention of this principle.

Accordingly, the participating States will refrain from any acts constituting a threat of force or direct or indirect use of force against another participating State. Likewise they will refrain from any manifestation of force for the purpose of inducing another participating State to renounce the full exercise of its sovereign rights. Likewise they will also refrain in their mutual relations from any act of reprisal by force.

No such threat or use of force will be employed as a means of settling disputes, or questions likely to give rise to disputes, between them.

III. *Inviolability of frontiers*

The participating States regard as inviolable all one another's frontiers as well as the frontiers of all States in Europe and therefore they will refrain now and in the future from assaulting these frontiers.

Accordingly, they will also refrain from any demand for, or act of seizure and usurpation of, part or all of the territory of any participating State.

IV. *Territorial integrity of States*

The participating States will respect the territorial integrity of each of the participating States.

Accordingly, they will refrain from any action inconsistent with the purposes and principles of the Charter of the United Nations against the territorial integrity, political independence or the unity of any participating State, and in particular from any such action constituting a threat or use of force.

The participating States will likewise refrain from making each other's territory the object of military occupation or other direct or indirect measures of force in contravention of international law, or the object of acquisition by means of such measures or the threat of them. No such occupation or acquisition will be recognized as legal.

V. *Peaceful settlement of disputes*

The participating States will settle disputes among them by peaceful means in such a manner as not to endanger international peace and security, and justice.

They will endeavour in good faith and a spirit of co-operation to reach a rapid and equitable solution on the basis of international law.

For this purpose they will use such means as negotiation, enquiry, mediation, conciliation, arbitration, judicial settlement or other peaceful means of their own choice including any settlement procedure agreed to in advance of disputes to which they are parties.

In the event of failure to reach a solution by any of the above peaceful means, the parties to a dispute will continue to seek a mutually agreed way to settle the dispute peacefully.

Participating States, parties to a dispute among them, as well as other participating States, will refrain from any action which might aggravate the situation to such a degree as to endanger the maintenance of international peace and security and thereby make a peaceful settlement of the dispute more difficult.

VI. *Non-intervention in internal affairs*

The participating States will refrain from any intervention, direct or indirect, individual or collective, in the internal or external affairs falling within the domestic jurisdiction of another participating State, regardless of their mutual relations.

They will accordingly refrain from any form of armed intervention or threat of such intervention against another participating State.

They will likewise in all circumstances refrain from any other act of military, or of political, economic or other coercion designed to subordinate to their own interest the exercise by another participating State of the rights inherent in its sovereignty and thus to secure advantages of any kind.

Accordingly, they will, *inter alia,* refrain from direct or indirect assistance to terrorist activities or to subversive or other activities directed towards the violent overthrow of the regime of another participating State.

VII. *Respect for human rights and fundamental freedoms, including the freedom of thought, conscience, religion or belief*

The participating States will respect human rights and fundamental freedoms, including the freedom of thought, conscience, religion or belief, for all without distinction as to race, sex, language or religion.

They will promote and encourage the effective exercise of civil, political, economic, social, cultural and other rights and freedoms all of which derive from the inherent dignity of the human person and are essential for his free and full development.

Within this framework the participating States will recognize and respect the freedom of the individual to profess and practise, alone or in community with others, religion or belief, acting in accordance with the dictates of his own conscience.

The participating States on whose territory national minorities exist will respect the right of persons belonging to such minorities to equality before the law, will afford them the full opportunity for the actual enjoyment of human rights and fundamental freedoms and will, in this manner, protect their legitimate interests in this sphere.

The participating States recognize the universal significance of human rights and fundamental freedoms, respect for which is an essential factor for the peace, justice and well-being necessary to ensure the development of friendly relations and co-operation among themselves as among all States.

They will constantly respect these rights and freedoms in their mutual relations and will endeavour jointly and separately, including in co-operation with the United Nations, to promote universal and effective respect for them.

They confirm the right of the individual to know and act upon his rights and duties in this field.

In the field of human rights and fundamental freedoms, the participating States will act in conformity with the purposes and principles of the Charter of the United Nations and with the Universal Declaration of Human Rights. They will also fulfil their obligations as set forth in the international declarations and agreements in this field, including *inter alia* the International Convenants on Human Rights, by which they may be bound.

VIII. *Equal rights and self-determination of peoples*

The participating States will respect the equal rights of peoples and their right to self-determination, acting at all times in conformity with the purposes and principles of the Charter of the United Nations and with the relevant norms of international law, including those relating to territorial integrity of States.

By virtue of the principle of equal rights and self-determination of peoples, all peoples always have the right, in full freedom, to determine, when and as they wish, their internal and external political status, without external interference, and to pursue as they wish their political, economic, social and cultural development.

The participating States reaffirm the universal significance of respect for and effective exercise of equal rights and self-determination of peoples for the development of friendly relations among themselves as among all

States; they also recall the importance of the elimination of any form of violation of this principle.

IX. *Co-operation among States*

The participating States will develop their co-operation with one another and with all States in all fields in accordance with the purposes and principles of the Charter of the United Nations. In developing their co-operation, the participating States will place special emphasis on the fields as set forth within the framework of the Conference on Security and Co-operation in Europe, with each of them making its contribution in conditions of full equality.

They will endeavour, in developing their co-operation as equals, to promote mutual understanding and confidence, friendly and good-neighbourly relations among themselves, international peace, security and justice. They will equally endeavour, in developing their co-operation, to improve the well-being of peoples and contribute to the fulfilment of their aspirations through, *inter alia*, the benefits resulting from increased mutual knowledge and from progress and achievement in the economic, scientific, technological, social, cultural and humanitarian fields. They will take steps to promote conditions favourable to making these benefits available to all; they will take into account the interest of all in the narrowing of differences in the levels of economic development, and in particular the interest of developing countries throughout the world.

They confirm that governments, institutions, organizations and persons have a relevant and positive role to play in contributing towards the achievement of these aims of their co-operation.

They will strive, in increasing their co-operation as set forth above, to develop closer relations among themselves on an improved and more enduring basis for the benefit of peoples.

X. *Fulfilment in good faith of obligations under international law*

The participating States will fulfil in good faith their obligations under international law, both those obligations arising from the generally recognized principles and rules of international law and those obligations arising from treaties or other agreements, in conformity with international law, to which they are parties.

In exercising their sovereign rights, including the right to determine their laws and regulations, they will conform with their legal obligations under international law; they will furthermore pay due regard to and implement the provisions in the Final Act of the Conference on Security and Co-operation in Europe.

The participating States confirm that, in the event of a conflict between the obligations of the members of the United Nations under the Charter of the United Nations and their obligations under any treaty or other international agreement, their obligations under the Charter will prevail, in accordance with Article 103 of the Charter of the United Nations.

All the principles set forth above are of primary significance and, accordingly, they will be equally and unreservedly applied, each of them being interpreted taking into account the others.

The participating States express their determination fully to respect and apply these principles, as set forth in the present Declaration, in all aspects, to their mutual relations and co-operation in order to ensure to each participating State the benefits resulting from the respect and application of these principles by all.

The participating States, paying due regard to the principles above and, in particular, to the first sentence of the tenth principle, "Fulfilment in good faith of obligations under international law", note that the present Declaration does not affect their rights and obligations, nor the corresponding treaties and other agreements and arrangements.

The participating States express the conviction that respect for these principles will encourage the development of normal and friendly relations and the progress of co-operation among them in all fields.

They also express the conviction that respect for these principles will encourage the development of political contacts among them which in turn would contribute to better mutual understanding of their positions and views.

The participating States declare their intention to conduct their relations with all other States in the spirit of the principles contained in the present Declaration.

b. ***Matters related to giving effect to certain of the above principles***

i. The participating States,

Reaffirming that they will respect and give effect to refraining from the threat or use of force and convinced of the necessity to make it an effective norm of international life,

Declare that they are resolved to respect and carry out, in their relations with one another, *inter alia,* the following provisions which are in conformity with the Declaration on Principles Guiding Relations between Participating States:

– to give effect and expression, by all the ways and forms which they consider appropriate, to the duty to refrain from the threat or use of force in their relations with one another;

– to refrain from any use of armed forces, inconsistent with the purposes and principles of the Charter of the United Nations and the provisions of the Declaration on Principles Guiding Relations between Participating States, against another participating State, in particular from invasion of or attack on its territory;

– to refrain from any manifestation of force for the purpose of inducing another participating State to renounce the full exercise of its sovereign rights;

– to refrain from any act of economic coercion designed to subordinate to their own interest the exercise by another participating State of the rights inherent in its sovereignty and thus to secure advantages of any kind;

– to take effective measures which by their scope and by their nature constitute steps towards the ultimate achievement of general and complete disarmament under strict and effective international control;

– to promote, by all means which each of them considers appropriate, a climate of confidence and respect among peoples consonant with their duty to refrain from propaganda for wars of aggression or for any threat or use of force, inconsistent with the purposes of the United Nations and with the Declaration on Principles Guiding Relations between Participating States, against another participating State;

– to make every effort to settle exclusively by peaceful means any dispute between them, the continuance of which is likely to endanger the maintenance of international peace and security in Europe, and to seek, first of all, a solution through the peaceful means set forth in Article 33 of the United Nations Charter;

– to refrain from any action which could hinder the peaceful settlement of disputes between the participating States.

ii. The participating States,

Reaffirming their determination to settle their disputes as set forth in the Principle of Peaceful Settlement of Disputes;

Convinced that the peaceful settlement of disputes is a complement to refraining from the threat or use of force, both being essential though not exclusive factors for the maintenance and consolidation of peace and security;

Desiring to reinforce and to improve the methods at their disposal for the peaceful settlement of disputes,

1. Are resolved to pursue the examination and elaboration of a generally acceptable method for the peaceful settlement of disputes aimed at complementing existing methods, and to continue to this end to work upon

the "Draft Convention on a European System for the Peaceful Settlement of Disputes" submitted by Switzerland during the second stage of the Conference on Security and Co-operation in Europe, as well as other proposals relating to it and directed towards the elaboration of such a method;

2. Decide that, on the invitation of Switzerland, a meeting of experts of all the participating States will be convoked in order to fulfil the mandate described in paragraph 1 above within the framework and under the procedures of the follow-up to the conference laid down in the chapter "Follow-up to the Conference";

3. This meeting of experts will take place after the meeting of the representatives appointed by the Ministers of Foreign Affairs of the participating States, scheduled according to the chapter "Follow-up to the Conference" for 1977; the results of the work of this meeting of experts will be submitted to Governments.

(...)

Co-operation in humanitarian and other fields

The participating States,

Desiring to contribute to the strengthening of peace and understanding among peoples and to the spiritual enrichment of the human personality without distinction as to race, sex, language or religion;

Conscious that increased cultural and educational exchanges, broader dissemination of information, contacts between people and the solution of humanitarian problems will contribute to the attainment of these aims;

Determined therefore to co-operate among themselves, irrespective of their political, economic and social systems, in order to create better conditions in the above fields, to develop and strengthen existing forms of co-operation and to work out new ways and means appropriate to these aims;

Convinced that this co-operation should take place in full respect for the principles guiding relations among participating States as set forth in the relevant document,

Have adopted the following:

1. ***Human contacts***

The participating States,

Considering the development of contacts to be an important element in the strengthening of friendly relations and trust among peoples;

Affirming, in relation to their present effort to improve conditions in this area, the importance they attach to humanitarian considerations;

Desiring in this spirit to develop, with the continuance of *détente,* further efforts to achieve continuing progress in this field;

And conscious that the questions relevant hereto must be settled by the States concerned under mutually acceptable conditions,

Make it their aim to facilitate freer movement and contacts, individually and collectively, whether privately or officially, among persons, institutions and organizations of the participating States, and to contribute to the solution of the humanitarian problems that arise in that connexion;

Declare their readiness to these ends to take measures which they consider appropriate and to conclude agreements or arrangements among themselves, as may be needed; and

Express their intention now to proceed to the implementation of the following:

a. *Contacts and regular meetings on the basis of family ties*

In order to promote further development of contacts on the basis of family ties, the participating States will favourably consider applications for travel with the purpose of allowing persons to enter or leave their territory temporarily, and on a regular basis if desired, in order to visit members of their families.

Applications for temporary visits to meet members of their families will be dealt with without distinction as to the country of origin or destination: existing requirements for travel documents and visas will be applied in this spirit. The preparation and issue of such documents and visas will be effected within reasonable time-limits, cases of urgent necessity – such as serious illness or death – will be given priority treatment. They will take such steps as may be necessary to ensure that the fees for official travel documents and visas are acceptable.

They confirm that the presentation of an application concerning contacts on the basis of family ties will not modify the rights and obligations of the applicant or of members of his family.

b. *Reunification of families*

The participating States will deal in a positive and humanitarian spirit with the applications of persons who wish to be reunited with members of their family, with special attention being given to requests of an urgent character – such as requests submitted by persons who are ill or old.

They will deal with applications in this field as expeditiously as possible.

They will lower, where necessary, the fees charged in connexion with these applications to ensure that they are at a moderate level.

Applications for the purpose of family reunification which are not granted may be renewed at the appropriate level and will be reconsidered at reasonably short intervals by the authorities of the country of residence or destination, whichever is concerned; under such circumstances fees will be charged only when applications are granted.

Persons whose applications for family reunification are granted may bring with them or ship their household and personal effects; to this end the participating States will use all possibilities provided by existing regulations.

Until members of the same family are reunited, meetings and contacts between them may take place in accordance with the modalities for contacts on the basis of family ties.

The participating States will support the efforts of Red Cross and Red Crescent Societies concerned with the problems of family reunification.

They confirm that the presentation of an application concerning family reunification will not modify the rights and obligations of the applicant or of members of his family.

The receiving participating State will take appropriate care with regard to employment for persons from other participating States who take up permanent residence in that State in connexion with family reunification with its citizens and see that they are afforded opportunities equal to those enjoyed by its own citizens for education, medical assistance and social security.

c. *Marriage between citizens of different States*

The participating States will examine favourably and on the basis of humanitarian considerations requests for exit or entry permits from persons who have decided to marry a citizen from another participating State.

The processing and issuing of the documents required for the above purposes and for the marriage will be in accordance with the provisions accepted for family reunification.

In dealing with requests from couples from different participating States, once married, to enable them and the minor children of their marriage to transfer their permanent residence to a State in which either one is normally a resident, the participating States will also apply the provisions accepted for family reunification.

d. *Travel for personal or professional reasons*

The participating States intend to facilitate wider travel by their citizens for personal or professional reasons and to this end they intend in particular:
- gradually to simplify and to administer flexibly the procedures for exit and entry;
- to ease regulations concerning movement of citizens from the other participating States in their territory, with due regard to security requirements.

They will endeavour gradually to lower, where necessary, the fees for visas and official travel documents.
They intend to consider, as necessary, means – including, in so far as appropriate, the conclusion of multilateral or bilateral consular conventions or other relevant agreements or understandings – for the improvement of arrangements to provide consular services, including legal and consular assistance.

They confirm that religious faiths, institutions and organizations, practising within the constitutional framework of the participating States, and their representatives can, in the field of their activities, have contacts and meetings among themselves and exchange information.

e. *Improvement of conditions for tourism on an individual or collective basis*

The participating States consider that tourism contributes to a fuller knowledge of the life, culture and history of other countries, to the growth of understanding among peoples, to the improvement of contacts and to the broader use of leisure. They intend to promote the development of tourism, on an individual or collective basis and, in particular, they intend:
- to promote visits to their respective countries by encouraging the provision of appropriate facilities and the simplification and expediting of necessary formalities relating to such visits;

– to increase, on the basis of appropriate agreements or arrangements where necessary, co-operation in the development of tourism, in particular by considering bilaterally possible ways to increase information relating to travel to other countries and to the reception and service of tourists, and other related questions of mutual interest.

f. *Meetings among young people*

The participating States intend to further the development of contacts and exchanges among young people by encouraging:

– increased exchanges and contacts on a short- or long-term basis among young people working, training or undergoing education through bilateral or multilateral agreements or regular programmes in all cases where it is possible;

– study by their youth organizations of the question of possible agreements relating to frameworks of multilateral youth co-operation;

– agreements or regular programmes relating to the organization of exchanges of students, of international youth seminars, of courses of professional training and foreign language study;

– the further development of youth tourism and the provision to this end of appropriate facilities;

– the development, where possible, of exchanges, contacts and co-operation on a bilateral or multilateral basis between the organizations which represent wide circles of young people working, training or undergoing education;

– awareness among youth of the importance of developing mutual understanding and of strengthening friendly relations and confidence among peoples.

g. *Sport*

In order to expand existing links and co-operation in the field of sport, the participating States will encourage contacts and exchanges of this kind, including sports meetings and competitions of all sorts, on the basis of the established international rules, regulations and practice.

h. *Expansion of contacts*

By way of further developing contacts among governmental institutions and non-governmental organizations and associations, including women's organizations, the participating States will facilitate the convening of meetings as well as travel by delegations, groups and individuals.

2. ***Information***

The participating States,

Conscious of the need for an ever wider knowledge and understanding of the various aspects of life in other participating States;

Acknowledging the contribution of this process to the growth of confidence between peoples;

Desiring, with the development of mutual understanding between the participating States and with the further improvement of their relations, to continue further efforts towards progress in field;

Recognizing the importance of the dissemination of information from the other participating States and of a better acquaintance with such information;

Emphasizing therefore the essential and influential role of the press, radio, television, cinema and news agencies and of the journalists working in these fields,

Make it their aim to facilitate the freer and wider dissemination of information of all kinds, to encourage co-operation in the field of information and the exchange of information with other countries, and to improve the conditions under which journalists from one participating State exercise their profession in another participating State; and

Express their intention in particular:

a. *Improvement of the circulation or access to, and exchange of information*

i. Oral information
To facilitate the dissemination of oral information through the encouragement of lectures and lecture tours by personalities and specialists from

the other participating States, as well as exchanges of opinions at round table meetings, seminars, symposia, summer schools, congresses and other bilateral and multilateral meetings.

ii. Printed information

To facilitate the improvement of the dissemination, on their territory, of newspapers and printed publications, periodical and non-periodical, from the other participating States. For this purpose:

– they will encourage their competent firms and organizations to conclude agreements and contracts designed gradually to increase the quantities and the number of titles of newspapers and publications imported from the other participating States. These agreements and contracts should in particular mention the speediest conditions of delivery and the use of the normal channels existing in each country for the distribution of its own publications and newspapers, as well as forms and means of payment agreed between the parties making it possible to achieve the objectives aimed at by these agreements and contracts;

– where necessary, they will take appropriate measures to achieve the above objectives and to implement the provisions contained in the agreements and contracts.

To contribute to the improvement of access by the public to periodical and non-periodical printed publications imported on the basis indicated above. In particular:

– they will encourage an increase in the number of places where these publications are on sale;

– they will facilitate the availability of these periodical publications during congresses, conferences, official visits and other international events and to tourists during the season;

– they will develop the possibilities for taking out subscriptions according to the modalities particular to each country;

– they will improve the opportunities for reading and borrowing these publications in large public libraries and their reading rooms as well as in university libraries.

They intend to improve the possibilities for acquaintance with bulletins of official information issued by diplomatic missions and distributed by those missions on the basis of arrangements acceptable to the interested parties.

iii. Filmed and broadcast information

To promote the improvement of the dissemination of filmed and broadcast information. To this end:

– they will encourage the wider showing and broadcasting of a greater variety of recorded and filmed information from the other participating States, illustrating the various aspects of life in their countries and received on the basis of such agreements or arrangements as may be necessary between the organizations and firms directly concerned;
– they will facilitate the import by competent organizations and firms of recorded audiovisual material from the other participating States.

The participating States note the expansion in the dissemination of information broadcast by radio and express the hope for the continuation of this process, so as to meet the interest of mutual understanding among peoples and the aims set forth by this Conference.

b. *Co-operation in the field of information*

To encourage co-operation in the field of information on the basis of short- or long- term agreements or arrangements. In particular:

– they will favour increased co-operation among mass media organizations, including press agencies, as well as among publishing houses and organizations;
– they will favour co-operation among public or private, national or international radio and televhrhon organizations, in particular through the exchange of both live and recorded radio and television programmes, and through the joint production and the broadcasting and distribution of such programmes;
– they will encourage meetings and contacts both between journalists' organizations and between journalists from the participating States;

– they will view favourably the possibilities of arrangements between periodical publications as well as between newspapers from the participating States, for the purpose of exchanging and publishing articles;
– they will encourage the exchange of technical information as well as the organization of joint research and meetings devoted to the exchange of experience and views between experts in the field of the press, radio and television.

c. *Improvement of working conditions for journalists*

The participating States, desiring to improve the conditions under which journalists from one participating State exercise their profession in another participating State, intend in particular to:

– examine in a favourable spirit and within a suitable and reasonable time-scale requests from journalists for visas;
– grant to permanently accredited journalists of the participating States, on the basis of arrangements, multiple entry and exit visas for specified periods;
– facilitate the issue to accredited journalists of the participating States of permits for stay in the country of temporary residence and, if and when these are necessary, of other official papers which it is appropriate for them to have;
– ease, on a basis of reciprocity, procedures for arranging travel by journalists of the participating States in the country where they are exercising their profession, and to provide progressively greater opportunities for such travel, subject to the observance of regulations relating to the existence of areas closed for security reasons;
– ensure that requests by such journalists for such travel receive, in so far as possible, an expeditious response, taking into account the time-scale of the request;
– increase the opportunities for journalists of the participating States to communicate personally with their sources, including organizations and official institutions;
– grant to journalists of the participating States the right to import, subject only to its being taken out again, the technical equipment

(photographic, cinematographic, tape recorder, radio and television) necessary for the exercise of their profession[1];

– enable journalists of the other participating States, whether permanently or temporarily accredited, to transmit completely, normally and rapidly by means recognized by the participating States to the information organs which they represent, the results of their professional activity, including tape recordings and undeveloped film, for the purpose of publication or of broadcasting on the radio or television.

The participating States reaffirm that the legitimate pursuit of their professional activity will neither render journalists liable to expulsion nor otherwise penalize them. If an accredited journalist is expelled, he will be informed of the reasons for this act and may submit an application for re-examination of his case.

3. *Co-operation and exchanges in the field of culture*

The participating States,

Considering that cultural exchanges and co-operation contribute to a better comprehension among people and among peoples, and thus promote a lasting understanding among States;

Confirming the conclusions already formulated in this field at the multilateral level, particularly at the Intergovernmental Conference on Cultural Policies in Europe, organized by Unesco in Helsinki in June 1972, where interest was manifested in the active participation of the broadest possible social groups in an increasingly diversified cultural life;

---

1. While recognizing that appropriate local personnel are employed by foreign journalists in many instances, the participating States note that the above provisions would be applied, subject to the observance of the appropriate rules, to persons from the other participating States, who are regularly and professionally engaged as technicians, photographers or cameramen of the press, radio, television or cinema.

Desiring, with the development of mutual confidence and the further improvement of relations between the participating States, to continue further efforts toward progress in this field;

Disposed in this spirit to increase substantially their cultural exchanges, with regard both to persons and to cultural works, and to develop among them an active co-operation, both at the bilateral and multilateral level, in all the fields of culture;

Convinced that such a development of their mutual relations will contribute to the enrichment of the respective cultures, while respecting the originality of each, as well as to the reinforcement among them of a consciousness of common values, while continuing to develop cultural co-operation with other countries of the world,

Declare that they jointly set themselves the following objectives:

a. to develop the mutual exchange of information with a view to a better knowledge of respective cultural achievements;
b. to improve the facilities for the exchange and for the dissemination of cultural property;
c. to promote access by all to respective cultural achievements;
d. to develop contacts and co-operation among persons active in the field of culture;
e. to seek new fields and forms of cultural co-operation;

Thus give expression to their common will to take progressive, coherent and long-term action in order to achieve the objectives of the present declaration; and

Express their intention now to proceed to the implementation of the following:

Extension of relations

To expand and improve at the various levels co-operation and links in the field of culture, in particular by:

– concluding, where appropriate, agreements on a bilateral or multilateral basis, providing for the extension of relations among competent State institutions and non-governmental organizations in the field of culture, as well as among people engaged in cultural activities, taking into account the need both for flexibility and the fullest possible use of existing agreements, and bearing in mind that agreements and also other arrangements constitute important means of developing cultural co-operation and exchanges;
– contributing to the development of direct communication and co-operation among relevant State institutions and non-governmental organizations, including, where necessary, such communication and co-operation carried out on the basis of special agreements and arrangements;
– encouraging direct contacts and communications among persons engaged in cultural activities, including, where necessary, such contacts and communications carried out on the basis of special agreements and arrangements.

Mutual knowledge

Within their competence to adopt, on a bilateral and multilateral level, appropriate measures which would give their peoples a more comprehensive and complete mutual knowledge of their achievements in the various fields of culture, and among them:

– to examine jointly, if necessary with the assistance of appropriate international organizations, the possible creation in Europe and the structure of a bank of cultural data, which would collect information from the participating countries and make it available to its correspondents on their request, and to convene for this purpose a meeting of experts from interested States;
– to consider, if necessary, in conjunction with appropriate international organisations, ways of compiling in Europe an inventory of documentary films of a cultural or scientific nature from the participating States;
– to encourage more frequent book exhibitions and to examine the possibility of organizing periodically in Europe a large-scale exhibition of books from the participating States;

– to promote the systematic exchange, between the institutions concerned and publishing houses, of catalogues of available books as well as of pre-publication material which will include, as far as possible, all forthcoming publications; and also to promote the exchange of material between firms publishing encyclopaedias, with a view to improving the presentation of each country;
– to examine jointly questions of expanding and improving exchanges of information in the various fields of culture, such as theatre, music, library work as well as the conservation and restoration of cultural property.

Exchanges and dissemination

To contribute to the improvement of facilities for exchanges and the dissemination of cultural property, by appropriate means, in particular by:

– studying the possibilities for harmonizing and reducing the charges relating to international commercial exchanges of books and other cultural materials, and also for new means of insuring works of art in foreign exhibitions and for reducing the risks of damage or loss to which these works are exposed by their movement;

– facilitating the formalities of customs clearance, in good time for programmes of artistic events, of the works of art, materials and accessories appearing on lists agreed upon by the organizers of these events;

– encouraging meetings among representatives of competent organizations and relevant firms to examine measures within their field of activity - such as the simplification of orders, time-limits for sending supplies and modalities of payment – which might facilitate international commercial exchanges of books;

– promoting the loan and exchange of films among their film institutes and film libraries;

– encouraging the exchange of information among interested parties concerning events of a cultural character foreseen in the participating States, in fields where this is most appropriate, such as music, theatre and the plastic and graphic arts, with a view to contributing to the compilation and publication of a calendar of such events, with the assistance, where necessary, of the appropriate international organizations;

– encouraging a study of the impact which the foreseeable development, and a possible harmonization among interested parties, of the technical means used for the dissemination of culture might have on the development of cultural co-operation and exchanges, while keeping in view the preservation of the diversity and originality of their respective cultures;

– encouraging, in the way they deem appropriate, within their cultural policies, the further development of interest in the cultural heritage of the other participating States, conscious of the merits and the value of each culture;

– endeavouring to ensure the full and effective application of the international agreements and conventions on copyrights and on circulation of cultural property to which they are party or to which they may decide in the future to become party.

Access

To promote fuller mutual access by all to the achievements – works, experiences and performing arts – in the various fields of culture of their countries, and to that end to make the best possible efforts, in accordance with their competence, more particularly:

– to promote wider dissemination of books and artistic works, in particular by such means as:

- – facilitating, while taking full account of the international copyright conventions to which they are party, international contacts and communications between authors and publishing houses as well as other cultural institutions, with a view to a more complete mutual access to cultural achievements;
- – recommending that, in determining the size of editions, publishing houses take into account also the demand from the other participating States, and that rights of sale in other participating States be granted, where possible, to several sales organizations of the importing countries, by agreement between interested partners;

- encouraging competent organizations and relevant firms to conclude agreements and contracts and contributing, by this means, to a gradual increase in the number and diversity of works by authors from the other participating States available in the original and in translation in their libraries and bookshops;
- promoting, where deemed appropriate, an increase in the number of sales outlets where books by authors from the other participating States, imported in the original on the basis of agreements and contracts, and in translation, are for sale;
- promoting, on a wider scale, the translation of works in the sphere of literature and other fields of cultural activity, produced in the languages of the other participating States, especially from the less widely-spoken languages, and the publication and dissemination of the translated works by such measures as:

• encouraging more regular contacts between interested publishing houses;
• developing their efforts in the basic and advanced training of translators;
• encouraging, by appropriate means, the publishing houses of their countries to publish translations;
• facilitating the exchange between publishers and interested institutions of lists of books which might be translated;
• promoting between their countries the professional activity and co-operation of translators;
• carrying out joint studies on ways of further promoting translations and their dissemination;

- improving and expanding exchanges of books, bibliographies and catalogue cards between libraries;

- to envisage other appropriate measures which would permit, where necessary by mutual agreement among interested parties, the facilitation of access to their respective cultural achievements, in particular in the field of books;

- to contribute by appropriate means to the wider use of the mass media in order to improve mutual acquaintance with the cultural life of each;

– to seek to develop the necessary conditions for migrant workers and their families to preserve their links with their national culture, and also to adapt themselves to their new cultural environment;

– to encourage the competent bodies and enterprises to make a wider choice and effect wider distribution of full-length and documentary films from the other participating States, and to promote more frequent non-commercial showings, such as premières, film weeks and festivals, giving due consideration to films from countries whose cinematographic works are less well known;

– to promote, by appropriate means, the extension of opportunities for specialists from the other participating States to work with materials of a cultural character from film and audio-visual archives, within the framework of the existing rules for work on such archival materials;

– to encourage a joint study by interested bodies, where appropriate with the assistance of the competent international organizations, of the expediency and the conditions for the establishment of a repertory of their recorded television programmes of a cultural nature, as well as of the means of viewing them rapidly in order to facilitate their selection and possible acquisition.

Contacts and co-operation

To contribute, by appropriate means, to the development of contacts and co-operation in the various fields of culture, especially among creative artists and people engaged in cultural activities, in particular by making efforts to:

– promote for persons active in the field of culture, travel and meetings including, where necessary, those carried out on the basis of agreements, contracts or other special arrangements and which are relevant to their cultural co-operation;

– encourage in this way contacts among creative and performing artists and artistic groups with a view to their working together, making known their works in other participating States or exchanging views on topics relevant to their common activity;

– encourage, where necessary through appropriate arrangements, exchanges of trainees and specialists and the granting of scholarships for basic and advanced training in various fields of culture such as the arts and architecture, museums and libraries, literary studies and translation, and contribute to the creation of favourable conditions of reception in their respective institutions;

– encourage the exchange of experience in the training of organizers of cultural activities as well as of teachers and specialists in fields such as theatre, opera, ballet, music and fine arts;

– continue to encourage the organization of international meetings among creative artists, especially young creative artists, on current questions of artistic and literary creation which are of interest for joint study;

– study other possibilities for developing exchanges and co-operation among persons active in the field of culture, with a view to a better mutual knowledge of the cultural life of the participating States.

Fields and forms of co-operation

To encourage the search for new fields and forms of cultural co-operation, to these ends contributing to the conclusion among interested parties, where necessary, of appropriate agreements and arrangements, and in this context to promote:

– joint studies regarding cultural policies, in particular in their social aspects, and as they relate to planning, town-planning, educational and environmental policies, and the cultural aspects of tourism;

– the exchange of knowledge in the realm of cultural diversity, with a view to contributing thus to a better understanding by interested parties of such diversity where it occurs;

– the exchange of information and, as may be appropriate, meetings of experts, the elaboration and execution of research programmes and projects, as well as their joint evaluation, and the dissemination of the results, on the subjects indicated above;

– such forms of cultural co-operation and development of such joint projects as:

– international events in the fields of the plastic and graphic arts, cinema, theatre, ballet, music, folklore, etc., book fairs and exhibitions, joint performances of operatic and dramatic works, as well as performances given by soloists, instrumental ensembles, orchestras, choirs and other artistic groups, including those composed of amateurs, paying due attention to the organization of international cultural youth events and the exchange of young artists;

– the inclusion of works by writers and composers from the other participating States in the repertoires of soloists and artistic ensembles;

– the preparation, translation and publication of articles, studies and monographs, as well as of low-cost books and of artistic and literary collections, suited to making better known respective cultural achievements, envisaging for this purpose meetings among experts and representatives of publishing houses;

– the co-production and the exchange of films and of radio and television programmes, by promoting, in particular, meetings among producers, technicians and representatives of the public authorities with a view to working out favourable conditions for the execution of specific joint projects and by encouraging, in the field of co-production, the establishment of international filming teams;

– the organization of competitions for architects and town-planners, bearing in mind the possible implementation of the best projects and the formation, where possible, of international teams;

– the implementation of joint projects for conserving, restoring and showing to advantage works of art, historical and archaeological monuments and sites of cultural interest, with the help, in appropriate cases, of international organizations of a governmental or non-governmental character as well as of private institutions – competent and active in these fields – envisaging for this purpose:

• periodic meetings of experts of the interested parties to elaborate the necessary proposals, while bearing in mind the need to consider these questions in a wider social and economic context;

- the publication in appropriate periodicals of articles designed to make known and to compare, among the participating States, the most significant achievements and innovations;
- a joint study with a view to the improvement and possible harmonization of the different systems used to inventory and catalogue the historical monuments and places of cultural interest in their countries;
- the study of the possibilities for organizing international courses for the training of specialists in different disciplines relating to restoration.

National minorities or regional cultures

The participating States, recognizing the contribution that national minorities or regional cultures can make to co-operation among them in various fields of culture, intend, when such minorities or cultures exist within their territory, to facilitate this contribution, taking into account the legitimate interests of their members.

4. *Co-operation and exchanges in the field of education*

The participating States,

Conscious that the development of relations of an international character in the fields of education and science contributes to a better mutual understanding and is to the advantage of all peoples as well as to the benefit of future generations;

Prepared to facilitate, between organizations, institutions and persons engaged in education and science, the further development of exchanges of knowledge and experience as well as of contacts, on the basis of special arrangements where these are necessary;

Desiring to strengthen the links among educational and scientific establishments and also to encourage their co-operation in sectors of common interest, particularly where the levels of knowledge and resources require efforts to be concerted internationally; and

Convinced that progress in these fields should be accompanied and supported by a wider knowledge of foreign languages,

Express to these ends their intention in particular:

a. *Extension of relations*

To expand and improve at the various levels co-operation and links in the fields of education and science, in particular by:

– concluding, where appropriate, bilateral or multilateral agreements providing for co-operation and exchanges among State institutions, non-governmental bodies and persons engaged in activities in education and science, bearing in mind the need both for flexibility and the fuller use of existing agreements and arrangements;

– promoting the conclusion of direct arrangements between universities and other institutions of higher education and research, in the framework of agreements between governments where appropriate;

– encouraging among persons engaged in education and science direct contacts and communications, including those based on special agreements or arrangements where these are appropriate.

b. *Access and exchanges*

To improve access, under mutually acceptable conditions, for students, teachers and scholars of the participating States to each other's educational, cultural and scientific institutions, and to intensify exchanges among these institutions in all areas of common interest, in particular by:

– increasing the exchange of information on facilities for study and courses open to foreign participants, as well as on the conditions under which they will be admitted and received;

– facilitating travel between the participating States by scholars, teachers and students for purposes of study, teaching and research as well as for improving knowledge of each other's educational, cultural and scientific achievements;

– encouraging the award of scholarships for study, teaching and research in their countries to scholars, teachers and students of other participating States;

– establishing, developing or encouraging programmes providing for the broader exchange of scholars, teachers and students, including the organization of symposia, seminars and collaborative projects, and the exchanges of educational and scholarly information such as university publications and materials from libraries;

– promoting the efficient implementation of such arrangements and programmes by providing scholars, teachers and students in good time with more detailed information about their placing in universities and institutes and the programmes envisaged for them by granting them the opportunity to use relevant scholarly, scientific and open archival materials; and by facilitating their travel within the receiving State for the purpose of study or research as well as in the form of vacation tours on the basis of the usual procedures;

– promoting a more exact assessment of the problems of comparison and equivalence of academic degrees and diplomas by fostering the exchange of information on the organization, duration and content of studies, the comparison of methods of assessing levels of knowledge and academic qualifications, and, where feasible, arriving at the mutual recognition of academic degrees and diplomas either through governmental agreements, where necessary, or direct arrangements between universities and other institutions of higher learning and research;

– recommending, moreover, to the appropriate international organizations that they should intensify their efforts to reach a generally acceptable solution to the problems of comparison and equivalence between academic degrees and diplomas.

c. *Science*

Within their competence to broaden and improve co-operation and exchanges in the field of science, in particular:

To increase, on a bilateral or multilateral basis, the exchange and dissemination of scientific information and documentation by such means as:

– making this information more widely available to scientists and research workers of the other participating States through, for instance, participation in international information-sharing programmes or through other appropriate arrangements;

– broadening and facilitating the exchange of samples and other scientific materials used particularly for fundamental research in the fields of natural sciences and medicine;

– inviting scientific institutions and universities to keep each other more fully and regularly informed about their current and contemplated research work in fields of common interest.

To facilitate the extension of communications and direct contacts between universities, scientific institutions and associations as well as among scientists and research workers, including those based where necessary on special agreements or arrangements, by such means as:

– further developing exchanges of scientists and research workers and encouraging the organization of preparatory meetings or working groups on research topics of common interest;

– encouraging the creation of joint teams of scientists to pursue research projects under arrangements made by the scientific institutions of several countries;

– assisting the organization and successful functioning of international conferences and seminars and participation in them by their scientists and research workers;

– furthermore envisaging, in the near future, a "Scientific Forum" in the form of a meeting of leading personalities in science from the participating States to discuss interrelated problems of common interest concerning current and future developments in science, and to promote the expansion of contacts, communications and the exchange of information between scientific institutions and among scientists;

– foreseeing, at an early date, a meeting of experts representing the participating States and their national scientific institutions, in order to prepare such a "Scientific Forum" in consultation with appropriate international organizations, such as Unesco and the ECE;

– considering in due course what further steps might be taken with respect to the "Scientific Forum".

To develop in the field of scientific research, on a bilateral or multilateral basis, the co-ordination of programmes carried out in the participating States and the organization of joint programmes, especially in the areas mentioned below, which may involve the combined efforts of scientists and in certain cases the use of costly or unique equipment. The list of subjects in these areas is illustrative; and specific projects would have to be determined subsequently by the potential partners in the participating States, taking account of the contribution which could be made by appropriate international organizations and scientific institutions:

– exact and natural sciences, in particular fundamental research in such fields as mathematics, physics, theoretical physics, geophysics, chemistry, biology, economy and astronomy;

– medicine, in particular basic research into cancer and cardiovascular diseases, studies on the diseases endemic in the developing countries, as well as medico-social research with special emphasis on occupational diseases, the rehabilitation of the handicapped and the care of mothers, children and the elderly;

– the humanities and social sciences, such as history, geography, philosophy, psychology, pedagogical research, linguistics, sociology, the legal, political and economic sciences; comparative studies on social, socio-economic and cultural phenomena which are of common interest to the participating States, especially the problems of human environment and urban development; and scientific studies on the methods of conserving and restoring monuments and works of art.

d. *Foreign languages and civilizations*

To encourage the study of foreign languages and civilizations as an important means of expanding communication among peoples for their better acquaintance with the culture of each country, as well as for the strengthening of international co-operation; to this end to stimulate, within their competence, the further development and improvement of foreign language teaching and the diversification of choice of languages taught at various levels, paying due attention to less widely-spread or studied languages, and in particular:

– to intensify co-operation aimed at improving the teaching of foreign languages through exchanges of information and experience concerning the development and application of effective modern teaching methods and technical aids, adapted to the needs of different categories of students, including methods of accelerated teaching; and to consider the possibility of conducting, on a bilateral or multilateral basis, studies of new methods of foreign language teaching;

– to encourage co-operation between institutions concerned, on a bilateral or multilateral basis, aimed at exploiting more fully the resources of modern educational technology in language teaching, for example through comparative studies by their specialists and, where agreed, through exchanges or transfer of audio-visual materials, of materials used for preparing textbooks, as well as of information about new types of technical equipment used for teaching languages;

– to promote the exchange of information on the experience acquired in the training of language teachers and to intensify exchanges on a bilateral basis of language teachers and students as well as to facilitate their participation in summer courses in languages and civilizations, wherever these are organized;

– to encourage co-operation among experts in the field of lexicography with the aim of defining the necessary terminological equivalents, particularly in the scientific and technical disciplines, in order to facilitate relations among scientific institutions and specialists;

– to promote the wider spread of foreign language study among the different types of secondary education establishments and greater possibilities of choice between an increased number of European languages; and in this context to consider, wherever appropriate, the possibilities for developing the recruitment and training of teachers as well as the organization of the student groups required;

– to favour, in higher education, a wider choice in the languages offered to language students and greater opportunities for other students to study various foreign languages; also to facilitate, where desirable, the organization of courses in languages and civilizations, on the basis of special arrangements as necessary, to be given by foreign lecturers, particularly from European countries having less widely-spread or studied languages;

– to promote, within the framework of adult education, the further development of specialized programmes, adapted to various needs and interests, for teaching foreign languages to their own inhabitants and the languages of host countries to interested adults from other countries; in this context to encourage interested institutions to co-operate, for example, in the elaboration of programmes for teaching by radio and television and by accelerated methods, and also, where desirable, in the definition of study objectives for such programmes, with a view to arriving at comparable levels of language proficiency;

– to encourage the association, where appropriate, of the teaching of foreign languages with the study of the corresponding civilizations and also to make further efforts to stimulate interest in the study of foreign languages, including relevant out-of-class activities.

e. *Teaching methods*

To promote the exchange of experience, on a bilateral or multilateral basis, in teaching methods at all levels of education, including those used in permanent and adult education, as well as the exchange of teaching materials, in particular by:

– further developing various forms of contacts and co-operation in the different fields of pedagogical science, for example through comparative or joint studies carried out by interested institutions or through exchanges of information on the results of teaching experiments;

– intensifying exchanges of information on teaching methods used in various educational systems and on results of research into the processes by which pupils and students acquire knowledge, taking account of relevant experience in different types of specialized education;

– facilitating exchanges of experience concerning the organization and functioning of education intended for adults and recurrent education, the relationships between these and other forms and levels of education, as well as concerning the means of adapting education, including vocational and technical training, to the needs of economic and social development in their countries;

– encouraging exchanges of experience in the education of youth and adults in international understanding, with particular reference to those major problems of mankind whose solution calls for a common approach and wider international co-operation;

– encouraging exchanges of teaching materials – including school textbooks, having in mind the possibility of promoting mutual knowledge and facilitating the presentation of each country in such books – as well as exchanges of information on technical innovations in the field of education.

National minorities or regional cultures

The participating States, recognizing the contribution that national minorities or regional cultures can make to co-operation among them in various fields of education, intend, when such minorities or cultures exist within their territory, to facilitate this contribution, taking into account the legitimate interests of their members.

Follow-up to the Conference

The participating States,

Having considered and evaluated the progress made at the Conference on Security and Co-operation in Europe;

Considering further that, within the broader context of the world, the Conference is an important part of the process of improving security and developing co-operation in Europe and that its results will contribute significantly to this process;

Intending to implement the provisions of the Final Act of the Conference in order to give full effect to its results and thus to further the process of improving security and developing co-operation in Europe;

Convinced that, in order to achieve the aims sought by the Conference, they should make further unilateral, bilateral and multilateral efforts and continue, in the appropriate forms set forth below, the multilateral process initiated by the Conference,

1. Declare their resolve, in the period following the Conference, to pay due regard to and implement the provisions of the Final Act of the Conference:

a. unilaterally, in all cases which lend themselves to such action;
b. bilaterally, by negotiations with other participating States;
c. multilaterally, by meetings of experts of the participating States, and also within the framework of existing international organizations, such as the United Nations Economic Commission for Europe and Unesco, with regard to educational, scientific and cultural co-operation;

2. Declare furthermore their resolve to continue the multilateral process initiated by the Conference:

a. by proceeding to a thorough exchange of views both on the implementation of the provisions of the Final Act and of the tasks defined by the Conference, as well as, in the context of the questions dealt with by the latter, on the deepening of their mutual relations, the improvement of security and the development of co-operation in Europe, and the development of the process of *détente* in the future;
b. by organizing to these ends meetings among their representatives, beginning with a meeting at the level of representatives appointed by the Ministers of Foreign Affairs. This meeting will define the appropriate modalities for the holding of other meetings which could include further similar meetings and the possibility of a new Conference;

3. The first of the meetings indicated above will be held at Belgrade in 1977. A preparatory meeting to organize this meeting will be held at Belgrade on 15 June 1977. The preparatory meeting will decide on the date, duration, agenda and other modalities of the meeting of representatives appointed by the Ministers of Foreign Affairs.

2. Concluding Document of the Vienna Meeting on the follow-up to the Conference

Vienna, 15 January 1989

(Extracts)

Questions relating to security in Europe

The participating States express their determination:

– to promote co-operation and dialogue among them, to ensure the effective exercise of human rights and fundamental freedoms and to facilitate contacts and communication between people;

(...)

Principles

1. The participating States reaffirm their commitment to all ten principles of the Final Act's Declaration on Principles Guiding Relations between participating States and their determination to respect them and put them into practice. The participating States reaffirm that all these principles are of primary significance and, accordingly, will be equally and unreservedly applied, each of them being interpreted taking into account the others.

2. They stress that respect for and full application of these principles as well as strict compliance with all CSCE commitments deriving from them are of great political importance and essential for building confidence and security as well as for the development of their friendly relations and of their co-operation in all fields.

3. In this context, they confirm that they will respect each other's right freely to choose and develop their political, social, economic and cultural systems as well as their right to determine their laws, regulations, prac-

tices and policies. In exercising these rights, they will ensure that their laws, regulations, practices and policies conform with their obligations under international law and are brought into harmony with the provisions of the Declaration on Principles and other CSCE commitments.

4. They also confirm that, by virtue of the principle of equal rights and self-determination of peoples and in conformity with the relevant provisions of the Final Act, all peoples always have the right, in full freedom, to determine, when and as they wish, their internal and external political status, without external interference, and to pursue as they wish their political, economic, social and cultural development.

5. They confirm their commitment strictly and effectively to observe the principle of the territorial integrity of States. They will refrain from any violation of this principle and thus from any action aimed by direct or indirect means, in contravention of the purposes and principles of the Charter of the United Nations, other obligations under international law or the provisions of the Final Act, at violating the territorial integrity, political independence or the unity of a State. No actions or situations in contravention of this principle will be recognized as legal by the participating States.

6. The participating States confirm their commitment to the principle of peaceful settlement of disputes, convinced that it is an essential complement to the duty of States to refrain from the threat or use of force, both being essential factors for the maintenance and consolidation of peace and security. They express their determination to pursue continuous efforts to examine and elaborate, on the basis of the relevant provisions of the Final Act and the Madrid Concluding Document and taking into account the reports of the meetings of experts in Montreux and Athens, a generally acceptable method for the peaceful settlement of disputes aimed at complementing existing methods. In this context they accept, in principle, the mandatory involvement of a third party when a dispute cannot be settled by other peaceful means.

7. In order to ensure the progressive implementation of this commitment, including, as a first step, the mandatory involvement of a third party in

the settlement of certain categories of disputes, they decide to convene a meeting of experts in Valletta from 15 January to 8 February 1991 to establish a list of such categories and the related procedures and mechanisms. This list would be subject to subsequent gradual extension. The meeting will also consider the possibility of establishing mechanisms for arriving at binding third-party decisions. The next CSCE follow-up meeting will assess the progress achieved at the meeting of experts. The agenda, timetable and other organizational modalities are set out in Annex I.

8. The participating States unreservedly condemn, as criminal, all acts, methods and practices of terrorism, wherever and by whomever committed, including those which jeopardize friendly relations among States and their security, and agree that terrorism cannot be justified under any circumstances.

9. They express their determination to work for the eradication of terrorism both bilaterally and through multilateral co-operation, particularly in such international fora as the United Nations, the International Civil Aviation Organization and the International Maritime Organization and in accordance with the relevant provisions of the Final Act and the Madrid Concluding Document.

10. Convinced of the need to combine measures at a national level with reinforced international co-operation, the participating States express their intention:

10.1. to pursue a policy of firmness in response to terrorist demands;

10.2. to reinforce and develop bilateral and multilateral co-operation among themselves in order to prevent and combat terrorism as well as to increase efficiency in existing co-operation at the bilateral level or in the framework of groups of States including, as appropriate, through the exchange of information.

(...)

11. They confirm that they will respect human rights and fundamental freedoms, including the freedom of thought, conscience, religion or belief, for all without distinction as to race, sex, language or religion. They also confirm the universal significance of human rights and fundamental freedoms, respect for which is an essential factor for the peace, justice and security necessary to ensure the development of friendly relations and co-operation among themselves, as among all States.

12. They express their determination to guarantee the effective exercise of human rights and fundamental freedoms, all of which derive from the inherent dignity of the human person and are essential for his free and full development. They recognize that civil, political, economic, social, cultural and other rights and freedoms are all of paramount importance and must be fully realized by all appropriate means.

13. In this context they will:

13.1. develop their laws, regulations and policies in the field of civil, political, economic, social, cultural and other human rights and fundamental freedoms and put them into practice in order to guarantee the effective exercise of these rights and freedoms;

13.2. consider acceding to the International Covenant on Civil and Political Rights, the International Covenant on Economic, Social and Cultural Rights, the Optional Protocol to the Covenant on Civil and Political Rights and other relevant international instruments, if they have not yet done so;

13.3. publish and disseminate the text of the Final Act, of the Madrid Concluding Document and of the present Document as well as those of any relevant international instruments in the field of human rights, in order to ensure the availability of these documents in their entirety, to make them known as widely as possible and to render them accessible to all individuals in their countries, in particular through public library systems;

13.4. effectively ensure the right of the individual to know and act upon his rights and duties in this field, and to that end publish and make accessible all laws, regulations and procedures relating to human rights and fundamental freedoms;

13.5. respect the right of their citizens to contribute actively, individually or in association with others, to the promotion and protection of human rights and fundamental freedoms;

13.6. encourage in schools and other educational institutions consideration of the promotion and protection of human rights and fundamental freedoms;

13.7. ensure human rights and fundamental freedoms to everyone within their territory and subject to their jurisdiction, without distinction of any kind such as race, colour, sex, language, religion, political or other opinion, national or social origin, property, birth or other status;

13.8. ensure that no individual exercising, expressing the intention to exercise or seeking to exercise these rights and freedoms or any member of his family, will as a consequence be discriminated against in any manner;

13.9. ensure that effective remedies as well as full information about them are available to those who claim that their human rights and fundamental freedoms have been violated; they will, *inter alia,* effectively apply the following remedies:

– the right of the individual to appeal to executive, legislative, judicial or administrative organs;
– the right to a fair and public hearing within a reasonable time before an independent and impartial tribunal, including the right to present legal arguments and to be represented by legal counsel of one's choice;
– the right to be promptly and officially informed of the decision taken on any appeal, including the legal grounds on which this decision was based. This information will be provided as a rule in writing and, in any

event, in a way that will enable the individual to make effective use of further available remedies.

14. The participating States recognize that the promotion of economic, social, cultural rights as well as of civil and political rights is of paramount importance for human dignity and for the attainment of the legitimate aspirations of every individual. They will therefore continue their efforts with a view to achieving progressively the full realization of economic, social and cultural rights by all appropriate means, including in particular by the adoption of legislative measures. In this context they will pay special attention to problems in the areas of employment, housing, social security, health, education and culture. They will promote constant progress in the realization of all rights and freedoms within their countries, as well as in the development of relations among themselves and with other States, so that everyone actually enjoys to the full his economic, social and cultural rights as well as his civil and political rights.

15. The participating States confirm their determination to ensure equal rights of men and women. Accordingly, they will take all measures necessary, including legislative measures, to promote equally effective participation of men and women in political, economic, social and cultural life. They will consider the possibility of acceding to the Convention on the Elimination of All Forms of Discrimination against Women, if they have not yet done so.

16. In order to ensure the freedom of the individual to profess and practise religion or belief, the participating States will, *inter alia:*

16.1. take effective measures to prevent and eliminate discrimination against individuals or communities on the grounds of religion or belief in the recognition, exercise and enjoyment of human rights and fundamental freedoms in all fields of civil, political, economic, social and cultural life, and to ensure the effective equality between believers and non-believers;

16.2. foster a climate of mutual tolerance and respect between believers of different communities as well as between believers and non-believers;

16.3. grant upon their request to communities of believers, practising or prepared to practise their faith within the constitutional framework of their States, recognition of the status provided for them in their respective countries;

16.4. respect the right of these religious communities to:

- establish and maintain freely accessible places of worship or assembly;
- organize themselves according to their own hierarchical and institutional structure;
- select, appoint and replace their personnel in accordance with their respective requirements and standards as well as with any freely accepted arrangements between them and their State;
- solicit and receive voluntary financial and other contributions;

16.5. engage in consultations with religious faiths, institutions and organizations in order to achieve a better understanding of the requirements of religious freedom;

16.6. respect the right of everyone to give and receive religious education in the language of his choice, whether individually or in association with others;

16.7. in this context respect, *inter alia*, the liberty of parents to ensure the religious and moral education of their children in conformity with their own convictions;

16.8. allow the training of religious personnel in appropriate institutions;

16.9. respect the right of individual believers and communities of believers to acquire, possess and use sacred books, religious publications in the language of their choice and other articles and materials related to the practice of religion or belief;

16.10. allow religious faiths, institutions and organizations to produce, import and disseminate religious publications and materials;

16.11. favourably consider the interest of religious communities to participate in public dialogue, including through the mass media.

17. The participating States recognize that the exercise of the above-mentioned rights relating to the freedom of religion or belief may be subject only to such limitations as are provided by law and consistent with their obligations under international law and with their international commitments. They will ensure in their laws and regulations and in their application the full and effective exercise of the freedom of thought, conscience, religion or belief.

18. The participating States will exert sustained efforts to implement the provisions of the Final Act and of the Madrid Concluding Document pertaining to national minorities. They will take all the necessary legislative, administrative, judicial and other measures and apply the relevant international instruments by which they may be bound to ensure the protection of human rights and fundamental freedoms of persons belonging to national minorities within their territory. They will refrain from any discrimination against such persons and will contribute to the realization of their legitimate interests and aspirations in the field of human rights and fundamental freedoms.

19. They will protect and create conditions for the promotion of the ethnic, cultural, linguistic and religious identity of national minorities on their territory. They will respect the free exercise of rights by persons belonging to such minorities and ensure their full equality with others.

20. The participating States will respect fully the right of everyone:

– to freedom of movement and residence within the borders of each State; and
– to leave any country, including his own, and to return to his country.

21. The participating States will ensure that the exercise of the above-mentioned rights will not be subject to any restrictions except those which are provided by law and are consistent with their obligations under

international law, in particular the International Covenant on Civil and Political Rights, and with their international commitments, in particular the Universal Declaration of Human Rights. These restrictions have the character of exceptions. The participating States will ensure that these restrictions are not abused and are not applied in an arbitrary manner, but in such a way that the effective exercise of these rights is ensured.

22. In this context they will allow all refugees who so desire to return in safety to their homes.

23. The participating States will:

23.1. ensure that no one will be subjected to arbitrary arrest, detention or exile;

23.2. ensure that all individuals in detention or incarceration will be treated with humanity and with respect for the inherent dignity of the human person;

23.3. observe the United Nations Standard Minimum Rules for the Treatment of Prisoners as well as the United Nations Code of Conduct for Law Enforcement Officials;

23.4. prohibit torture and other cruel, inhuman or degrading treatment or punishment and take effective legislative, administrative, judicial and other measures to prevent and punish such practices;

23.5. consider acceding to the Convention against Torture and other Cruel, Inhuman or Degrading Treatment or Punishment, if they have not yet done so;

23.6. protect individuals from any psychiatric or other medical practices that violate human rights and fundamental freedoms and take effective measures to prevent and punish such practices.

24. With regard to the question of capital punishment, the participating States note that capital punishment has been abolished in a number of

them. In participating States where capital punishment has not been abolished, sentence of death may be imposed only for the most serious crimes in accordance with the law in force at the time of the commission of the crime and not contrary to their international commitments. This question will be kept under consideration. In this context, the participating States will co-operate within relevant international organizations.

(...)

26. They confirm that governments, institutions, organizations and persons have a relevant positive role to play in contributing to the achievement of the aims of their co-operation and to the full realization of the Final Act. To that end they will respect the right of persons to observe and promote the implementation of CSCE provisions and to associate with others for this purpose. They will facilitate direct contacts and communication among these persons, organizations and institutions within and between participating States and remove, where they exist, legal and administrative impediments inconsistent with the CSCE provisions. They will also take effective measures to facilitate access to information on the implementation of CSCE provisions and to facilitate the free expression of views on these matters.

(...)

Co-operation in humanitarian and other fields

The participating States,

Considering that co-operation in humanitarian and other fields is an essential factor for the development of their relations;

Agreeing that their co-operation in these fields should take place in full respect for the principles guiding relations between participating States as set forth in the Final Act as well as for the provisions in the Madrid Concluding Document and in the present Document pertaining to those principles;

Confirming that, in implementing the provisions concerning co-operation in humanitarian and other fields in the framework of their laws and regulations, they will ensure that those laws and regulations conform with their obligations under international law and are brought into harmony with their CSCE commitments;

Recognizing that the implementation of the relevant provisions of the Final Act and of the Madrid Concluding Document requires continuous and intensified efforts;

Have adopted and will implement the following:

Human contacts

1. In implementing the human contacts provisions of the Final Act, the Madrid Concluding Document and the present Document, they will fully respect their obligations under international law as referred to in the sub-chapter of the present Document devoted to principles, in particular that everyone shall be free to leave any country, including his own, and to return to his country, as well as their international commitments in this field.

2. They will ensure that their policies concerning entry into their territories are fully consistent with the aims set out in the relevant provisions of the Final Act, the Madrid Concluding Document and the present Document.

3. They will take the necessary steps to find solutions as expeditiously as possible, but in any case within six months, to all applications based on the human contacts provisions of the Final Act and the Madrid Concluding Document, outstanding at the conclusion of the Vienna Follow-up Meeting.

4. Thereafter they will conduct regular reviews in order to ensure that all applications based on the human contacts provisions of the Final Act and of the other aforementioned CSCE documents are being dealt with in a manner consistent with those provisions.

5. They will decide upon applications relating to family meetings in accordance with the Final Act and the other aforementioned CSCE documents in as short a time as possible and in normal practice within one month.

6. In the same manner they will decide upon applications relating to family reunification or marriage between citizens of different States, in normal practice within three months.

7. In dealing favourably with applications relating to family meetings, they will take due account of the wishes of the applicant, in particular on the timing and sufficiently long duration of such meetings, and on travelling together with other members of his family for joint family meetings.

8. In dealing favourably with applications relating to family meetings, they will also allow visits to and from more distant relatives.

9. In dealing favourably with applications relating to family reunification or marriage between citizens of different States, they will respect the wishes of the applicants on the country of destination ready to accept them.

10. They will pay particular attention to the solution of problems involving the reunification of minor children with their parents. In this context and on the basis of the relevant provisions of the Final Act and of the other aforementioned CSCE documents, they will ensure:

– that an application for this purpose submitted while the child is a minor will be dealt with favourably and expeditiously in order to effect the reunification without delay; and
– that adequate arrangements are made to protect the interests and welfare of the children concerned.

11. They will consider the scope for gradually reducing and eventually eliminating any requirements which might exist for travellers to obtain local currency in excess of actual expenditure, giving priority to persons travelling for the purpose of family meetings. They will accord such

persons the opportunity in practice to bring in or to take out with them personal possessions or gifts.

12. They will pay immediate attention to applications for travel of an urgent humanitarian nature and deal with them favourably as follows:

– they will decide within three working days upon applications relating to visits to a seriously ill or dying family member, travel to attend the funeral of a family member or travel by those who have a proven need of urgent medical treatment or who can be shown to be critically or terminally ill;
– they will decide as expeditiously as possible upon applications relating to travel by those who are seriously ill or by the elderly, and other travel of an urgent humanitarian nature.

They will intensify efforts by their local, regional and central authorities concerned with the implementation of the above, and ensure that charges for giving priority treatment to such applications do not exceed costs actually incurred.

13. In dealing with applications for travel for family meetings, family reunification or marriage between citizens of different States, they will ensure that acts or omissions by members of the applicant's family do not adversely affect the rights of the applicant as set forth in the relevant international instruments.

14. They will ensure that all documents necessary for applications based on the human contacts provisions of the Final Act and of the other aforementioned CSCE documents are easily accessible to the applicant. The documents will remain valid throughout the application procedure. In the event of a renewed application, the documents already submitted by the applicant in connection with previous applications will be taken into consideration.

15. They will simplify practices and gradually reduce administrative requirements for applications based on the human contacts provisions of the Final Act and of the other aforementioned CSCE documents.

16. They will ensure that, when applications based on the human contacts provisions of the Final Act and of the other aforementioned CSCE documents are refused for reasons specified in the relevant international instruments, the applicant is promptly provided in writing with an official notification of the grounds on which the decision was based. As a rule and in all cases where the applicant so requests, he will be given the necessary information about the procedure for making use of any effective administrative or judicial remedies against the decision available to him as envisaged in the above-mentioned international instruments. In cases where exit for permanent settlement abroad is involved, this information will be provided as part of the official notification foreseen above.

17. If in this context an individual's application for travel abroad has been refused for reasons of national security, they will ensure that, within strictly warranted time-limits, any restriction on that individual's travel is as short as possible and is not applied in an arbitrary manner. They will also ensure that the applicant can have the refusal reviewed within six months and, should the need arise, at regular intervals thereafter so that any changes in the circumstances surrounding the refusal, such as time elapsed since the applicant was last engaged in work or duties involving national security, are taken into account. Before individuals take up such work or duties they will be formally notified if and how this could affect applications they might submit for such travel.

18. Within one year of the conclusion of the Vienna Follow-up Meeting they will publish and make easily accessible, where this has not already been done, all their laws and statutory regulations concerning movement by individuals within their territory and travel between States.

19. In dealing favourably with applications based on the human contacts provisions of the Final Act and of the other aforementioned CSCE documents, they will ensure that these are dealt with in good time in order, *inter alia,* to take due account of important family, personal or professional considerations significant for the applicant.

20. They will deal favourably with applications for travel abroad without distinction of any kind, such as race, colour, sex, language, religion,

political or other opinion, national or social origin, property, birth, age or other status. They will ensure that any refusal does not affect applications submitted by other persons.

21. They will further facilitate travel on an individual or collective basis for personal or professional reasons and for tourism, such as travel by delegations, groups and individuals. To this end they will reduce the time for the consideration of applications for such travel to a minimum.

22. They will give serious consideration to proposals for concluding agreements on the issuing of multiple entry visas and the reciprocal easing of visa processing formalities, and consider possibilities for the reciprocal abolition of entry visas on the basis of agreements between them.

23. They will consider adhering to the relevant multilateral instruments as well as concluding complementary or other bilateral agreements, if necessary, in order to improve arrangements for ensuring effective consular, legal and medical assistance for citizens of other participating States temporarily on their territory.

24. They will take any necessary measures to ensure that citizens of other participating States temporarily on their territory for personal or professional reasons, *inter alia,* for the purpose of participating in cultural, scientific and educational activities, are afforded appropriate personal safety, where this is not already the case.

25. They will facilitate and encourage the establishment and maintenance of direct personal contacts between their citizens as well as between representatives of their institutions and organizations through travel between States and other means of communication.

26. They will facilitate such contacts and co-operation among their peoples through such measures as direct sports exchanges on a local and regional level, the unimpeded establishment and implementation of town-twinning arrangements, as well as student and teacher exchanges.

27. They will encourage the further development of direct contacts between young people, as well as between governmental and non-governmental youth and student organizations and institutions; the conclusion between such organisations and institutions of bilateral and multilateral arrangements and programmes; and the holding on a bilateral and multilateral basis of educational, cultural and other events and activities by and for young people.

28. They will make further efforts to facilitate travel and tourism by young people, *inter alia,* by recommending to those of their railway authorities which are members of the International Union of Railways (UIC) that they expand the Inter-Rail system to cover all their European networks and by recommending to those of their railway authorities which are not members of the UIC that they consider establishing similar facilities.

29. In accordance with the Universal Postal Convention and the International Telecommunication Convention, they will:

– guarantee the freedom of transit of postal communication;
– ensure the rapid and unhindered delivery of correspondence, including personal mail and parcels;
– respect the privacy and integrity of postal and telephone communications; and
– ensure the conditions necessary for rapid and uninterrupted telephone calls, including the use of international direct dialling systems, where they exist, and their development.

30. They will encourage direct personal contacts between the citizens of their States, *inter alia*, by facilitating individual travel within their countries and by allowing foreigners to meet their citizens as well as, when invited to do so, to stay in private homes.

31. They will ensure that the status of persons belonging to national minorities or regional cultures on their territories is equal to that of other citizens with regard to human contacts under the Final Act and the other aforementioned CSCE documents and that these persons can establish and maintain such contacts through travel and other means of com-

munication, including contacts with citizens of other States with whom they share a common national origin or cultural heritage.

32. They will allow believers, religious faiths and their representatives, in groups or on an individual basis, to establish and maintain direct personal contacts and communication with each other, in their own and other countries, *inter alia*, through travel, pilgrimages and participation in assemblies and other religious events. In this context and commensurate with such contacts and events, those concerned will be allowed to acquire, receive and carry with them religious publications and objects related to the practice of their religion or belief.

(...)

Information

34. They will continue efforts to contribute to an ever wider knowledge and understanding of life in their States, thus promoting confidence between peoples.

They will make further efforts to facilitate the freer and wider dissemination of information of all kinds, to encourage co-operation in the field of information and to improve the working conditions for journalists.

In this connection and in accordance with the International Covenant on Civil and Political Rights, the Universal Declaration of Human Rights and their relevant international commitments concerning seeking, receiving and imparting information of all kinds, they will ensure that individuals can freely choose their sources of information. In this context they will:

– ensure that radio services operating in accordance with the ITU Radio Regulations can be directly and normally received in their States; and
– allow individuals, institutions and organizations, while respecting intellectual property rights, including copyright, to obtain, possess, reproduce and distribute information material of all kinds.

To these ends they will remove any restrictions inconsistent with the above-mentioned obligations and commitments.

35. They will take every opportunity offered by modern means of communication, including cable and satellites, to increase the freer and wider dissemination of information of all kinds. They will also encourage co-operation and exchanges between their relevant institutions, organizations and technical experts, and work towards the harmonization of technical standards and norms. They will bear in mind the effects of these modern means of communication on their mass media.

36. They will ensure in practice that official information bulletins can be freely distributed on their territory by the diplomatic and other official missions and consular posts of the other participating States.

37. They will encourage radio and television organizations, on the basis of arrangements between them, to broadcast live, especially in the organizing countries, programmes and discussions with participants from different States and to broadcast statements of and interviews with political and other personalities from the participating States.

38. They will encourage radio and television organizations to report on different aspects of life in other participating States and to increase the number of telebridges between their countries.

39. Recalling that the legitimate pursuit of journalists' professional activity will neither render them liable to expulsion nor otherwise penalize them, they will refrain from taking restrictive measures such as withdrawing a journalist's accreditation or expelling him because of the content of the reporting of the journalist or of his information media.

40. They will ensure that, in pursuing this activity, journalists, including those representing media from other participating States, are free to seek access to and maintain contacts with public and private sources of information and that their need for professional confidentiality is respected.

41. They will respect the copyright of journalists.

42. On the basis of arrangements between them, where necessary, and for the purpose of regular reporting, they will grant accreditation, where it is required, and multiple entry visas to journalists from other participating States, regardless of their domicile. On this basis they will reduce to a maximum of two months the period for issuing both accreditation and multiple entry visas to journalists.

43. They will facilitate the work of foreign journalists by providing relevant information, on request, on matters of practical concern, such as import regulations, taxation and accommodation.

44. They will ensure that official press conferences and, as appropriate, other similar official press events are also open to foreign journalists, upon accreditation, where this is required.

45. They will ensure in practice that persons belonging to national minorities or regional cultures on their territories can disseminate, have access to and exchange information in their mother tongue.

46. They agree to convene an Information Forum to discuss improvement of the circulation of, access to and exchange of information, co-operation in the field of information and the improvement of working conditions for journalists.

(...)

Human dimension of the CSCE

The participating States,

Recalling the undertaking entered into in the Final Act and in other CSCE documents concerning respect for all human rights and fundamental freedoms, human contacts and other issues of a related humanitarian character;

Recognizing the need to improve the implementation of their CSCE commitments and their co-operation in these areas which are hereafter referred to as the "human dimension of the CSCE",

Have, on the basis of the principles and provisions of the Final Act and of other relevant CSCE documents, decided:

1. to exchange information and respond to requests for information and to representations made to them by other participating States on questions relating to the human dimension of the CSCE. Such communications may be forwarded through diplomatic channels or be addressed to any agency designated for these purposes;

2. to hold bilateral meetings with other participating States that so request, in order to examine questions relating to the human dimension of the CSCE, including situations and specific cases, with a view to resolving them. The date and place of such meetings will be arranged by mutual agreement through diplomatic channels;

3. that any participating State which deems it necessary may bring situations and cases in the human dimension of the CSCE, including those which have been raised at the bilateral meetings described in paragraph 2, to the attention of other participating States through diplomatic channels;

4. that any participating State which deems it necessary may provide data on the exchanges of information and the responses to its requests for information and to representations (paragraph 1) and on the results of the bilateral meetings (paragraph 2), including information concerning situations and specific cases, at the meetings of the Conference on the Human Dimension as well as at the main CSCE follow-up meetings.

The participating States decide further to convene a Conference on the Human Dimension of the CSCE in order to achieve further progress concerning respect for all human rights and fundamental freedoms, human contacts and other issues of a related humanitarian character. The

Conference will hold three meetings before the next CSCE follow-up meeting.

The Conference will:

– review developments in the human dimension of the CSCE, including the implementation of the relevant CSCE commitments;
– evaluate the functioning of the procedures described in paragraphs 1 to 4 and discuss the information provided according to paragraph 4;
– consider practical proposals for new measures aimed at improving the implementation of the commitments relating to the human dimension of the CSCE and enhancing the effectiveness of the procedures described in paragraphs 1 to 4.

On the basis of these proposals, the Conference will consider adopting new measures.

3. **Document of the Copenhagen Meeting of the Conference on the Human Dimension of the CSCE**

Copenhagen, 29 June 1990

The representatives of the participating States of the Conference on Security and Co-operation in Europe (CSCE), Austria, Belgium, Bulgaria, Canada, Cyprus, Czechoslovakia, Denmark, Finland, France, the German Democratic Republic, the Federal Republic of Germany, Greece, the Holy See, Hungary, Iceland, Ireland, Italy, Liechtenstein, Luxembourg, Malta, Monaco, the Netherlands, Norway, Poland, Portugal, Romania, San Marino, Spain, Sweden, Switzerland, Turkey, the Union of Soviet Socialist Republics, the United Kingdom, the United States of America and Yugoslavia, met in Copenhagen from 5 to 29 June 1990, in accordance with the provisions relating to the Conference on the Human Dimension of the CSCE contained in the Concluding Document of the Vienna Follow-up Meeting of the CSCE.

The representative of Albania attended the Copenhagen Meeting as observer.

The first Meeting of the Conference was held in Paris from 30 May to 23 June 1989.

The Copenhagen Meeting was opened and closed by the Minister for Foreign Affairs of Denmark.

The formal opening of the Copenhagen Meeting was attended by Her Majesty the Queen of Denmark and His Royal Highness the Prince Consort.

Opening statements were made by Ministers and Deputy Ministers of the participating States.

At a special meeting of the Ministers for Foreign Affairs of the participating States of the CSCE on 5 June 1990, convened on the invitation of the Minister for Foreign Affairs of Denmark, it was agreed to convene a preparatory committee in Vienna on 10 July 1990 to prepare a summit meeting in Paris of their Heads of State or Government.

The participating States welcome with great satisfaction the fundamental political changes that have occurred in Europe since the first Meeting of the Conference on the Human Dimension of the CSCE in Paris in 1989. They note that the CSCE process has contributed significantly to bringing about these changes and that these developments in turn have greatly advanced the implementation of the provisions of the Final Act and of the other CSCE documents.

They recognize that pluralistic democracy and the rule of law are essential for ensuring respect for all human rights and fundamental freedoms, the development of human contacts and the resolution of other issues of a related humanitarian character. They therefore welcome the commitment expressed by all participating States to the ideals of democracy and political pluralism as well as their common determination to build democratic societies based on free elections and the rule of law.

At the Copenhagen Meeting the participating States held a review of the implementation of their commitments in the field of the human dimension. They considered that the degree of compliance with the commitments contained in the relevant provisions of the CSCE documents had shown a fundamental improvement since the Paris Meeting. They also expressed the view, however, that further steps are required for the full realization of their commitments relating to the human dimension.

The participating States express their conviction that full respect for human rights and fundamental freedoms and the development of societies based on pluralistic democracy and the rule of law are prerequisites for progress in setting up the lasting order of peace, security, justice and co-operation that they seek to establish in Europe. They therefore reaffirm their commitment to implement fully all provisions of the Final Act and of the other CSCE documents relating to the human dimension and undertake to build on the progress they have made.

They recognize that co-operation among themselves, as well as the active involvement of persons, groups, organizations and institutions, will be essential to ensure continuing progress towards their shared objectives.

In order to strengthen respect for and enjoyment of human rights and fundamental freedoms, to develop human contacts and to resolve issues of a related humanitarian character, the participating States agree on the following:

I.

1. The participating States express their conviction that the protection and promotion of human rights and fundamental freedoms is one of the basic purposes of government, and reaffirm that the recognition of these rights and freedoms constitutes the foundation of freedom, justice and peace.

2. They are determined to support and advance those principles of justice which form the basis of the rule of law. They consider that the rule of law does not mean merely a formal legality which assures regularity and consistency in the achievement and enforcement of democratic order, but justice based on the recognition and full acceptance of the supreme value of the human personality and guaranteed by institutions providing a framework for its fullest expression.

3. They reaffirm that democracy is an inherent element of the rule of law. They recognize the importance of pluralism with regard to political organizations.

4. They confirm that they will respect each other's right freely to choose and develop, in accordance with international human rights standards, their political, social, economic and cultural systems. In exercising this right, they will ensure that their laws, regulations, practices and policies conform with their obligations under international law and are brought into harmony with the provisions of the Declaration on Principles and other CSCE commitments.

5. They solemnly declare that among those elements of justice which are essential to the full expression of the inherent dignity and of the equal and inalienable rights of all human beings are the following:

5.1. free elections that will be held at reasonable intervals by secret ballot or by equivalent free voting procedure, under conditions which ensure in practice the free expression of the opinion of the electors in the choice of their representatives;

5.2. a form of government that is representative in character, in which the executive is accountable to the elected legislature or the electorate;

5.3. the duty of the government and public authorities to comply with the constitution and to act in a manner consistent with law;

5.4. a clear separation between the State and political parties; in particular, political parties will not be merged with the State;

5.5. the activity of the government and the administration, as well as that of the judiciary, will be exercised in accordance with the system established by law. Respect for that system must be ensured;

5.6. military forces and the police will be under the control of and accountable to the civil authorities;

5.7. human rights and fundamental freedoms will be guaranteed by law and in accordance with their obligations under international law;

5.8. legislation, adopted at the end of a public procedure, and regulations will be published, that being the condition for their applicability. Those texts will be accessible to everyone;

5.9. all persons are equal before the law and are entitled without any discrimination to the equal protection of the law. In this respect, the law will prohibit any discrimination and guarantee to all persons equal and effective protection against discrimination on any ground;

5.10. everyone will have an effective means of redress against administrative decisions, so as to guarantee respect for fundamental rights and ensure legal integrity;

5.11. administrative decisions against a person must be fully justifiable and must as a rule indicate the usual remedies available;

5.12. the independence of judges and the impartial operation of the public judicial service will be ensured;

5.13. the independence of legal practitioners will be recognized and protected, in particular as regards conditions for recruitment and practice;

5.14. the rules relating to criminal procedure will contain a clear definition of powers in relation to prosecution and the measures preceding and accompanying prosecution;

5.15. any person arrested or detained on a criminal charge will have the right, so that the lawfulness of his arrest or detention can be decided, to be brought promptly before a judge or other officer authorized by law to exercise this function;

5.16. in the determination of any criminal charge against him, or of his rights and obligations in a suit at law, everyone will be entitled to a fair and public hearing by a competent, independent and impartial tribunal established by law;

5.17. any person prosecuted will have the right to defend himself in person or through prompt legal assistance of his own choosing or, if he does not have sufficient means to pay for legal assistance, to be given it free when the interests of justice so require;

5.18. no one will be charged with, tried for or convicted of any criminal offence unless the offence is provided for by a law which defines the elements of the offence with clarity and precision;

5.19. everyone will be presumed innocent until proved guilty according to law;

5.20. considering the important contribution of international instruments in the field of human rights to the rule of law at a national level, the participating States reaffirm that they will consider acceding to the International Covenant on Civil and Political Rights, the International Covenant on Economic, Social and Cultural Rights and other relevant international instruments, if they have not yet done so;

5.21. in order to supplement domestic remedies and better to ensure that the participating States respect the international obligations they have undertaken, the participating States will consider acceding to a regional or global international convention concerning the protection of human rights, such as the European Convention on Human Rights or the Optional Protocol to the International Covenant on Civil and Political Rights, which provide for procedures of individual recourse to international bodies.

6. The participating States declare that the will of the people, freely and fairly expressed through periodic and genuine elections, is the basis of the authority and legitimacy of all government. The participating States will accordingly respect the right of their citizens to take part in the governing of their country, either directly or through representatives freely chosen by them through fair electoral processes. They recognize their responsibility to defend and protect, in accordance with their laws, their international human rights obligations and their international commitments, the democratic order freely established through the will of the people against the activities of persons, groups or organizations that engage in or refuse to renounce terrorism or violence aimed at the overthrow of that order or of that of another participating State.

7. To ensure that the will of the people serves as the basis of the authority of government, the participating States will:

7.1. hold free elections at reasonable intervals, as established by law;

7.2. permit all seats in at least one chamber of the national legislature to be freely contested in a popular vote;

7.3. guarantee universal and equal suffrage to adult citizens;

7.4. ensure that votes are cast by secret ballot or by equivalent free voting procedure, and that they are counted and reported honestly with the official results made public;

7.5. respect the right of citizens to seek political or public office, individually or as representatives of political parties or organizations, without discrimination;

7.6. respect the right of individuals and groups to establish, in full freedom, their own political parties or other political organizations and provide such political parties and organizations with the necessary legal guarantees to enable them to compete with each other on a basis of equal treatment before the law and by the authorities;

7.7. ensure that law and public policy work to permit political campaigning to be conducted in a fair and free atmosphere in which neither administrative action, violence nor intimidation bars the parties and the candidates from freely presenting their views and qualifications, or prevents the voters from learning and discussing them or from casting their vote free of fear of retribution;

7.8. provide that no legal or administrative obstacle stands in the way of unimpeded access to the media on a non-discriminatory basis for all political groupings and individuals wishing to participate in the electoral process;

7.9. ensure that candidates who obtain the necessary number of votes required by law are duly installed in office and are permitted to remain in office until their term expires or is otherwise brought to an end in a manner that is regulated by law in conformity with democratic parliamentary and constitutional procedures.

8. The participating States consider that the presence of observers, both foreign and domestic, can enhance the electoral process for States in which elections are taking place. They therefore invite observers from any other CSCE participating States and any appropriate private institutions and organizations who may wish to do so to observe the course of their national election proceedings, to the extent permitted by law. They will also endeavour to facilitate similar access for election proceedings held below the national level. Such observers will undertake not to interfere in the electoral proceedings.

II.

9. The participating States reaffirm that:

9.1. everyone will have the right to freedom of expression including the right to communication. This right will include freedom to hold opinions and to receive and impart information and ideas without interference by public authority and regardless of frontiers. The exercise of this right may be subject only to such restrictions as are prescribed by law and are consistent with international standards. In particular, no limitation will be imposed on access to, and use of means of reproducing documents of any kind, while respecting, however, rights relating to intellectual property, including copyright;

9.2. everyone will have the right of peaceful assembly and demonstration. Any restrictions which may be placed on the exercise of these rights will be prescribed by law and consistent with international standards;

9.3. the right of association will be guaranteed. The right to form and – subject to the general right of a trade union to determine its own membership – freely to join a trade union will be guaranteed. These rights will exclude any prior control. Freedom of association for workers, including the right to strike, will be guaranteed, subject to limitations prescribed by law and consistent with international standards;

9.4. everyone will have the right to freedom of thought, conscience and religion. This right includes freedom to change one's religion or belief and freedom to manifest one's religion or belief, either alone or in community with others, in public or in private, through worship, teaching, practice and observance. The exercise of these rights may be subject only to such restrictions as are prescribed by law and are consistent with international standards;

9.5. they will respect the right of everyone to leave any country, including his own, and to return to his country, consistent with a State's international obligations and CSCE commitments. Restrictions on this right will have the character of very rare exceptions, will be considered necessary only if they respond to a specific public need, pursue a legitimate aim and are proportionate to that aim, and will not be abused or applied in an arbitrary manner;

9.6. everyone has the right peacefully to enjoy his property either on his own or in common with others. No one may be deprived of his property except in the public interest and subject to the conditions provided for by law and consistent with international commitments and obligations.

10. In reaffirming their commitment to ensure effectively the rights of the individual to know and act upon human rights and fundamental freedoms, and to contribute actively, individually or in association with others, to their promotion and protection, the participating States express their commitment to:

10.1. respect the right of everyone, individually or in association with others, to seek, receive and impart freely views and information on human rights and fundamental freedoms, including the rights to disseminate and publish such views and information;

10.2. respect the rights of everyone, individually or in association with others, to study and discuss the observance of human rights and fundamental freedoms and to develop and discuss ideas for improved protection of human rights and better means for ensuring compliance with international human rights standards;

10.3. ensure that individuals are permitted to exercise the right to association, including the right to form, join and participate effectively in non-governmental organizations which seek the promotion and protection of human rights and fundamental freedoms, including trade unions and human rights monitoring groups;

10.4. allow members of such groups and organizations to have unhindered access to and communication with similar bodies within and outside their countries and with international organizations, to engage in exchanges, contacts and co-operation with such groups and organizations and to solicit, receive and utilize for the purpose of promoting and protecting human rights and fundamental freedoms voluntary financial contributions from national and international sources as provided for by law.

11. The participating States further affirm that, where violations of human rights and fundamental freedoms are alleged to have occurred, the effective remedies available include:

11.1. the right of the individual to seek and receive adequate legal assistance;

11.2. the right of the individual to seek and receive assistance from others in defending human rights and fundamental freedoms, and to assist others in defending human rights and fundamental freedoms;

11.3. the right of individuals or groups acting on their behalf to communicate with international bodies with competence to receive and consider information concerning allegations of human rights abuses.

12. The participating States, wishing to ensure greater transparency in the implementation of the commitments undertaken in the Vienna Concluding Document under the heading of the human dimension of the CSCE, decide to accept as a confidence-building measure the presence of observers sent by participating States and representatives of non-governmental organizations and other interested persons at proceedings before courts as provided for in national legislation and international law;

it is understood that proceedings may only be held in camera in the circumstances prescribed by law and consistent with obligations under international law and international commitments.

13. The participating States decide to accord particular attention to the recognition of the rights of the child, his civil rights and his individual freedoms, his economic, social and cultural rights, and his right to special protection against all forms of violence and exploitation. They will consider acceding to the Convention on the Rights of the Child, if they have not yet done so, which was opened for signature by States on 26 January 1990. They will recognize in their domestic legislation the rights of the child as affirmed in the international agreements to which they are parties.

14. The participating States agree to encourage the creation, within their countries, of conditions for the training of students and trainees from other participating States, including persons taking vocational and technical courses. They also agree to promote travel by young people from their countries for the purpose of obtaining education in other participating States and to that end to encourage the conclusion, where appropriate, of bilateral and multilateral agreements between their relevant governmental institutions, organizations and educational establishments.

15. The participating States will act in such a way as to facilitate the transfer of sentenced persons and encourage those participating States which are not Parties to the Convention on the Transfer of Sentenced Persons, signed at Strasbourg on 21 November 1983, to consider acceding to the convention.

16. The participating States:

16.1. reaffirm their commitment to prohibit torture and other cruel, inhuman or degrading treatment or punishment, to take effective legislative, administrative, judicial and other measures to prevent and punish such practices, to protect individuals from any psychiatric or other medical practices that violate human rights and fundamental freedoms and to take effective measures to prevent and punish such practices;

16.2. intend, as a matter of urgency, to consider acceding to the Convention against Torture and Other Cruel, Inhuman or Degrading Treatment or Punishment, if they have not yet done so, and recognizing the competences of the Committee against Torture under Articles 21 and 22 of the convention and withdrawing reservations regarding the competence of the committee under Article 20;

16.3. stress that no exceptional circumstances whatsoever, whether a state of war or a threat of war, internal political instability or any other public emergency, may be invoked as a justification of torture;

16.4. will ensure that education and information regarding the prohibition against torture are fully included in the training of law enforcement personnel, civil or military, medical personnel, public officials and other persons who may be involved in the custody, interrogation or treatment of any individual subjected to any form of arrest, detention or imprisonment;

16.5. will keep under systematic review interrogation rules, instructions, methods and practices as well as arrangements for the custody and treatment of persons subjected to any form of arrest, detention or imprisonment in any territory under their jurisdiction, with a view to preventing any cases of torture;

16.6. will take up with priority for consideration and for appropriate action, in accordance with the agreed measures and procedures for the effective implementation of the commitments relating to the human dimension of the CSCE, any cases of torture and other inhuman or degrading treatment or punishment made known to them through official channels or coming from any other reliable source of information;

16.7. will act upon the understanding that preserving and guaranteeing the life and security of any individual subjected to any form of torture and other inhuman or degrading treatment or punishment will be the sole criterion in determining the urgency and priorities to be accorded in taking appropriate remedial action; and, therefore, the consideration of any cases of torture and other inhuman or degrading treatment or punishment within the framework of any other international body or mechanism may not be invoked as a reason for refraining from consideration and appropriate action in accordance with the agreed measures and procedures for the effective implementation of the commitments relating to the human dimension of the CSCE.

17. The participating States:

17.1. recall the commitment undertaken in the Vienna Concluding Document to keep the question of capital punishment under consideration and to co-operate within relevant international organizations;

17.2. recall, in this context, the adoption by the General Assembly of the United Nations, on 15 December 1989, of the Second Optional Protocol to the International Covenant on Civil and Political Rights, aiming at the abolition of the death penalty;

17.3. note the restrictions and safeguards regarding the use of the death penalty which have been adopted by the international community, in particular Article 6 of the International Covenant on Civil and Political Rights;

17.4. note the provisions of the Sixth Protocol to the European Convention for the Protection of Human Rights and Fundamental Freedoms, concerning the abolition of the death penalty;

17.5. note recent measures taken by a number of participating States towards the abolition of capital punishment;

17.6. note the activities of several non-governmental organizations on the question of the death penalty;

17.7. will exchange information within the framework of the Conference on the Human Dimension on the question of the abolition of the death penalty and keep that question under consideration;

17.8. will make available to the public information regarding the use of the death penalty.

18. The participating States:

18.1. note that the United Nations Commission on Human Rights has recognized the right of everyone to have conscientious objections to military service;

18.2. note recent measures taken by a number of participating States to permit exemption from compulsory military service on the basis of conscientious objections;

18.3. note the activities of several non-governmental organizations on the question of conscientious objections to compulsory military service;

18.4. agree to consider introducing, where this has not yet been done, various forms of alternative service, which are compatible with the reasons for conscientious objection, such forms of alternative service being in principle of a non-combatant or civilian nature, in the public interest and of a non-punitive nature;

18.5. will make available to the public information on this issue;

18.6. will keep under consideration, within the framework of the Conference on the Human Dimension, the relevant questions related to the exemption from compulsory military service, where it exists, of individuals on the basis of conscientious objections to armed service, and will exchange information on these questions.

19. The participating States affirm that freer movement and contacts among their citizens are important in the context of the protection and

promotion of human rights and fundamental freedoms. They will ensure that their policies concerning entry into their territories are fully consistent with the aims set out in the relevant provisions of the Final Act, the Madrid Concluding Document and the Vienna Concluding Document. While reaffirming their determination not to recede from the commitments contained in CSCE documents, they undertake to implement fully and improve present commitments in the field of human contacts, including on a bilateral and multilateral basis. In this context they will:

19.1. strive to implement the procedures for entry into their territories, including the issuing of visas and passport and customs control, in good faith and without unjustified delay. Where necessary, they will shorten the waiting time for visa decisions, as well as simplify practices and reduce administrative requirements for visa applications;

19.2. ensure, in dealing with visa applications, that these are processed as expeditiously as possible in order, *inter alia*, to take due account of important family, personal or professional considerations, especially in cases of an urgent, humanitarian nature;

19.3. endeavour, where necessary, to reduce fees charged in connection with visa applications to the lowest possible level.

20. The participating States concerned will consult and, where appropriate, co-operate in dealing with problems that might emerge as a result of the increased movement of persons.

21. The participating States recommend the consideration, at the next CSCE follow-up meeting in Helsinki, of the advisability of holding a meeting of experts on consular matters.

22. The participating States reaffirm that the protection and promotion of the rights of migrant workers have their human dimension. In this context, they:

22.1. agree that the protection and promotion of the rights of migrant workers are the concern of all participating States and that as such they should be addressed within the CSCE process;

22.2. reaffirm their commitment to implement fully in their domestic legislation the rights of migrant workers provided for in international agreements to which they are parties;

22.3. consider that, in future international instruments concerning the rights of migrant workers, they should take into account the fact that this issue is of importance for all of them;

22.4. express their readiness to examine, at future CSCE meetings, the relevant aspects of the further promotion of the rights of migrant workers and their families.

23. The participating States reaffirm their conviction expressed in the Vienna Concluding Document that the promotion of economic, social and cultural rights as well as of civil and political rights is of paramount importance for human dignity and for the attainment of the legitimate aspirations of every individual. They also reaffirm their commitment taken in the Document of the Bonn Conference on Economic Co-operation in Europe to the promotion of social justice and the improvement of living and working conditions. In the context of continuing their efforts with a view to achieving progressively the full realization of economic, social and cultural rights by all appropriate means, they will pay special attention to problems in the areas of employment, housing, social security, health, education and culture.

24. The participating States will ensure that the exercise of all the human rights and fundamental freedoms set out above will not be subject to any restrictions except those which are provided by law and are consistent with their obligations under international law, in particular the International Covenant on Civil and Political Rights, and with their international commitments, in particular the Universal Declaration of Human Rights. These restrictions have the character of exceptions. The participating States will ensure that these restrictions are not abused and are

not applied in an arbitrary manner, but in such a way that the effective exercise of these rights is ensured.

Any restriction on rights and freedoms must, in a democratic society, relate to one of the objectives of the applicable law and be strictly proportionate to the aim of that law.

25. The participating States confirm that any derogations from obligations relating to human rights and fundamental freedoms during a state of public emergency must remain strictly within the limits provided for by international law, in particular the relevant international instruments by which they are bound, especially with respect to rights from which there can be no derogation. They also reaffirm that:

25.1. measures derogating from such obligations must be taken in strict conformity with the procedural requirements laid down in those instruments;

25.2. the imposition of a state of public emergency must be proclaimed officially, publicly and in accordance with the provisions laid down by the law;

25.3. measures derogating from obligations will be limited to the extent strictly required by the exigencies of the situation;

25.4. such measures will not discriminate solely on the grounds of race, colour, sex, language, religion, social origin or of belonging to a minority.

III.

26. The participating States recognize that vigorous democracy depends on the existence as an integral part of national life of democratic values and practices as well as an extensive range of democratic institutions. They will therefore encourage, facilitate and, where appropriate, support practical co-operative endeavours and the sharing of information, ideas and expertise among themselves and by direct contacts and co-operation

between individuals, groups and organizations in areas including the following:

– constitutional law, reform and development;
– electoral legislation, administration and observations;
– establishment and management of courts and legal systems;
– the development of an impartial and effective public service where recruitment and advancement are based on a merit system;
– law enforcement;
– local government and decentralisation;
– access to information and protection of privacy;
– developing political parties and their role in pluralistic societies;
– free and independent trade unions;
– co-operative movements;
– developing other forms of free associations and public interest groups;
– journalism, independent media, and intellectual and cultural life;
– the teaching of democratic values, institutions and practices in educational institutions and the fostering of an atmosphere of free enquiry.

Such endeavours may cover the range of co-operation encompassed in the human dimension of the CSCE, including training, exchange of information, books and instructional materials, co-operative programmes and projects, academic and professional exchanges and conferences, scholarships, research grants, provisions of expertise and advice, business and scientific contacts and programmes.

27. The participating States will also facilitate the establishment and strengthening of independent national institutions in the area of human rights and the rule of law, which may also serve as focal points for co-ordination and collaboration between such institutions in the participating States. They propose that co-operation be encouraged between parliamentarians from participating States, including through existing interparliamentary associations and, *inter alia*, through joint commissions, television debates involving parliamentarians, meetings and round-table discussions. They will also encourage existing institutions, such as organizations within the United Nations system and the Council of Europe, to continue and expand the work they have begun in this area.

28. The participating States recognize the important expertise of the Council of Europe in the field of human rights and fundamental freedoms and agree to consider further ways and means to enable the Council of Europe to make a contribution to the human dimension of the CSCE. They agree that the nature of this contribution could be examined further in a future CSCE forum.

29. The participating States will consider the idea of convening a meeting or seminar of experts to review and discuss co-operative measures designed to promote and sustain viable democratic institutions in participating States, including comparative studies of legislation in participating States in the area of human rights and fundamental freedoms, *inter alia* drawing upon the experience acquired in this area by the Council of Europe and the activities of the Commission "Democracy through law".

IV.

30. The participating States recognize that the questions relating to national minorities can only be satisfactorily resolved in a democratic political framework based on the rule of law, with a functioning independent judiciary. This framework guarantees full respect for human rights and fundamental freedoms, equal rights and status for all citizens, the free expression of all their legitimate interests and aspirations, the implementation of legal rules that place effective restraints on the abuse of governmental power, political pluralism and social intolerance.

They also recognize the important role of non-governmental organizations, including political parties, trade unions, human rights organizations and religious groups, in the promotion of tolerance, cultural diversity and the resolution of questions relating to national minorities.

They further reaffirm that respect for the rights of persons belonging to national minorities as part of universally recognized human rights is an essential factor for peace, justice, stability and democracy in the participating States.

31. Persons belonging to national minorities have the right to exercise fully and effectively their human rights and fundamental freedoms without any discrimination and in full equality before the law.

The participating States will adopt, where necessary, special measures for the purpose of ensuring to persons belonging to national minorities full equality with the other citizens in the exercise and enjoyment of human rights and fundamental freedoms.

32. To belong to a national minority is a matter of a person's individual choice and no disadvantage may arise from the exercise of such choice.

Persons belonging to national minorities have the right freely to express, preserve and develop their ethnic, cultural, linguistic or religious identity and to maintain and develop their culture in all its aspects, free of any attempts at assimilation against their will. In particular, they have the right:

32.1. to use freely their mother tongue in private as well as in public;

32.2. to establish and maintain their own educational, cultural and religious institutions, organizations or associations, which can seek voluntary financial and other contributions as well as public assistance, in conformity with national legislation;

32.3. to profess and practise their religion, including the acquisition, possession and use of religious materials, and to conduct religious educational activities in their mother tongue;

32.4. to establish and maintain unimpeded contacts among themselves within their country as well as contacts across frontiers with citizens of other States with whom they share a common ethnic or national origin, cultural heritage or religious beliefs;

32.5. to disseminate, have access to and exchange information in their mother tongue;

32.6. to establish and maintain organizations or associations within their country and to participate in international non-governmental organizations.

Persons belonging to national minorities can exercise and enjoy their rights individually as well as in community with other members of their group. No disadvantage may arise for a person belonging to a national minority on account of the exercise or non-exercise of any such rights.

33. The participating States will protect the ethnic, cultural, linguistic and religious identity of national minorities on their territory and create conditions for the promotion of that identity. They will take the necessary measures to that effect after due consultations, including contacts with organizations or associations of such minorities, in accordance with the decision-making procedures of each State.

Any such measures will be in conformity with the principles of equality and non-discrimination with respect to the other citizens of the participating State concerned.

34. The participating States will endeavour to ensure that persons belonging to national minorities, notwithstanding the need to learn the official language or languages of the State concerned, have adequate opportunities for instruction of their mother tongue or in their mother tongue, as well as, wherever possible and necessary, for its use before public authorities, in conformity with applicable national legislation.

In the context of the teaching of history and culture in educational establishments, they will also take account of the history and culture of national minorities.

35. The participating States will respect the right of persons belonging to national minorities to effective participation in public affairs, including participation in the affairs relating to the protection and promotion of the identity of such minorities.

The participating States note the efforts undertaken to protect and create conditions for the promotion of the ethnic, cultural, linguistic and religious identity of certain national minorities by establishing, as one of the possible means to achieve these aims, appropriate local or autonomous administrations corresponding to the specific historical and territorial circumstances of such minorities and in accordance with the policies of the State concerned.

36. The participating States recognize the particular importance of increasing constructive co-operation among themselves on questions relating to national minorities. Such co-operation seeks to promote mutual understanding and confidence, friendly and good-neighbourly relations, international peace, security and justice.

Every participating State will promote a climate of mutual respect, understanding, co-operation and solidarity among all persons living on its territory, without distinction as to ethnic or national origin or religion, and will encourage the solution of problems through dialogue based on the principles of the rule of law.

37. None of these commitments may be interpreted as implying any right to engage in any activity or perform any action in contravention of the purposes and principles of the Charter of the United Nations, other obligations under international law or the provisions of the Final Act, including the principle of territorial integrity of States.

38. The participating States, in their efforts to protect and promote the rights of persons belonging to national minorities, will fully respect their undertakings under existing human rights conventions and other relevant international instruments and consider adhering to the relevant conventions, if they have not yet done so, including those providing for a right of complaint by individuals.

39. The participating States will co-operate closely in the competent international organizations to which they belong, including the United Nations and, as appropriate, the Council of Europe, bearing in mind

their ongoing work with respect to questions relating to national minorities.

They will consider convening a meeting of experts for a thorough discussion of the issue of national minorities.

40. The participating States clearly and unequivocally condemn totalitarianism, racial and ethnic hatred, anti-Semitism, xenophobia and discrimination against anyone, as well as persecution on religious and ideological grounds. In this context, they also recognize the particular problems of Roma (Gypsies).

They declare their firm intention to intensify the efforts to combat these phenomena in all their forms and therefore will:

40.1. take effective measures, including the adoption, in conformity with their constitutional systems and their international obligations, of such laws as may be necessary, to provide protection against any acts that constitute incitement to violence against persons or groups based on national, racial, ethnic or religious discrimination, hostility or hatred, including anti-Semitism;

40.2. commit themselves to take appropriate and proportionate measures to protect persons or groups who may be subject to threats or acts of discrimination, hostility or violence as a result of their racial, ethnic, cultural, linguistic and religious identity, and to protect their property;

40.3. take effective measures, in conformity with their constitutional systems, at the national, regional and local levels to promote understanding and tolerance, particularly in the fields of education, culture and information;

40.4. endeavour to ensure that the objectives of education include special attention to the problem of racial prejudice and hatred and to the development of respect for different civilizations and cultures;

40.5. recognize the right of the individual to effective remedies and endeavour to recognize, in conformity with national legislation, the right of interested persons and groups to initiate and support complaints against acts of discrimination, including racist and xenophobic acts;

40.6. consider adhering, if they have not yet done so, to the international instruments which address the problem of discrimination and ensure full compliance with the obligations therein, including those relating to the submission of periodic reports;

40.7. consider, also, accepting those international mechanisms which allow States and individuals to bring communications relating to discrimination before international bodies.

V.

41. The participating States reaffirm their commitment to the human dimension of the CSCE and emphasize its importance as an integral part of a balanced approach to security and co-operation in Europe. They agree that the Conference on the Human Dimension of the CSCE and the human dimension mechanism described in the section on the human dimension of the CSCE of the Vienna Concluding Document have demonstrated their value as methods of furthering their dialogue and co-operation and assisting in the resolution of relevant specific questions. They express their conviction that these should be continued and developed as part of an expanding CSCE process.

42. The participating States recognize the need to enhance further the effectiveness of the procedures described in paragraphs 1 to 4 of the section on the human dimension of the CSCE of the Vienna Concluding Document and with this aim decide:

42.1. to provide in as short a time as possible, but no later than four weeks, a written response to requests for information and to representations made to them in writing by other participating States under paragraph 1;

42.2. that the bilateral meetings, as contained in paragraph 2, will take place as soon as possible, as a rule within three weeks of the date of the request;

42.3. to refrain, in the course of a bilateral meeting held under paragraph 2, from raising situations and cases not connected with the subject of the meeting, unless both sides have agreed to do so.

43. The participating States examined practical proposals for new measures aimed at improving the implementation of the commitments relating to the human dimension of the CSCE. In this regard, they considered proposals related to the sending of observers to examine situations and specific cases, the appointment of rapporteurs to investigate and suggest appropriate solutions, the setting up of a Committee on the Human Dimension of the CSCE, greater involvement of persons, organizations and institutions in the human dimension mechanism and further bilateral and multilateral efforts to promote the resolution of relevant issues.

They decide to continue to discuss thoroughly in subsequent relevant CSCE fora these and other proposals designed to strengthen the human dimension mechanism, and to consider adopting, in the context of the further development of the CSCE process, appropriate new measures. They agree that these measures should contribute to achieving further effective progress, enhance conflict prevention and confidence in the field of the human dimension of the CSCE.

44. The representatives of the participating States express their profound gratitude to the people and Government of Denmark for the excellent organization of the Copenhagen Meeting and the warm hospitality extended to the delegations which participated in the meeting.

45. In accordance with the provisions relating to the Conference on the Human Dimension of the CSCE contained in the Concluding Document of the Vienna Follow-up Meeting of the CSCE, the third Meeting of the Conference will take place in Moscow from 10 September to 4 October 1991.

4. Charter of Paris for a New Europe

Paris, 21 November 1990

A new era of democracy, peace and unity

We, the Heads of State or Government of the States participating in the Conference on Security and Co-operation in Europe, have assembled in Paris at a time of profound change and historic expectations. The era of confrontation and division of Europe has ended. We declare that henceforth our relations will be founded on respect and co-operation.

Europe is liberating itself from the legacy of the past. The courage of men and women, the strength of the will of the peoples and the power of the ideas of the Helsinki Final Act have opened a new era of democracy, peace and unity in Europe.

Ours is a time for fulfilling the hopes and expectations our peoples have cherished for decades: steadfast commitment to democracy based on human rights and fundamental freedoms; prosperity through economic liberty and social justice; and equal security for all our countries.

The Ten Principles of the Final Act will guide us towards this ambitious future, just as they have lighted our way towards better relations for the past fifteen years. Full implementation of all CSCE commitments must form the basis for the initiatives we are now taking to enable our nations to live in accordance with their aspirations.

Human rights, democracy and rule of law

We undertake to build, consolidate and strengthen democracy as the only system of government of our nations. In this endeavour, we will abide by the following:

Human rights and fundamental freedoms are the birthright of all human beings, are inalienable and are guaranteed by law. Their protection and promotion is the first responsibility of government. Respect for them is an essential safeguard against an over-mighty State. Their observance and full exercise are the foundation of freedom, justice and peace.

Democratic government is based on the will of the people, expressed regularly through free and fair elections. Democracy has as its foundation respect for the human person and the rule of law. Democracy is the best safeguard of freedom of expression, tolerance of all groups of society and equality of opportunity for each person.

Democracy, with its representative and pluralist character, entails accountability to the electorate, the obligation of public authorities to comply with the law and justice administered impartially. No one will be above the law.

We affirm that, without discrimination, every individual has the right to:

freedom of thought, conscience and religion or belief, freedom of expression, freedom of association and peaceful assembly, freedom of movement;

no one will be:

subject to arbitrary arrest or detention, subject to torture or other cruel, inhuman or degrading treatment or punishment;

everyone also has the right:

to know and act upon his rights, to participate in free and fair elections, to a fair and public trial if charged with an offence, to own property alone or in association and to exercise individual enterprise, to enjoy his economic, social and cultural rights.

We affirm that the ethnic, cultural, linguistic and religious identity of national minorities will be protected and that persons belonging to national minorities have the right freely to express, preserve and develop that identity without any discrimination and in full equality before the law.

We will ensure that everyone will enjoy recourse to effective remedies, national or international, against any violation of his rights.

Full respect for these precepts is the bedrock on which we will seek to construct the new Europe.

Our States will co-operate and support each other with the aim of making democratic gains irreversible.

Economic liberty and responsibility

Economic liberty, social justice and environmental responsibility are indispensable for prosperity.

The free will of the individual, excercised in democracy and protected by the rule of law, forms the necessary basis for successful economic and social development. We will promote economic activity which respects and upholds human dignity.

Freedom and political pluralism are necessary elements in our common objective of developing market economies towards sustainable economic growth, prosperity, social justice, expanding employment and efficient use of economic resources. The success of the transition to market economy by countries making efforts to this effect is important and in the interest of us all. It will enable us to share a higher level of prosperity which is our common objective. We will co-operate to this end.

Preservation of the environment is a shared responsibility of all our nations. While supporting national and regional efforts in this field, we must also look to the pressing need for joint action on a wider scale.

Friendly relations among participating States

Now that a new era is dawning in Europe, we are determined to expand and strengthen friendly relations and co-operation among the States of Europe, the United States of America and Canada, and to promote friendship among our peoples.

To uphold and promote democracy, peace and unity in Europe, we solemnly pledge our full commitment to the Ten Principles of the Helsinki Final Act. We affirm the continuing validity of the Ten Principles and our determination to put them into practice. All the principles apply equally and unreservedly, each of them being interpreted taking into account the others. They form the basis for our relations.

In accordance with our obligations under the Charter of the United Nations and commitments under the Helsinki Final Act, we renew our pledge to refrain from the threat or use of force against the territorial integrity or political independence of any State, or from acting in any other manner inconsistent with the principles or purposes of those documents. We recall that non-compliance with obligations under the Charter of the United Nations constitutes a violation of international law.

We reaffirm our commitment to settle disputes by peaceful means. We decide to develop mechanisms for the prevention and resolution of conflicts among the participating States.

With the ending of the division of Europe, we will strive for a new quality in our security relations while fully respecting each other's freedom of choice in that respect. Security is indivisible and the security of every participating State is inseparably linked to that of all the others. We therefore pledge to co-operate in strengthening confidence and security among us and in promoting arms control and disarmament.

We welcome the Joint Declaration of Twenty-Two States on the improvement of their relations.

Our relations will rest on our common adherence to democratic values and to human rights and fundamental freedoms. We are convinced that, in order to strengthen peace and security among our States, the advancement of democracy and respect for and effective exercise of human rights are indispensable. We reaffirm the equal rights of peoples and their right to self-determination in conformity with the Charter of the United Nations and with the relevant norms of international law, including those relating to territorial integrity of States.

We are determined to enhance political consultation and to widen co-operation to solve economic, social, environmental, cultural and humanitarian problems. This common resolve and our growing interdependence will help to overcome the mistrust of decades, to increase stability and to build a united Europe.

We want Europe to be a source of peace, open to dialogue and to co-operation with other countries, welcoming exchanges and involved in the search for common responses to the challenges of the future.

Security

Friendly relations among us will benefit from the consolidation of democracy and improved security.

We welcome the signature of the Treaty on Conventional Armed Forces in Europe by twenty-two participating States, which will lead to lower levels of armed forces. We endorse the adoption of a substantial new set of confidence- and security-building measures which will lead to increased transparency and confidence among all participating States. These are important steps towards enhanced stability and security in Europe.

The unprecedented reduction in armed forces resulting from the Treaty on Conventional Armed Forces in Europe, together with new approaches to security and co-operation within the CSCE process, will lead to a new perception of security in Europe and a new dimension in our relations. In this context we fully recognize the freedom of States to choose their own security arrangements.

Unity

Europe, whole and free, is calling for a new beginning. We invite our peoples to join in this great endeavour.

We note with great satisfaction the Treaty on the Final Settlement with respect to Germany signed in Moscow on 12 September 1990 and sincerely welcome the fact that the German people have united to become one State, in accordance with the principles of the Final Act of the Conference on Security and Co-operation in Europe and in full accord with their neighbours. The establishment of the national unity of Germany is an important contribution to a just and lasting order of peace for a united, democratic Europe, aware of its responsibility for stability, peace and co-operation.

The participation of both North American and European States is a fundamental characteristic of the CSCE; it underlies its past achievements and is essential to the future of the CSCE process. An abiding adherence to shared values and our common heritage are the ties which bind us together. With all the rich diversity of our nations, we are united in our commitment to expand our co-operation in all fields. The challenges confronting us can only be met by common action, co-operation and solidarity.

The CSCE and the world

The destiny of our nations is linked to that of all other nations. We support fully the United Nations and the enhancement of its role in promoting international peace, security and justice. We reaffirm our commitment to the principles and purposes of the United Nations as enshrined in the Charter and condemn all violations of these principles. We recognize with satisfaction the growing role of the United Nations in world affairs and its increasing effectiveness, fostered by the improvement in relations among our States.

Aware of the dire needs of a great part of the world, we commit ourselves to solidarity with all other countries. Therefore, we issue a call from Paris today to all the nations of the world. We stand ready to join with any and all States in common efforts to protect and advance the community of fundamental human values.

Guidelines for the future

Proceeding from our firm commitment to the full implementation of all CSCE principles and provisions, we now resolve to give a new impetus to a balanced and comprehensive development of our co-operation in order to address the needs and aspirations of our peoples.

Human dimension

We declare our respect for human rights and fundamental freedoms to be irrevocable. We will fully implement and build upon the provisions relating to the human dimension of the CSCE.

Proceeding from the Document of the Copenhagen Meeting of the Conference on the Human Dimension, we will co-operate to strengthen democratic institutions and to promote the application of the rule of law. To that end, we decide to convene a seminar of experts in Oslo from 4 to 15 November 1991.

Determined to foster the rich contribution of national minorities to the life of our societies, we undertake further to improve their situation. We reaffirm our deep conviction that friendly relations among our peoples, as well as peace, justice, stability and democracy, require that the ethnic, cultural, linguistic and religious identity of national minorities be protected and conditions for the promotion of that identity be created. We declare that questions related to national minorities can only be satisfactorily resolved in a democratic political framework. We further acknowledge that the rights of persons belonging to national minorities must be fully respected as part of universal human rights. Being aware of the urgent need for increased co-operation on, as well as better protection of, national minorities, we decide to convene a meeting of experts on national minorities to be held in Geneva from 1 to 19 July 1991.

We express our determination to combat all forms of racial and ethnic hatred, anti-Semitism, xenophobia and discrimination against anyone as well as persecution on religious and ideological grounds.

In accordance with our CSCE commitments, we stress that free movement and contacts among our citizens as well as the free flow of information and ideas are crucial for the maintenance and development of free societies and flourishing cultures. We welcome increased tourism and visits among our countries.

The human dimension mechanism has proved its usefulness, and we are consequently determined to expand it to include new procedures involving, *inter alia*, the services of experts or a roster of eminent persons experienced in human rights issues which could be raised under the mechanism. We shall provide, in the context of the mechanism, for individuals to be involved in the protection of their rights. Therefore, we undertake to develop further our commitments in this respect, in particular at the Moscow Meeting of the Conference on the Human Dimension, without prejudice to obligations under existing international instruments to which our States may be parties.

We recognize the important contribution of the Council of Europe to the promotion of human rights and the principles of democracy and the rule of law as well as to the development of cultural co-operation. We welcome moves by several participating States to join the Council of Europe and adhere to its European Convention on Human Rights. We welcome as well the readiness of the Council of Europe to make its experience available to the CSCE.

Security

The changing political and military environment in Europe opens new possibilities for common efforts in the field of military security. We will build on the important achievements attained in the Treaty on Conventional Armed Forces in Europe and in the Negotiations on Confidence- and Security-building Measures. We undertake to continue the CSBM negotiations under the same mandate, and to seek to conclude them no later than the Follow-up Meeting of the CSCE to be held in Helsinki in 1992. We also welcome the decision of the participating States concerned to continue the CFE negotiation under the same mandate and to seek to conclude it no later than the Helsinki Follow-up Meeting. Following a period for national preparations, we look forward to a more structured co-operation among all participating States on security matters, and to discussions and consultations among the thirty-four participating States aimed at establishing by 1992, from the conclusion of the Helsinki Follow-up Meeting, new negotiations on disarmament and confidence and security building open to all participating States.

We call for the earliest possible conclusion of the Convention on an effectively verifiable, global and comprehensive ban on chemical weapons, and we intend to be original signatories to it.

We reaffirm the importance of the Open Skies initiative and call for the successful conclusion of the negotiations as soon as possible.

Although the threat of conflict in Europe has diminished, other dangers threaten the stability of our societies. We are determined to co-operate in defending democratic institutions against activities which violate the independence, sovereign equality or territorial integrity of the participating States. These include illegal activities involving outside pressure, coercion and subversion.

We unreservedly condemn, as criminal, all acts, methods and practices of terrorism and express our determination to work for its eradication both bilaterally and through multilateral co-operation. We will also join together in combating illicit trafficking in drugs.

Being aware that an essential complement to the duty of States to refrain from the threat or use of force is the peaceful settlement of disputes, both being essential factors for the maintenance and consolidation of international peace and security, we will not only seek effective ways of preventing, through political means, conflicts which may yet emerge, but also define, in conformity with international law, appropriate mechanisms for the peaceful resolution of any disputes which may arise. Accordingly, we undertake to seek new forms of co-operation in this area, in particular a range of methods for the peaceful settlement of disputes, including mandatory third-party involvement. We stress that full use should be made in this context of the opportunity of the Meeting on the Peaceful

Settlement of Disputes which will be convened in Valletta at the beginning of 1991. The Council of Ministers for Foreign Affairs will take into account the report of the Valletta Meeting.

Economic co-operation

We stress that economic co-operation based on market economy constitutes an essential element of our relations and will be instrumental in the construction of a prosperous and united Europe. Democratic institutions and economic liberty foster economic and social progress, as recognized in the Document of the Bonn Conference on Economic Co-operation, the results of which we strongly support.

We underline that co-operation in the economic field, science and technology is now an important pillar of the CSCE. The participating States should periodically review progress and give new impulses in these fields.

We are convinced that our overall economic co-operation should be expanded, free enterprise encouraged and trade increased and diversified according to GATT rules. We will promote social justice and progress and further the welfare of our peoples. We recognize in this context the importance of effective policies to address the problem of unemployment.

We reaffirm the need to continue to support democratic countries in transition towards the establishment of a market economy and the creation of the basis for self-sustained economic and social growth, as already undertaken by the Group of twenty-four countries. We further underline the necessity of their increased integration, involving the acceptance of disciplines as well as benefits, into the international economic and financial system.

We consider that increased emphasis on economic co-operation within the CSCE process should take into account the interests of developing participating States.

We recall the link between respect for and promotion of human rights and fundamental freedoms and scientific progress. Co-operation in the field of science and technology will play an essential role in economic and social development. Therefore, it must evolve towards a greater sharing of appropriate scientific and technological information and knowledge with a view to overcoming the technological gap which exists among the participating States. We further encourage the participating States to work together in order to develop human potential and the spirit of free enterprise.

We are determined to give the necessary impetus to co-operation among our States in the fields of energy, transport and tourism for economic and social development. We welcome, in particular, practical steps to create optimal conditions for the economic and rational development of energy resources, with due regard for environmental considerations.

We recognize the important role of the European Community in the political and economic development of Europe. International economic organizations such as the United Nations Economic Commission for Europe (ECE), the Bretton Woods Institutions, the Organisation for Economic Co-operation and Development (OECD), the European Free Trade Association (EFTA) and the International Chamber of Commerce (ICC) also have a significant task in promoting economic co-operation, which will be further enhanced by the establishment of the European Bank for Reconstruction and Development (EBRD). In order to pursue our objectives, we stress the necessity for effective co-ordination of the activities of these organizations and emphasize the need to find methods for all our States to take part in these activities.

Environment

We recognize the urgent need to tackle the problems of the environment and the importance of individual and co-operative efforts in this area. We pledge to intensify our endeavours to protect and improve our environment in order to restore and maintain a sound ecological balance in air, water and soil. Therefore, we are determined to make full use of the CSCE as a framework for the formulation of common environmental commitments and objectives, and thus to pursue the work reflected in the report of the Sofia Meeting on the Protection of the Environment.

We emphasize the significant role of a well-informed society in enabling the public and individuals to take initiatives to improve the environment. To this end, we commit ourselves to promoting public awareness and education on the environment as well as the public reporting of the environmental impact of policies, projects and programmes.

We attach priority to the introduction of clean and low-waste technology, being aware of the need to support countries which do not yet have their own means for appropriate measures.

We underline that environmental policies should be supported by appropriate legislative measures and administrative structures to ensure their effective implementation.

We stress the need for new measures providing for the systematic evaluation of compliance with the existing commitments and, moreover, for the development of more ambitious commitments with regard to notification and exchange of information about the state of the environment and potential environmental hazards. We also welcome the creation of the European Environment Agency (EEA).

We welcome the operational activities, problem-oriented studies and policy reviews in various existing international organizations engaged in the protection of the environment, such as the United Nations Environment Programme (UNEP), the United Nations Economic Commission for Europe (ECE) and the Organisation for Economic Co-operation and Development (OECD). We emphasize the need for strengthening their co-operation and for their efficient co-ordination.

Culture

We recognize the essential contribution of our common European culture and our shared values in overcoming the division of the continent. Therefore, we underline our attachment to creative freedom and to the protection and promotion of our cultural and spiritual heritage, in all its richness and diversity.

In view of the recent changes in Europe, we stress the increased importance of the Cracow Symposium and we look forward to its consideration of guidelines for intensified co-operation in the field of culture. We invite the Council of Europe to contribute to this symposium.

In order to promote greater familiarity amongst our peoples, we favour the establishment of cultural centres in cities of other participating States, as well as increased co-operation in the audio-visual field and wider exchange in music, theatre, literature and the arts.

We resolve to make special efforts in our national policies to promote better understanding, in particular among young people, through cultural exchanges, co-operation in all fields of education and, more specifically, through teaching and training in the languages of other participating States. We intend to consider first results of this action at the Helsinki Follow-up Meeting in 1992.

Migrant workers

We recognize that the issues of migrant workers and their families legally residing in host countries have economic, cultural and social aspects as well as their human dimension. We reaffirm that the protection and promotion of their rights, as well as the implementation of relevant international obligations, is our common concern.

Mediterranean

We consider that the fundamental political changes that have occurred in Europe have a positive relevance to the Mediterranean region. Thus, we will continue efforts to strengthen security and co-operation in the Mediterranean as an important factor for stability in Europe. We welcome the report of the Palma de Mallorca Meeting on the Mediterranean, the results of which we all support.

We are concerned with the continuing tensions in the region, and renew our determination to intensify efforts towards finding just, viable and lasting solutions, through peaceful means, to outstanding crucial problems, based on respect for the principles of the Final Act.

We wish to promote favourable conditions for a harmonious development and diversification of relations with the non-participating Mediterranean States. Enhanced co-operation with these States will be pursued with the aim of promoting economic and social development and thereby enhancing stability in the region. To this end, we will strive together with these countries towards a substantial narrowing of the prosperity gap between Europe and its Mediterranean neighbours.

Non-governmental organizations

We recall the major role that non-governmental organizations, religious and other groups and individuals have played in the achievement of the objectives of the CSCE and will further facilitate their activities for the implementation of the CSCE commitments by the participating States. These organizations, groups and individuals must be involved in an appropriate way in the activities and new structures of the CSCE in order to fulfil their important tasks.

New structures and institutions of the CSCE process

Our common efforts to consolidate respect for human rights, democracy and the rule of law, to strengthen peace and to promote unity in Europe require a new quality of political dialogue and co-operation and thus development of the structures of the CSCE.

The intensification of our consultations at all levels is of prime importance in shaping our future relations. To this end, we decide on the following:

We, the Heads of State or Government, shall meet next time in Helsinki on the occasion of the CSCE Follow-up Meeting 1992. Thereafter, we will meet on the occasion of subsequent follow-up meetings.

Our Ministers for Foreign Affairs will meet, as a Council, regularly and at least once a year. These meetings will provide the central forum for political consultations within the CSCE process. The Council will consider issues relevant to the Conference on Security and Co-operation in Europe and take appropriate decisions.

The first meeting of the Council will take place in Berlin.

A Committee of Senior Officials will prepare the meetings of the Council and carry out its decisions. The Committee will review current issues and may take appropriate decisions, including in the form of recommendations to the Council.

Additional meetings of the representatives of the participating States may be agreed upon to discuss questions of urgent concern.

The Council will examine the development of provisions for convening meetings of the Committee of Senior Officials in emergency situations.

Meetings of other Ministers may also be agreed by the participating States.

In order to provide administrative support for these consultations we establish a Secretariat in Prague.

Follow-up meetings of the participating States will be held, as a rule, every two years to allow the participating States to take stock of developments, review the implementation of their commitments and consider further steps in the CSCE process.

We decide to create a Conflict Prevention Centre in Vienna to assist the Council in reducing the risk of conflict.

We decide to establish an Office for Free Elections in Warsaw to facilitate contacts and the exchange of information on elections within participating States.

Recognizing the important role parliamentarians can play in the CSCE process, we call for greater parliamentary involvement in the CSCE, in particular through the creation of a CSCE parliamentary assembly, involving members of parliaments from all participating States. To this end, we urge that contacts be pursued at parliamentary level to discuss the field of activities, working methods and rules of procedure of such CSCE parliamentary structure, drawing on existing experience and work already undertaken in this field.

We ask our Ministers for Foreign Affairs to review this matter on the occasion of their first meeting as a Council.

Procedural and organizational modalities relating to certain provisions contained in the Charter of Paris for a New Europe are set out in the Supplementary Document which is adopted together with the Charter of Paris.

We entrust to the Council the further steps which may be required to ensure the implementation of decisions contained in the present document, as well as in the Supplementary Document, and to consider further efforts for the strengthening of security and co-operation in Europe. The Council may adopt any amendment to the Supplementary Document which it may deem appropriate.

The original of the Charter of Paris for a New Europe, drawn up in English, French, German, Italian, Russian and Spanish, will be transmitted to the Government of the French Republic, which will retain it in its archives. Each of the participating States will receive from the Government of the French Republic a true copy of the Charter of Paris.

The text of the Charter of Paris will be published in each participating State, which will disseminate it and make it known as widely as possible.

The Government of the French Republic is requested to transmit to the Secretary General of the United Nations the text of the Charter of Paris for a New Europe which is not eligible for registration under Article 102 of the Charter of the United Nations, with a view to its circulation to all the members of the Organization as an official document of the United Nations.

The Government of the French Republic is also requested to transmit the text of the Charter of Paris to all the other international organizations mentioned in the text.

Sales agents for publications of the Council of Europe

AUSTRALIA
Hunter Publications
58A, Gipps Street
AUS-3066 COLLINGWOOD, Victoria

AUSTRIA
Gerold und Co.
Graben 31
A-1011 VIENNA 1

BELGIUM
La Librairie européenne SA
244, rue de la Loi
B-1040 BRUSSELS

CANADA
Renouf Publishing Company Limited
1294 Algoma Road
CDN-OTTAWA ONT K1B 3W8

CYPRUS
MAM
The House of the Cyprus Book
PO Box 1722
CY-NICOSIA

DENMARK
Munksgaard
Book and Subscription Service
PO Box 2148
DK-1016 COPENHAGEN K

FINLAND
Akateeminen Kirjakauppa
Keskuskatu 1
PO Box 218
SF-00381 HELSINKI

GERMANY
Verlag Dr. Hans Heger
Herderstraße 56
Postfach 20 13 63
D-5300 BONN

GREECE
Librairie Kauffmann
Mavrokordatou 9, GR-ATHENS 106 78

ICELAND
Bókabúd Máls og menningar
Laugavegi 18
IS-REYKJAVIK 101

IRELAND
Government Stationery Office
Office of Public Works
Government Supplies Agency
4-5 Harcourt Road
IRL-DUBLIN 2

ITALY
Libreria Commissionaria Sansoni
Via Duca di Calabria, 1/1
Casella Postale 552
I-50125 FLORENCE

LUXEMBOURG
Librairie Bourbon
(Imprimerie Saint-Paul)
11, rue Bourbon
L-1249 LUXEMBOURG

MALAYSIA
Library Building
University of Malaya
PO Box 1127
Jalan Pantai Baru
59700 KUALA LUMPUR

NETHERLANDS
InOr-publikaties
PO Box 202
NL-7480 AE HAAKSBERGEN

Sdu Uitgeverij Plantijnstraat
Christoffel Plantijnstraat 2
PO Box 20014
NL-2500 EA THE HAGUE

NEW ZEALAND
GP Publications Ltd
33 The Esplanade
PO Box 33-900 Petone
NZ-WELLINGTON

NORWAY
Akademika, A/S Universitetsbokhandel
PO Box 84
Blindern
N-0314 OSLO

PAKISTAN
Tayyab MS Commercial Services
PO Box 16006
A-2/3, Usman Ghani Road
Manzoor Colony
PAK-KARACHI-44

PORTUGAL
Livraria Portugal
Rua do Carmo, 70
P-1200 LISBON

SPAIN
Mundi-Prensa Libros SA
Castelló 37
E-28001 MADRID

Llibreria de la Generalitat
Rambla dels Estudis, 118
E-08002 BARCELONA

Llibreria de la Generalitat de Catalunya
Gran Via Jaume I, 38
E-17001 GIRONA

Libreria internacional AEDOS
Concejo de Ciento, 391
E-08009 BARCELONA

SWEDEN
Aktiebolaget CE Fritzes
Regeringsgatan 12
Box 163 56
S-10327 STOCKHOLM

SWITZERLAND
Buchhandlung Heinimann & Co.
Kirchgasse 17
CH-8001 ZURICH

Librairies Payot et Naville SA
Case postale 3212
30, rue des Côtes-de-Montbenon
CH-1002 LAUSANNE

TAIWAN – HONG KONG
SINGAPORE
Mappamundi Taiwan
7 Fl. 258, Nanking E. Rd.
Sec. 3 Taipei
TAIWAN ROC

TURKEY
Librairie Haset Kitapevi AS
469, Istiklâl Caddesi
Beyoglu
TR-ISTANBUL

UNITED KINGDOM
HMSO
Agency Section
51 Nine Elms Lane
GB-LONDON SW8 5DR

UNITED STATES and CANADA
Manhattan Publishing Company
1 Croton Point Avenue, PO Box 650
CROTON, NY 10520

STRASBOURG
Mésange SA
Groupe Berger-Levrault
23, place Broglie
F-67081 STRASBOURG Cedex